COMPASSIONATE EDUCATION

A Prolegomena for Radical Schooling

Khen Lampert

Copyright © 2003 by
University Press of America,® Inc.
4501 Forbes Boulevard
Suite 200
Lanham, Maryland 20706
UPA Acquisitions Department (301) 459-3366

PO Box 317
Oxford
OX2 9RU, UK

British Library Cataloging in Publication Information Available

Library of Congress Control Number: 2003108920
ISBN 0-7618-2641-6 (paperback : alk. ppr.)

⊚™ The paper used in this publication meets the minimum
requirements of American National Standard for Information
Sciences—Permanence of Paper for Printed Library Materials,
ANSI Z39.48—1984

Contents

IV. The Idea of Radical Compassion

V. Alternative Schooling

Preface

Dialogue cannot exist, however, in the absence of profound love for the world and for people. The meaning of the world, which is an act of creation and re-creation, is not possible if it is not infused with love. Love is at the same time the foundation of dialogue and dialogue itself. It thus necessarily the task of responsible Subjects and cannot exist in a relation of domination. Domination reveals the pathology of love: sadism in the dominator and masochism in the dominated. Because love is an act of courage, not of fear, love is commitment to others. No matter where the oppressed are found, the act of love is commitment to their cause—the cause of liberation.

Paulo Freire, *Pedagogy of the Oppressed*

The term "compassionate education" is used in three different senses in this book: First, it is education that is driven by empathy and love for others, education that is committed to the interests of the other, even if this is at the expense of self-interest. Second, this is active political education that is directed at the emancipation of man, education that stands in defiance of the modern educational ideal of shaping the individual according to an external social model. And third, this is education that is committed to alleviate people's pain, to addressing their distress and alienation. Compassionate education is grounded in the concrete act of giving others presence, which constitutes the epistemological and ethical foundation of dialogic education. This act requires of the educator that she discard her own consciousness and instead look at reality through the eyes of her pupil, feel his feelings, know his knowledge, and thereby give them legitimacy.

The educational, humanistic, liberal, and radical theories are all flooded with declarations on the importance of empathy, mercy, and love. The educational relationship preferred by many educational theorists (even prior to Freire) is the dialogic relationship or, at the very least, a relationship of guidance. However, it seems that the abysmal school reality leaves humaneness outside and that the technocratic achievement-oriented educational practice presents the dialogic relationship as naïve and wasteful and as a method whose appropriate social place is in welfare and psychology, not in education, whose objectives are cognitive. Needless to say, the primary victims of the industrialization, efficiency, and professionalization trends in education are those children who in any event are not destined to succeed in the public school systems, who begin at school their biographies of social rejection, who live a life of distress at school.

The decision to write a book that presents the rationale of working with children in distress at the school was made over a bowl of soup in a tourist restaurant in Prague in November 2001, during a short vacation with my good friend and colleague, Gadi Avidan. Perhaps it was being far away from home, the cold Czech autumn scenery, and the taste of the homemade soup that awoke in us the desire to write. Our first thought was to try to write a sort of summary of twenty-two years of working together in underprivileged neighborhoods with children and youth—from working with street gangs and delinquents, to coordinating and running community projects, to our present work as co-directors of the *Karev* Program for Involvement in Education. The Program is an educational enrichment project that is intended to advance schools and communities in underprivileged areas in Israel (Jewish and Arab) and to foster equal opportunities in education.

In this framework, we established a system of personal mentoring for children in distress in schools, which has been operating for three years to change the hard reality of their lives and to try and influence in a meaningful way the school's language and world of imagery by effecting institutional change.

From an external perspective, it seemed to be a relatively easy prospect to present the ideological concept by which we work, an ideology that is supposedly "left-wing educational", whose principles appear in great detail in the critical pedagogy. We did not anticipate any particular difficulty in presenting the innovative methodology we developed of working in the area between the existing disciplines of education and therapy. We most certainly did not foresee any difficulty in presenting the practice we propose today as welfare and education practitioners, a practice of generative dialogue between children and adults, which we certainly did not invent, even though our version of it is unique.

But the reality turned out to be not quite so simple. When we sat down to write, it quickly became clear that there are significant gaps between the way in which we work and guide the wonderful and dedicated people who work with us and the way in which the educational endeavor is described in the critical literature as well as the constructive literature. We discovered that a collection of theoretical stances does not represent the overall narrative of life with children and that the force and vitality of the reality cannot be reduced into dry academic language. Thus, we decided to divide up the writing between us: I took upon myself to present the theoretical aspects of the world view, while Gadi took upon himself (along with Gish Amit, our colleague) the almost impossible task of creating a text of stories and conversations that illustrates for the reader the complexity and vitality of compassionate education.

This book is the first part of our project, and it focuses almost completely on the theoretical aspects (philosophical, sociological, educational) of the generative mentoring work—the only foundation that to our mind is legitimate to defend the possibility of education in general and public education specifically.

Khen Lampert, Tel Aviv, December 2002

Introduction

For many people, the time they spent at school is remembered as the best time of their lives. This book does not deal with those people. There also are people who remember school as the place where they received their training for life, and although it was not always easy, in the final analysis, it was worthwhile. This book does not deal with these people either. There are a few people who remember school as a protective, warm, loving place; as a safe harbor that afforded them a "fresh opportunity", where one or two adults recognized their abilities—these people will also remain outside the present discussion.

Instead, this book deals with people who experience school as a hard place. As a place in which a battle of survival is conducted. As a place that represents pain, helplessness, and feelings of frustration, fear, and disappointment. Some of them "survive" school and feel they have managed to stabilize their lives despite the tough experience. Others leave school alienated from society and from themselves, lacking confidence, untrusting of others, and with a lack of self-value that accompanies them throughout their lives, limits their freedom and ability to live full, creative lives.

This book considers the issue of children in distress at school. The term "distress" is used here in the broadest sense, implying both personal and social distress, alienation, hardship, suffering, anxiety, humiliation, etc., all of which characterize the experiences of some children in school, and these children tend to be from poorer neighborhoods, children of immigrants, from ethnic minorities, and so forth. The aim is to propose an alternative to the way in which schools cope with the phenomenon of distress. The proposed model is based on the belief that despite the fact that the school itself is one of the principal causes of distress, it is also the place with the greatest potential for finding an appropriate, humane response to a considerable part of this distress. Generally, this belief contradicts the way in which most teachers perceive both the school and themselves within the school—namely, as places that do not create distress. Even if they do, teachers certainly cannot deal with that distress.

The way in which I have chosen to relate to the distress of children in school is by examining a range of organizational, psychological, and functional difficulties experienced by the school and presenting them as factors that hinder the ability of the adults working there to take responsibility for the distress of a large segment of the children, by first feeling it and then easing it. My assumption is that this emasculation of educational work, accompanied by overt and covert rationalization, is not the legacy of malevolence, stupidity, or impotence on the part of those engaged in education. Rather, it is deeply rooted in the capitalist, politico-social structure of the industrial democracy. In this sense, schoolteachers are the victims of the very social process that turns the lives of some children into a living hell. A further assumption (which constitutes the *raison d'etre* for writing this book) is that the underlying structure of the educational endeavor as a whole includes a commitment to the well-being of children, as well as a genuine intention to promote that well-being, and that renouncing that commitment diminishes both the child and the adult, since both are deprived of the possibility of achieving meaningful human contact.

Distress

Beginning a critical discussion with a concept that stresses emotion, personal experience, and a mental state is not mere coincidence and is indicative of the importance of concrete human experience as the basis for any theoretical discussion of significance, particularly one proposing change. This experience, presented from the point of view or, more precisely, from the point of *feeling*, of the child, anchors the child's presence as an actual and feeling person, as a subject, at every stage of the discussion. It does not allow for an instrumental approach to children as objects or products and is intended to limit the reduction of the concept of "child" to generalities of operations or behaviors.

While defining "distress" as a concept that stresses the personal experience, on the one hand, and a universal, existential phenomenon, on the other, I conceive of distress also as a social phenomenon. Social distress is a feeling common to people from the lower socio-economic classes, manifested as a sense of lack of value, absence of usefulness, inability to work toward change, and alienation and detachment. In this sense, the distress I will refer to in this discussion is not only the existential, universal distress of people everywhere, but, more specifically, that of the child who lacks a sense of value, feels repressed and humiliated. Not surprisingly, this child is the child of the poorer classes, the working classes, the child of those who exist under duress, unemployment, immigration, and so forth. In this sense, distress is not simply a universal concept denoting individual experience, but, rather, is also a concrete concept denoting a general common denominator for a social class.

If we consider children's distress at school from the social perspective, we can identify a great deal of overlap and, in certain cases, even identity among three social groups. The one group is children who feel distress, alienation, isolation, and humiliation at school. The second group comprises children from poor families, members of the lower socio-economic class. The third group comprises children who simply do not succeed at school: they fail in their studies; they drop out of school; they do not continue beyond compulsory education; and they reach a point where they "hate" studying. In many cases, these three distinct groups are comprised of the same children (not of their own will).

In most of the sociological theories, scholars attempt to identity causal connections that explain this overlap and recommend a reduction of the two groups to the third group, presenting membership in the latter as the chief cause of membership in the other two. Thus, for instance, it can be claimed that poverty and economic distress are the main factors in psychological distress, on the one hand, and the social rejection manifested in the failure in social frameworks, on the other hand. An alternative explanation is that failure at school is the cause of the sense of alienation and humiliation experienced by the children and ultimately condemns those children to a life of economic and social failure.

What is important in the present discussion is the existence of an overlap between poverty and the lower socio-economic class, on the one hand, and academic failure, on the other, and the overlap of both of these with children's distress. By identifying this overlap, I seek to present the general social experience of children who have been condemned to social exclusion[1] and argue that this experience is reinforced and intensified by the school. At the same time, I will argue that, ironically, one of the key players in changing this experience is the school itself.

The manifestations of social ostracism for children are dramatic. One of the ways children shape and form their self-image, according to the approach presented below, is through their perceptions of themselves as reflected in the eyes of others. However, for a reflection of this sort to be real and significant, the child has to know somebody who sees him, recognizes him, feels his presence, and takes an interest in him. A person of this sort might become a "significant adult" for that child by being a person whose way of seeing the child enables the latter to form his or her self-image as a person of value, with the ability to function in a manner that is significant to others. One of the features of the psychosocial experience of poverty is the absence of a positive self-image, in the sense of "of being of value". This deficiency makes it difficult for the poor, the oppressed, the humiliated, to be significant adults, who feel they are worthy and capable of reflecting others, for their children, siblings, neighbors, etc. Hence, upon entering school, children from

---

[1] The expression "social exclusion" seems to have been coined by members of the "Fourth World". It relates mainly to people living in extreme poverty. A description of poor people's struggle for social recognition and the attempt to assist them in this struggle can be found in J.M. Rosenfeld, *Artisans of Democracy*, Univ. Press of America, Inc., Maryland, 2000.

lower-class families, despite their strong need to feel valued, can have a low, negative self-image or, alternatively, can lack any significant self-image. The question is: Can schools, as social institutions whose function is based on the meeting between adults and children, contribute positively to deprived children's sense of self-value, or do they work to reproduce social alienation?

The approach that serves as the backdrop for the present discussion views distress as a fundamental part of the social reality dictated by power structures, namely, the control and manipulation of the individual by society. The source of this distress is not the individual but, rather, society, which prevents the individual from constructing a self-image and attaining an existential state of being of value. The preventive process includes the exercise of institutional violence that clearly separates those who will take control of resources in the future from those who will be oppressed or will remain in the margins of society. The use of violence by society creates distress in the individual, an absence of self-esteem, a sense of alienation, anonymity, and despair, which, in certain cases, can lead to anti-social behavior as one of the expressions of violence against the institutions, against others, and against oneself. Among other things, we learn from children's feelings of distress about the overt and covert institutional violence that, in extreme cases, creates the distress, in other cases exacerbates it, and in yet other cases ignores it—thus forever perpetuating it.

Children
In the early 1980s, Postman argued that childhood had ceased to be a social category in the modern sense and that the postmodern era has set off processes of change that have eroded the decisiveness of the dichotomy between adults and children.[2] Postman's claim rests on the current era's rapid erosion of the relationship of authority between adults and children and the gradual

---

[2] N. Postman, *The Disappearance of Childhood*, Vintage Books, N.Y., 1982.

disappearance of the innocence and ignorance that separated children from adults in the past. Because adults have lost their authority over children (starting at home and continuing at school) and because in the computer age and cyber-age, knowledge has become the natural birthright of all, adult and child alike, and because children, in any event, have better access to this knowledge than their parents or teachers do, the firm foundation of differentiation between adults and children, adulthood and childhood, is fast vanishing.

My assumption is substantially different. To begin with, Postman's argument that the difference between adults and children is based on authority and knowledge is simply incorrect. The distinction between adulthood and childhood was and still is of a far broader nature: It is connected to the power adults hold (physical, economic, and political) vis-à-vis children, which they will not, and cannot, relinquish. It is connected to the strong protective instincts of parents toward their children.[3] It is linked to childhood's short chronology with a long future, as opposed to the adult's long history with a future that is getting progressively shorter. It is manifested in the projection of the reservoir of hopes of those born long ago (the hope of continuity, maybe even immortality, in the face of the approaching end and the hope for success and fulfillment through another person, the child) onto those who have recently arrived. And so much more: the many types of feelings and impulses that form the background to the distinction between child and adult, a distinction made by adults (as Postman correctly notes) and not by children. It is very likely that since the distinction between child and adult is not based on rational analysis, but on impulses and feelings, it cannot be theoretically justified. It may well be that adults, in order to justify their control of children, their imposing of their

---

[3] Postman quotes Lloyd de Mause who claimed that before the modern era, parents were not mentally prepared to protect and be compassionate toward their children (ibid. p. 8). I dispute this assertion, but cannot rebut it on a historical basis in the framework of the present discussion.

aspirations on children, and their negating of children's rights, use a rationalization that stresses elements such as authority and knowledge. It is also very likely that the postmodern era presages the disappearance of the rational justifications for differentiation, just as it negates the justifications for clinging to all the modern dichotomies.[4] However, none of this negates the need of adults to distinguish between themselves and children. Quite the contrary: the very absence of a justification for the distinction and the exposure of its irrational, instinctive, and emotional basis demonstrate its essentiality, its necessity, and, in my view, its assured continuity.

This not withstanding, Postman is most certainly correct in his observation of the disappearance of authority and the increased accessibility of knowledge. This discernment is of great significance to the discussion of children in the school context; for in contrast to parents, the school as a social institution (i.e., as an institution funded by the state) must have a clear definition of its target population and must justify the way in which it defines children, because this definition delineates the boundaries of the mandate that it takes upon itself and from which its activities derive. In other words, the school does define itself as a place of authority and knowledge, and this is in opposition to the children who have neither and are not supposed to have either. And because the justification for the institutional definition of the school is losing force in the present era, a reformulation of that definition is necessary, on a rational basis by which the school can justify its activity (in addition, of course, to the many good reasons for redefining the school, as I will argue below). In particular, a reconstruction of the concept of childhood is called

---

[4] My argument will be that in what is called postmodernism, there is an erosion of the classical dichotomies in philosophy, morality, and society indeed. Postmodernism, therefore, constitutes a threat to the individual's possibility of constructing a self-identity. The only dichotomy that remains decisive in the current era is the dichotomy between rich and poor, which persists, splendid in its isolation, and has become the sole parameter on which to base identity.

for, since under my claim, childhood will not disappear, just as the school will not be discarded.

But beyond the justification of definitions, it is important to recall that childhood is, in principle, different from adulthood:

(1) Children see the world differently from adults, both in level of perception and in interpretation of sensory data. Research has shown that the functioning of the sensory organs changes dramatically with the move from childhood to adulthood, both in the manner in which reality is perceived and in the way the perceived data are interpreted. Children see physical space differently from adults, as well as movement in that space (cars approaching, for instance). They feel heat and cold differently, hear differently, and "taste" differently: nothing tastes the same as it did when we were children. The child's interpretation of what we see is entirely different from that of the adult: a simple conversation with a child after watching a movie where you have both seen the same pictures and heard the same text is sufficient to understand the difference.

(2) Children feel different, in terms of both physical sensation and emotional feeling, from feelings of pleasure and pain, in which the physical and psychological ranges of children are generally narrower than those of adults (although there are many children who have experienced pain and starvation never experienced by many adults), to the different ways children respond to those feelings. Adults and children differ substantially in their abilities to express feelings. The adult has strong verbal capability (he simply has more words to express his feelings), but rigid inhibitions and defenses based on a long history of denial and repression, whereas the child tends to express her feelings in a non-verbal way, but those feelings are more exposed and accessible.

(3) Children think differently from adults. What interests children, i.e., the contents of their thought, is different in principle from what interests adults (despite many children thinking of themselves as being party to the adult world of content). At the same time, a child's way of thinking is different from an adult's

way of thinking—and it is not necessary to accept Piaget's problematic views characterizing children's thought in terms of its evolution toward abstract and logical thought (thus wreaking great harm to the possibility of recognizing children as creative and thinking beings). It is sufficient to remember that children live in a more humanized, more purposeful world with a different measure of possibilities for countering stumbling blocks (in the world of children, there is more room for magic, but greater fixedness in relation to words, for instance).

(4) Children's intentions are different from those of adults, both in the sense of having intentions toward different objects, an attribute that stems from the previous feature, since thinking is always intentional, always a thought about "something" (as Husserl showed us), as well as in the sense of the motivational basis for every action. Adults are motivated by different things (money, power, fear, status, etc.) than the forces that motivate children, as various psychologists have taught us (beginning with Freud and his daughter, to Erikson and Winnicott, through to Bandura).

At the foundation of this distinction between the world of children and the world of adults, which was first presented by Rousseau in the eighteenth century, is the assertion that children are not "little adults" and that they have their own world with unique dynamics and content. According to Rousseau, the attempt to "educate" children, in the sense of preparing them for the adult world, is not justified and, in any event, only will lead to repression. The only education that children should be given is "negative" education; they should be left to their own devices and not taught anything, until they reach the age when they are interested in learning (after the age of twelve).[5] Echoes of this view were strongly apparent in twentieth-century educational discourse, from the approach of "open education" to the various developmental theories that demand that school life be adapted to children's "normal" developmental format, with recognition of the uniqueness of childhood. Children need to be taught in the

---

[5] J.J. Rousseau, *Emile*, trans. W.H. Payne, Appleton, N.Y., 1912.

manner in which they think and feel and must not be put into a cognitive and emotional straight-jacket that will cause them frustration, which, in any event, would be inefficient since children are incapable of performing adult tasks and there is no way of forcing them to do what they are incapable of understanding.

This approach, which is present in the educational theses of various thinkers, including Piaget, Montessori, and Gardner, has, to a certain extent, affected schools, particularly the various curriculum reform programs and, to a lesser extent, the attempt to amend teaching methods. The main areas where change was of particular importance were: the manner in which schools define their goals and apply them; the organizational structure of the school and the way in which the lives of the children and adults in the school are conducted within that structure; and the meanings of these concepts for the relations between adults and children. All these usually change subject to the needs of the adults.

The claim that will be asserted below is that the shape children's lives take in school is almost entirely dictated by the view that children are little adults. In this sense, the entirety of school activity, to the extent that it is rational (namely, that it is derived from Idea), is bound to a mature and purposeful conception of children's lives. The sole justification of the entire school enterprise, for both the children and adults, is contingent on the future image of the school graduate as a desirable product of educational activity. Children at school are in fact "mortgaged" to the benefit of the future product, despite their period at school constituting a considerable part of their lives, and only getting longer. Schools' integration into their practices of developmental views—something that is supposed to lead to a change in fundamental attitudes vis-à-vis children—is translated into patterns of avoidance, rather than legitimization, of children's lives. In other words, children do not get sanctioning to function and live like children. Instead, they get academic assignments that have been adapted to children by taking into account what children are supposedly incapable of performing. Children have to travel down a long path of activities planned by adults, from sensor-motoric activities to cognitive exercises, which, from the perspective of the child, seem random and aimless, without receiving any explanation or perspective, since children are, of course, supposedly unable to make generalizations and "comprehend".

Indeed, the experience of childhood, in contrast to adulthood, is one of "I am incapable", and not an experience of potency. In this sense, it is apparent that liberal, humanitarian theory, aimed at changing the relationship vis-à-vis children and making them a goal of the educational endeavor in and of themselves, serves, in practice, as a yoke for the repression of children by justifying relating to them as "just children" or "still children".

Where the education system has allowed children to lead "childlike" lives is not at the center of the school experience, but, rather, at its margins. Children are supposed to play at recess between lessons (as play is a childlike, if not "childish", activity), and they are allowed to behave in an infantile manner (that is, not to defer gratification and to display frustration), although only within very specific limits. Moreover, the school is supposed to provide children with social frameworks in which they are given the opportunity to experience their peer groups, since, again, this is the "right" social framework for children. By contrast, the curriculum, the hard core of the school, is a matter of investment in the future: children are supposed to learn skills and subject-matter that will be of use to them as adults and will enable them to be productive citizens in society.

Underlying the position expounded here is a different view of the relationship between what is right for present and what is right from a forward-looking perspective. Under my view, it is precisely the social, emotional, and intellectual experience of interpersonal relations—between children and adults and among children—that is the experience taken from childhood into adult life. It is the formative experience of a person's life, shaping her self-image; it is the manner in which she is perceived by others, and it is destined to manifest itself in adulthood as the key to either freedom or repression and alienation. Thus, if the goal of the elementary school is to prepare children for their future lives, it must invest in interpersonal interaction, a sphere today considered marginal, at least in most of the schools investing efforts in scientific education or in promoting access to technology, the popular features of the curriculum in many elementary schools in industrialized democracies. After all, do any of us remember even a smattering of what we learnt in elementary school? As an activity intended to prepare the person for adult life, the school program is bound to fail miserably. The view that has prevailed in recent years in educational debate, that the curriculum, even if not important in terms of its contents, is reliable in terms of teaching the students skills, has also not proved itself, and for two reasons.

First, the skills the curriculum is supposed to teach—study habits, understanding texts, mathematical thinking, language skills, etc.—cannot be taught directly if the student lacks a self-image that enables the acquisition of these skills, and this sort of self-image can only be constructed by means of interactive, human contact.

Second, no consensus exists today as to the complete list of skills people need in a changing reality. It is very likely that skills that seem to us today to be essential will in the future (for the children the future means in another twenty years) become irrelevant. In any case, the ability of schools to adapt their curricula and "real-time" teaching will always lag a good few years behind the changing reality.

The one thing that elementary schools rightly consider important is teaching reading and writing skills. However, in contrast to the accepted school stance that language is a skill and reading and writing are a technique to be acquired, my view is that the acquisition of all aspects of language is paramount. It enables children to develop a self-image as active creators capable of shaping reality and to take advantage of possibilities (both fantasy and real), because it allows them to build meaningful personal biographies for themselves, not because it is the key to external objective knowledge of one sort or another.

The School

The humanistic liberal vision of the school, derived from modernity, proposes an education model based on ideals that totally contradict the idea of school as a source of distress. Under this model, the sources of distress are outside of the school, not inside: in the parental home (as psychologist have taught us); in the streets and neighborhood (as the sociologists have taught us); or perhaps due to too much exposure to television (as the media itself tells us). Indeed, the children themselves may be the source of their distress, as the socio-biologists and geneticists hint at, with their mapping of the human genome. What occurs in schools, under this logic, stands in complete contradiction to the feelings of distress of some of the children. School is an instrument of socialization; it is planned and even operates according to patterns that teach children discipline and boundaries, develop interpersonal communication, values, tolerance, and self-discipline, all of which are supposed to instill in children a sense of confidence, stability, and belonging. More and more, modern schools are organized and set up to allow children to express themselves and their personal talents and to offer them possibilities for realizing their potential and discovering areas of interest. All of these bolster the individual's sense of self-worth, reduce frustration, and generally reduce both the sense of distress and the need to display violent behavior. Since, under this approach, the source of children's distress is basically an external one, it is not the school's concern, nor does it fall in the school's sphere of responsibility beyond the extent to which it interferes in the school's functioning. Interference of this sort can occur in two areas. One is the study area: children who bring distress with them to school from the outside could find themselves in a mental state that makes it difficult for them to meet the school's standards. Consequently, the school has to refer them to professionals entrusted with treating the distress, namely, educational psychologists.

The second area in which children's distress can pose a problem for schools is where distress translates into violent behavior, which, in turn, creates further distress. It is precisely with regard to this that schools develop the myth of the link between distress and violent behavior, while repudiating any connection between the school itself and the creation of distress, on the one hand, and between the school and violence, on the other. The underlying structure of the school's distress myth is built on three claims, all three of which I will contest in the course of the book's discussion:

(1) There is no such thing as "school distress", in the sense of the source of the distress deriving from inside the school. All distress children feel that is translated into behavior (generally violent and directed at teachers, other children, and, sometimes, at themselves) that occurs in school originates from external sources. The coercion employed by schools, if at indeed employed, is merely a restraining response to that behavior intended to protect children and adults from other children or themselves.

(2) Even if school distress were to exist, we would not know how to cope with it. Teachers do not understand distress, nor do they have the tools to contend with its behavioral implications. They do not have the training for it and it is not their job; their main function is to teach.

(3) Even if we could cope with school distress, the powers that be would not let us do so. Coping with the distress of some of the children by means of legal and public restrictions requires many resources, both mental and material, that we do not have at our disposal. It entails, for instance, the investment of a tremendous amount of energy in a small number of children who are in distress, and no one, especially the parents of other children, will agree to the neglect of important work intended for everybody's benefit, in order to focus on a few children experiencing difficulties (generally those children whose parents' voices are seldom heard in the school).

My argument against these claims is that the school creates institutional violence that is employed against some (in fact a sizeable amount) of the children in the school. Teachers and professionals have the ability and knowledge to stop, or at least reduce, school violence, and that despite this necessitating a radical change in the structure of the school, the required resources are attainable.

The school's distress myth is supposedly based on a series of "objective" descriptions that create a paradigmatic structure that explains the reality in a fashion that serves positive and overt interests; namely, it rationalizes reality, thereby enabling a continuation of the existing situation by legitimizing inaction and rejecting any idea of change. In the context of this point, it is important to note that paradigms of this sort do not just describe reality; they also create it by systematically influencing the decision-making processes, allocation of resources, and construction of relationships that operate within the school's bounds. But what is more important is that this is a myth that affects children's minds and perpetuates an intolerable situation of anxiety, offense, humiliation, alienation, and despair.

From this understanding of distress as a social phenomenon, as presented above, emerges the connection between being poor and being in distress. Poverty is not merely a personal economic and psychological situation, but, primarily, a social situation originating in overt and covert processes of repression and, in industrialized democracies, institutional repression. However, does this mean that the school, the first significant social institution a child meets upon leaving home, is a violent institution that creates distress? Is there no basis for conceiving of the school as an institution that offers all children both equal opportunities and the moratorium and protection they need before encountering the social reality, as most teachers and parents view the school, for instance?

The answer, as will become apparent in the course of the discussion, is not at all simple. On the one hand, it is absolutely clear that school, insofar as it is understood as an instrument of social control, is an institution that employs force, manipulation, and institutional violence against the individual. As such, schools create distress in many children, particularly poor children. In the way they operate, schools display the most profound contradiction between the basic humanist tendency present in educational thinking and the reality of "a dehumanized and dehumanizing totality affecting both the oppressor and those they oppress", [6] as stated by Freire.

---

[6] P. Freire, *Pedagogy of the Oppressed*, trans. M.B. Ramos, Herder & Herder, New York, 1970, p. 32.

On the other hand, with respect to certain children, the school may be a venue of nurturing, growth, acquiring a self-image of being of value, of self-structuring, and manifesting talents. In many important respects, the school affords poor children and children from historically discriminated classes (immigrants, women, etc.) the opportunity for mobility and for extricating themselves from the class "decree". As such, the school might even constitute the basis for real social change. This optimistic view of the school as an institution possessing the potential for equality and freedom is disputed both by conservatives, who are advocates of maintaining the status quo in schools, and by the most vociferous critics of schools as well as by educational critics, who search for a way to reform schools so that, despite their being part of the ideological super-structure (namely, that they are intended to guarantee the interests of the upper classes), they will be able to fulfill the promise embodied in them to become places that offer personal and social freedom to all. The view presented below is based on a similar assumption.

Radical Schooling

Modern reality has created the school as a segregative social institution. As such, schools, although structured to nurture some of the children socially by slightly enabling mobility, are basically institutions that repress children. Yet the school is also an institution in which humanistic ideology is present and manifests itself in the self-image of the adults working in it. It is a workplace for people who visualize themselves as good, child-loving people, with a mission and commitment. There are two aspects of the significant disparity between the self-image of the adults working in schools and the severely repressive reality vis-à-vis some of the children. The one aspect is that the humanistic image itself inadvertently turns into an instrument of repression, in the sense that it does not allow the school to diagnose the problem and take responsibility for the creation of children's distress. The other aspect is that there is a patent need for people engaged in education to reduce the intolerable disparity between the image, the educational idea they would want associated with their work, and the grim, alienating, denigrating, violent, and thankless reality that they encounter daily in their workplace. This disparity frequently creates feelings of exasperation, helplessness, and impotence (often experienced by teachers) and appears unbridgeable.

The claim made below is that at its foundation, the educational endeavor includes a radical commitment to people, expressed as the willingness to actualize others—namely, the child as a complete person. This is a principle commitment, and it precedes all ideologies and specific worldviews. It is not an outcome of the humanistic ideology of modernity, but, rather, has as a universal, timeless existence based on our being human, i.e., on being creatures capable of compassion, self-determination, love, and realization only through other people. The historical problem is that the school, as a social institution, is not designed to promote the realization of human, educational contact. Modern schools were built as academic institutions intended to teach or, alternatively, as institutions intended to socialize the children of the upper classes. In this capacity, the modern school handled and is handling its task well.

However, we can now see on the horizon a turning point in the possibility of bridging the disparity referred to above, against the postmodern background, which, in social and personal terms, is a crisis reality. This reality is subverting both the superstructure that obligates the school to have aims, organizational structures, and pedagogy that serve power interests and the educational ideology of shaping the individual according to the desired model, the modern definition of education. In the postmodern situation, one cannot point to a universally agreed-upon desired model or a desired model that has been derived from a binding ideology from the era of "the end of all ideologies". This reality has produced an unusual situation in which, on the one hand, the school has immense freedom to conduct reform, change priorities, and restructure its activities, yet on the other hand, the school is exposed to a range of pressures, which vary from social pressure from parents and public leaders to economic pressure from the political establishment seeking to reduce education's dependence on public funding. There is also pressure from the education system itself, which tries to ensure its survival through desperate adherence to modernistic attitudes and their translation into patterns of activity that will guarantee its essentiality. These pressures tie the school down and preventing it from progressing.

Hence, the school of today is an institution at a crossroads. It faces the very real possibility of falling prey to the dominant forces of neocapitalism, viz.: free market forces, the global economy, privatization, and aggressive trading. This possibility, which is fast becoming relevant for many schools in the first and second worlds, means the transformation of the educational bond, namely, of the teacher-pupil relationship, into a client-provider relationship, effectively converting educational work into an industrialized activity of producing defined learning outputs. It also means abrogating education's definition of itself as "human contact", converting it into merely "the technology of teaching".

Against this possibility one can point to an alternative in the form of a radical return to the human source of educational endeavor, namely, to the teacher-pupil relationship as a relationship that represents an entire world of content, method, and feeling, a conscious world where the adults enable the children to recognize themselves as being of value for others, thereby learning to recognize that they themselves, the adults, have value.

This return is radical both in the sense that it draws attention to the primary basis of educational activity and in the sense that it necessitates a far-reaching change in the adult's work with children and in the moral structure of working in education. A return of this sort is conditional on the acknowledgment of a number of points: the distress of children as the foremost challenge facing the educator; the procedures by which the school creates, or, alternatively, maintains and does not prevent, that distress; personal contact as the basis of full self-realization and for creating a self-image of being of value—for the child and adult; the necessity of structural, organizational, and content changes in the school's work, in order to foster the teacher-pupil interaction.

The book is divided into five parts. In the first part, I will present what I call the school's myth of distress, aimed at rejecting the image of the school as a place that creates distress. I will consider first the various critical stances that attack the school and try to invalidate its positive self-image and then my stance, which accepts some of the criticism and further adds the claim that the very existence of the myth is itself a cause of distress.

In the second part, I will present what I call the "postmodern challenge" that schools are facing today. I will initially consider the postmodern intellectual position, revealing both its advantages in highlighting the non-actualization of modern values such as freedom, equality, and pluralism as well as its shortcomings, manifested as superficiality, submission, and nihilism. The significance of the postmodern analysis for schools is that it provides an intellectual challenge in the wake of the collapse of beliefs and intellectual paradigms that have guided modern education and according to which schools justify their activities. This challenge requires substantial reconstruction of the positions and values by means of which schools can devise a new image. In the second chapter of this part, I will consider postmodernism as a description of a social situation, arguing that the analysis of the processes that societies, mainly Western, are undergoing at the start of the third millennium points to a neocapitalist social existence that, on the one hand, has many innovations but, on the other hand, accentuates, reinforces, and preserves the general trends of modern capitalism. My argument will be that the challenge posed by neocapitalism to schools is to decide between submitting to the commercialization processes, globalization, and reification that characterize certain general trends and taking issue with them by attempting to define a different type of humane relating and educational activity within the school's realm.

The third part will be devoted to the type of educational activity that, in my view, could counter the overall trend of the denial of children's distress in schools, as well as being the key to contending with the general social trends of commercialization and alienation. I term this activity "generative mentoring", and it refers to a special type of intellectual encounter between child and adult, which is essentially the creation of a self-image of being of value. The discussion will focus on the psychological-epistemological aspects of self-image and on the difference between this image and other mental constructs like personal identity, as well as on the various ways in which generative mentoring could constitute a means to opening up social options for children in distress.

In the fourth part, I will present what I call the theory of radical compassion. This theory is based on the concept of compassion, as understood by eighteenth-century European (British) thinkers and, in contrast, by Buddhist intellectuals and practitioners. What emerges from these understandings is that compassion, in the sense of the ability to acknowledge the pain (and joy) of others, is a fundamental type of human awareness and constitutes a sort of anthropological definition of humanness exceeding the bounds of a specific feeling and, as such, is universal. Based on this analysis of compassion, I will add my contention with respect to people's ability to distinguish between containing, passive compassion, and active compassion, which obligates those who practice it to real, material action, to change the reality of a person in pain. I will attach the appellation "radical compassion" to this obligatory compassion and argue that it is awareness that ensures generative mentoring as a type of progressive educational activity that focuses on fully actualizing others and on attempting to alter reality for them.

In the fifth and final part, I will propose a number of ideas for formulating a school alternative that takes into account both the criticism and possibility of engaging in educational work based on radical compassion, as manifested in generative mentoring. This alternative advocates schools that see their purpose as promoting freedom and equality and working to reduce social disparities by adapting their curricula, organization, and internal communication to combat alienation, commercialization, and the social rejection of children.

The book, as a whole, deals with apprenticeship, and as such, it contains some aspects that deviate from specific times and places. At the same time, this is, in principle, a theoretical discussion, based on generalizations, sometimes crude, that, as is usually the case with generalizations, take specific stories, other realities, and additional perspectives out of the realms of the discussion. Therefore, it seems appropriate to limit the discussion to those areas where the link between the generalization and the concrete reality might make a contribution, enlighten, or assist understanding, criticism, and renewal.

The discussion in the book relates chiefly to schools, particularly elementary schools. This is not to say it is not relevant to high schools, for instance. On the contrary, I believe that the reader will find that a large part of the diagnoses and analyses do indeed apply to other institutions. However, my basic intention is to present a picture that is as close as possible to the initial, critical meetings of the child with the social institution, and these meetings generally take place in the first years of school. I do not hold the view that these first years are a time of shaping, certainly not the "final shaping". I believe that children, and people generally, can change endlessly and ceaselessly during the course of their lives. The problem does not lie with the children, but with the institutions, particularly with elementary school, which, in many important senses, seals the fate of children at very the moment they appear at its gates. Unfortunately, the possibilities of changing the way in which children are perceived by schools and, later, by other social institutions (including the family, for instance) are extremely limited. At the same time, the elementary school is an institution with wide freedom of movement, since it relies on sources of funding that do not demand "output" from it (i.e., academic performance by the children) with the same intensity and decisiveness they do with regard to high school, for instance. The elementary school is also a place that still engenders hope: many parents, including from immigrant and poverty-stricken families and from the working class, pin their hopes for a better future for their children on the school, even if they have despaired of improving themselves. These hopes, which still have force in the early years of school,

are due to be proved false over the course of time, when parents
will discover in their children manifestations of the reproduction
of alienation and despair.

The schools I had in mind while engaging in this discussion
are schools I know, with which my colleagues and I have worked
for many years, and the present book was written on the background of this familiarity and the many and varied experiences it
includes. These are mainly schools in deprived neighborhoods at
the end of the twentieth century and the beginning of the third
millennium. In my estimation, based on my personal familiarity
with the field and on the literature from around the world, these
schools share a very broad common denominator with public
schools in slums, particularly in the great metropolises of Western Europe and North America, but also in Australia, Eastern
Europe, Brazil, and South Africa. Accordingly, the concept
"school" as used in the book relates in principle to the elementary school in Western culture and in countries that regard themselves as part of or are trying to be annexed to the West, where
the education system was designed according to similar standards and objectives (either through European colonialism or as
a consequence of American commercial imperialism).

At the same time, it is important for me to add two reservations. The one reservation is connected to the differences between education systems and, hence, also to schools in different
countries. There are significant differences between the manner
in which poverty is related to in America and how it is related to
in Europe, for instance. These differences, which express themselves in legislation and in public policy on the allocation of resources, as well as in the ethos of the society in general, pro-
foundly affect schools. Western European schools' degree of
commitment and responsibility to a child's distress that is linked
to her economic background are substantially different from the
degree to which responsibility for this is felt and, therefore, expressed in American schools. Accordingly, someone familiar
with this type of difference might find that some of the critiques
that are very relevant to a school in one place are tantamount to
"charging through an open door" in another place.

The second reservation is connected to the fact that a generalization, by its very nature, discriminates against the exceptions to the rule. And in the case of schools, there are many such exceptions. There are wonderful and dedicated schools in which people devote their time and energy to the onerous task of coping with the cruel, absurd reality of children threatened with social rejection. These are schools that try to make far-reaching changes in their working methods, in the personal stances of the adults working in them, in their organizational structure, and mainly in the various ways in which they meet the children. And they do exist. In truth, these schools can teach us about the power of optimism, the value of determination, sacrifice, hope, and persistence, and although a substantial part of the criticism that appears in this book is not relevant to them, I see them in my mind's eye throughout the discussion.

Part I

The Myth of School Violence

Chapter 1

The Presence of the Myth

The myth of school violence states that a child in distress within the confines of the school is the victim of a violent reality emanating from outside the school. Hence, the discussion on this distress is, by its very nature, a discussion of violent behavior and its results.[7] Violence is the way in which children express their distress and, in doing so, cause distress to other children and to teachers. This is a logic that clearly differentiates between children's undesirable behavior within the confines of the school and their life outside school, where they live in a violent society. The exposure to television, violent computer games, and family violence from which many children suffer are the chief reasons for children's sense of distress. Ultimately it manifests itself in a series of violent modes of behavior that are causally connected and create added distress both for the violent children and for their friends and teachers, who become their victims. The predetermined pattern appears in the life of the school in the form of an inexorable slide into gradually deteriorating behavior: beginning with being defiant and disrespectful to teachers, to recalci-

---

[7] There are generally two different meanings to the term myth: One refers to an accepted view that is false, and the appellate myth indicates our intention to negate or reexamine it. The second meaning of myth is of a traditional story that has become part of discourse or the world of images of a culture, nd use of the term shows an intention to refer to tradition and culture. My use of the term relates principally to the first meaning, but, indirectly, also to the second.

trance and rebellion against authority, to violent communication, vandalism, and physical violence, and ending, according to this reasoning, in actual delinquency: theft, inflicting terror, extortion, and, in the older age-groups, drug use and even rape and murder. These latter phenomena are often linked to school dropout. The internal logic assumes a connection between children's distress in their relationships with their parents, expressed in stealing a friend's pencil in Grade 2, and the possibility of decline into serious delinquency at age fifteen due to detachment from the school's authority, which has destructive consequences for the individual's personality and behavior. However, the school itself does not create distress. It defends itself against the violent products of distress and attempts to protect the children against them. According to this logic, what is done inside the school stands in stark contrast to the external violence; school is a safe haven for children in distress, since it provides the normative option, which does not permit distress to be translated into violence.

Moreover, schools are operated by adults with professions and humanistic values, who have chosen education out of the belief in a better future, a just society, and have even undergone training for years in order to give children an education and imbue them with values. These good people do their utmost to alert children to, and prevent children from embarking on, the route of violence and dropping-out, explain that it necessarily leads to an unavoidable, linear sinking into tragedy. The problem is that in recent decades, there has been a significant increase in the scale and severity of violence imported into schools from the street and the home, with a parallel increase in parents' and children's awareness of their rights, which has significantly restricted the teachers' range of possible responses. This must all be seen against the background of the increased demand by the authorities and the public for teachers to do something about the mounting violence. The unavoidable consequences are severe burnout of the adults in schools, the inability and/or the absence of pedagogic tools to contend with discipline problems and violence, fear of imposing sanctions, and despair and foregoing of ideals. According to this logic, the process reaches a peak with the transformation of the teachers into the children's victims.

Putting aside for the moment the suspicion that humanistic ideals are *not* the heritage of educators, I wish to cast doubt on the correctness of the above theory and perhaps even question the very possibility of its existing in the context and situation prevailing in schools today. To this end I will attempt to explore the internal logic of the separation between the school and the distress of the children attending it:

(1) External source versus internal practice: The internal logic guiding the actions of the school derives solely from what is perceived as the good of the child and the good of society. Since people are social creatures, in at least some spheres, there is no significant contradiction between the two. This is learned in teacher's college; it exists in the pedagogic books and constitutes the cornerstone of educational thinking, which guides the educational process and from which it is apparently derived: that same range of activities to which every child is exposed when he or she starts school. The school's structured intentionalism presents itself as egalitarian, neutral, and tolerant. Even if this is sometimes mere false pretension and, instead, discrimination, abuse of authority, covert and overt racism, sexism, and so forth, are present in the school, the latter do not belong to the structural logic of the educational institution. Rather, they belong to an external phenomenon, a normal human problem of disparity between good intentions and the ability to apply them, a disparity between planning and execution. The real problem is that the school's intentional activity takes place in the framework of a violent, grim, and alienating reality. Children are sometimes the victims of violence at home and in the street and therefore imitate patterns of violent behavior they see on television, in the cinema, and video games. If they do not integrate well into the school framework for personal reasons—related to their personalities, homes, and/or the organic structure of their brains—the school is then faced with an objective difficulty to act in their best interests.

(2) Discipline and authority versus impulse, nature, and environment: Children beginning school arrive with a very meager

store of knowledge, no orderly work habits, a lack of discipline, and patterns of action and response that do not permit structured, reflective thinking, a condition for fulfilling their personal potentials. The school's structured work is intended to teach children skills, habits, and boundaries that will enable them to maximize their personal abilities as well as afford them the socialization needed to express those abilities at the social level and to shape them as exemplary productive, tax-paying citizens. To this end, the school employs a graded structure of tasks appropriate for children's developmental stages, a curriculum based on scientific rationalism, and enables them to develop abstract thinking and elucidation of theories—an accessible, intelligible body of knowledge and a series of instructions and rules of social behavior representing the wider culture, which assist the child to become "cultured". Being cultured, the child controls his or her impulses, is self-disciplined, and has the ability to communicate with others and think rationally. In this sense, modern schools strive to constitute an opposition to barbarism, interpreted as savagery, sentimentalism, absence of boundaries, absence of values, concreteness, and violence. Thus, it is highly likely that the school is required to exert a certain extent of force and restraint, interpreted by critics of schools as violence, which schools prefer to call "discipline" and is essential both to achieving minimal preliminary conditions for working with children and to "undoing" previous habits. Indeed, discipline and order are imperative for significant learning to take place. In certain cases, the setting of these norms and procedures may produce frustration, interpreted by some of the children some of the time as real distress. However, we have to distinguish between the exercise of reasonable force, intended to improve a situation and out of loyalty to the children themselves, and arbitrary violence, which is intended to humiliate, repress, and achieve the personal goals of the enforcer.

(3) Pressure as a means of positive formation: Educational activity presupposes the exertion of pressure because it is defined as a formative activity. Education is shaping a person according to a desired model, irrespective of the question: What is the desired model? It is clear that a measure of repression and coercion

is necessary to shape, to achieve a change. However, the exertion of pressure is not only repression and coercion, but a genuine contribution to the maturation process and preparation of each child for life, for life outside the school, in the family, in society, and at work induces many and complex pressure situations for people. Every school graduate will be required to handle tasks, decipher complex situations, respond to surprises, and cope with a turbulent life. In this sense, the school performs an important service for children when it prepares them to cope with situations that demand concentration, handling tasks, contending with objective procedures that appear arbitrary, competing with others, success in examinations, and so forth. Any interpretation of the pressures exerted on children by the school, as the creation of distress is no more than a distortion of reality and the presentation of the important preparation process provided by the school for the benefit of the children as an activity directed against them. Moreover, the children themselves, as part of their developmental process, demonstrate a need for competition, comparison with others, excellence, etc. These natural and/or cultural tendencies may become disastrous, an opening to violence, hostility, and frustration. The school's great advantage is precisely in the translation of those natural tendencies of children into practices of "positive competition", "equal opportunity", and "fair rules of the game".

(4) The connection between success at school and a normal life: The simplest claim (and the most mistaken) that differentiates between school and the sense of distress is that it is clear that the school does not create distress, but, rather, prevents it. The most convincing proof of this is to look at the difference between school graduates, or those who have been successful students, and school dropouts. The majority of graduates manage to conduct normal, orderly, and productive lives—a in other words, they live a "good life"—whereas a considerable proportion of the dropouts live hard, often violent lives, lives of distress. Thus, even if schools only succeed with some of the children, it follows that the school is a framework that combats distress and prevents distress in a systematic manner.

However, this logic is not just theoretical. It manifests itself in the way the school is built and in the way the teaching activities and curricula are derived from the overall conception. A school is a defined, stable place (generally built from concrete blocks); it is essentially loco-centric and radiates permanence and time-lessness. It is a shelter because it operates outside the reach of adult society and outside the bounds of the existential jungle and conducts itself according to its own laws. In other words, it is a kind of greenhouse protecting the children and enabling them to develop in conditions that suit them. To this end, the school re-cruits adults who have been professionally trained to nurture and teach children, whose training includes child psychology, spe-cially adapted teaching methods, amongst other things. A school is also a social institution. It meets the public criteria that justify its existence, as it is the most important place for the socializa-tion of the individual, for turning him or her into an educated person who is useful to society. It also accepts external scientific and objective criteria to examine its activities and achievements and, as such, serves as an example of a rational institution that fosters personal and social rationalism. The school's curriculum combines public consent, consensus with regard to the values and knowledge worthy of being taught, as well as the methods and academic criterion for examining this content. Despite hav-ing an important personal dimension, teaching activities strive for the maximum objectivity, uniformity, and effectiveness re-quired of a respectable social institution.

Furthermore, it is important to remember that a school is also a flexible institution, accepting the need to change, in accor-dance both with changes in society and with the development of scientific knowledge. Thus, it is evident that schools are opening their doors more and more to parents, who are becoming part-ners in the educational endeavor as part of the social changes in the functioning of the family and in the division of responsibility between society and school. It is also evident that the strict hier-archy that characterized the organizational structure of schools in the past is being tempered by structural changes intended to involve parents and teachers, while taking account of the chil-dren, in the decision-making processes. Schools are striving to renew themselves, to change their teaching methods, to get new ideas and adapt their curricula to innovations in science and to changing public (political) directives. Schools are also able to accept criticism, and most of the changes in recent years originate from this ability, particularly with respect to criticism of their commitment to children. Hence, schools have adopted disciplinary teaching tactics and practice alternative assessment methods; they try to offer children more choice; they have introduced consultation and specialist work, such as diagnostic experts and psychologists. All this is intended to meet the various needs of the children in an appropriate manner, in order to achieve both effectiveness and maximum humanity. This logic largely constitutes the aggregate of the self-image of the majority of people involved in education. It is the way in which teachers and, subsequently, many parents and children have perceived school.

In contrast to this logic presenting the modern school, with all its practices, in a positive light, over the years there has been a great deal of criticism challenging the above description of the school, presenting, instead, the hard, alienating, and violent visage of schools.

The most familiar criticism refers to the disparity between intentions and reality. The theory behind the criticism assumes that school activity does, indeed, rest on a basis of good intentions, but in practice, the school does not manage to offer a protective and nurturing learning environment for children, not even for some of them. We know that prejudice, racism, and chauvinism are present in today's schools, that a significant amount of the teachers are not suited to educational work, and that some of the procedures in the school are determined arbitrarily on the basis of power and interests. Schools do not succeed to integrate the various cultural and ethnic groups. There are many instances of abuse of authority and employment of violence by adults against children. A school's resources frequently do not correspond with the pedagogic planning, and the curriculum is outdated and does not prepare the children for life. Overall, the public school system does not meet the expectations it had of itself, neither in the normative sphere nor in the academic sphere. This line of criticism is well known to parents and decision-makers. It is part of the public discourse in the media in industrialized countries and, in a certain sense, the most effective criticism because in the past it dictated (and still dictates) most of the attempts at improvement and reform in the public education system.

Hyman and Snook[8] are examples of this type of criticism. They argue that the American school at the end of the twentieth century is a danger to children's physical and mental well-being, despite being less dangerous than the street. The dangers to which the child is exposed when attending school include abuse by adults. Hyman, who, for years, has been a determined opponent of corporal punishment in the American education system, rails against the fact that the despite significant advances in legislation and public opinion, corporal punishment still exists in a considerable number of schools in certain states in the United States. Worse yet, there are active advocates of this kind of punishment, who are employed primarily in schools in the neighborhoods of African-Americans, minorities, and the poor.[9] Moreover, many school children are in a state of physical distress, suffering from hunger, injuries, lack of sleep, and so forth. This distress is neglected by the relevant adults and does not receive suitable treatment in school.

No less perilous is the psychological danger of schools. Hyman and Snook report many cases of children who have suffered humiliation, avoidance, corporal punishment, ridicule from teachers, employment of pressure tactics, of psychological terror, to create a feeling of guilt and a feeling of "there is something wrong with me". In extreme cases, Hyman and Snook re-

---

[8] I.A. Hyman & P.A. Snook, *Dangerous Schools*, Jossey-Bass, San Francisco, 1999, use the expression "toxic schools", echoing the expression "toxic parents" coined by Susan Forward in the popular psychologist literature in the United States, which identifies demons and gremlins wherever injustice is done (and where a hefty compensation claim can be made).
[9] Ibid. pp. 41, 42.

port, children have reached crisis situations, some reaching the severity of post-traumatic syndrome, requiring prolonged external psychological treatment.[10] In many schools, double standards in the way teachers relate to children and the real injury to the children's natural sense of justice are detectable. The violence of certain teachers manifests itself in the common phenomenon of translating the teacher's helplessness with respect to an active, naughty child into the image of the child as a monster. This entitles teachers to drug children (Ritalin), fail them, and exclude them from school, as well as generally continue to mistreat them.

This important line of criticism is extremely influential. It induces parents to demand better protection for their children at school and exerts pressure on schools to be mindful of their obligations. It also allows parents and many schools to wash their hands of the problem and feel that "it doesn't happen here—we are just fine." The problem with this type of criticism is that it is only partial: it presents symptoms that appear starkly in certain places, particularly at the social margins, and does not manage to establish a more general claim. It ignores the general social processes and bases itself on humanistic school thinking as a possible description of reality impaired by untrained people and bureaucratic, opaque public machinery. The painful human drama endured by the children, as described in the criticism, does not reflect the rule. It represents the exception that proves the rule.

Another line of criticism takes a pedagogic tack. The public school is a learning framework constructed to socialize the individual—namely, to restrain, train, and shape him or her according to an externally determined model. Hence, by definition, school education as a formative educational activity entails the employment of violence by society on the individual. Schools do not intend to realize, nor can they afford to worry about realizing, the talents, abilities, and inclinations of every child, and the humanistic thinking merely cloaks a process of repression that

---

[10] Ibid. p. 53 *ff.*

detaches children from their authentic natures, eradicates their curiosity, and represses their creativity. As such, the school is a systematic creator of distress, particularly for talented, creative, and "special" children, who tend not to conform to the normative mediocrity imposed on them. However, this does not only apply to exceptional children. It is very likely that all children, were they not the victims of the school steamroller, would express a wealth of hidden talents.

This criticism does not distinguish between intention and implementation. On the contrary, it is precisely the school's success at implementing the outdated curriculum and the coercive teaching methods that presents the greatest threat to the individual. The criticism also does not distinguish between different pupils: the coercive processes apply to everyone, and the attempt to create uniformity, standardization, and equality are the root of the problem and the principal source of children's distress in school. This criticism has been well received in liberal circles and is mainly identified with the open stream of education, which strives to create coercion-free learning frameworks or to abolish frameworks altogether. It has been presented in the doctrines of educational thinkers from Tolstoy to Neal and of avowed liberals like Russell, who preached the abolition of institutional coercion on the individual in the name of individuation as an educational ideal.

A characteristic example of this line of criticism can be found in Postman's description of the school as a place where passive absorption is a more preferable response to ideas than is an active critical approach[11]. The former approach presumes that expressing an opinion is beyond the capabilities of school pupils and not something to concern them, and it characterizes memorizing as the supreme form of intellectual achievement and amassing unconnected facts as the goal of education. Public schools determine that the voice of authority is worthy of greater trust and appreciation than is self-judgment and that pupils' ideas are inconsequential. They avoid emotional feelings by arguing

---

[11] N. Postman & Ch. Weingartner, *Teaching as a Subversive Activity*, Delacorte Press, New York, 1975, pp. 31-32.

that they are not relevant to education; they take possession of knowledge and try to teach that there has always been a "right" answer to every question.

In the face of this school reality, critics have proposed various types of education alternatives based mainly on the self-directed learner, on natural curiosity, free choice of contents and strategies, creativity, and the pupil's total access to sources of knowledge. Also included is the scrapping of the hierarchy between teacher and pupil and its conversion into an instrumental relationship of information-provider and information-consumer.

The problem with this critique is primarily methodological. It does not differentiate between cause and effect, or, more precisely, it confuses the two. It describes the school reality well, but relates to it as a reason, as the cause of social ills, as a reality that dictates social mediocrity that impairs the ability of society to allow the individual to express his or her talents and so forth. However, it consistently avoids the imperceptible processes, the element of necessity in the school reality, the distressing fact that the school reality is the result of wider social and institutional processes and not of the malevolence of teachers or vague bureaucratic stupidity. Hence, the optimism exuded by the liberal critics with regard to the possibility of change is exaggerated; it ignores, first and foremost, the lack of any real possibility of achieving public education under the heading of "individuation" and the fact that the proposed liberal education has been and always will be beyond the reach of the lower classes.[12] Not surprisingly, when Postman and Weingartner proposed the liberal option as a "subversive alternative",[13] it was intended (they said) for middle-class children at high school and headed for academic study, not for the deprived members of society, who were in any event not going to have the benefit of an open, creative, enjoyable, and futuristic education.

---

[12] On this issue, see Kozol's critique in this Chapter, Section B.
[13]. This was after they suggested a physicalist explanatory model of social atrophy and the supposedly subversive possibility of schools forming a basis for anti-antrophy.

The most extreme expression of the line of criticism that views schools as the source of society's ills, as a cause and not an effect, was suggested by Ivan Illich. According to Illich, the modern school is not a framework for socializing the individual for society and, particularly, not for the community. It is socialization for the school itself, which, over the years, has become something of a robotic bureaucratic giant, with its own rules and internal logic and which demands of the children that they relinquish their personalities, uniqueness, curiosity, and desire to learn for "learning's sake" in order to accept a system of narratives and hierarchic rules of operation all intended to preserve and sustain the institution's existence. In fact, Illich claims, school is a "radical monopoly", that, like Coca Cola, not only bears the responsibility of providing the product ("Education"), but also creates the very need it is supposed to satisfy. It is the school that has created the myth of "Education" in industrialized societies and the belief that the school is the only place where the desired product—"Education"—can be acquired. The school also created the identification of "Education" with "education", thus expanding the scope of its monopoly, and distinguished between those who accept the teacher's definition of reality and those who get an "Education" outside the reach of the school and therefore are deemed as "uneducated". In this way the school created both the total dependence on them and the basis for social inequality. The school, according to Illich, is a place where no learning whatsoever takes place, because it creates confusion in the pupil between teaching and learning. It does not allow children to acquire skills because it operates according to a curriculum, and moreover, "If school is an unsuitable place for learning skills, it is worse than that for everything concerned with education."[14] "Education" according to Illich is learning for its own sake, which has been exchanged for learning about school for its own sake.

---

[14] Ivan Illich, "Why We Must Abolish Schooling", *New York Review of Books*, July 2, 1970; "Schooling, the Ritual Process", *New York Review of Books*, December 3, 1970.

Illich's educational alternative is the abolition of schools and the transfer of the entire educational process to the community. In the community envisioned by Illich, every child will be given maximum access to the information sources by way of a community education service (libraries, laboratories, museums, etc.). The pupil will receive a list of skilled experts for whom he or she can apprentice. The pupils will be part of the community communications network that will transfer and share information and will also offer the possibility to benefit from an adult-child encounter, similar to apprenticeship with an expert.

This critique raises two problems: One, which I have already stressed, is the confusion of cause with effect. The school is not a creator of society, and it bears no resemblance to a radical monopoly like Coca Cola (which does, indeed, shape society and create inequality and over-consumerism). Schools are outmoded social institutions that exist within the growing disparity between their self-image and the reality they inhabit and attempt, with quite meager resources, to continue to survive in a reality in which they are becoming less and less relevant. This is not the threatening, monstrous giant Illich described. Illich's second mistake concerns the alternative. The more appealing it is made to look (and I have to admit that except for the encounter between the youngster and the adult, I cannot see much appeal in it), the further removed it becomes from reality.

Where exactly can communities of this sort be found? And even if they do exist, how will they organize themselves to provide the described education services? And what if the members of the community are not Illich sympathizers and do not believe in self-direction and apprenticeship? In order to create a process at the end of which a community education autonomy will be built, a far more complex vision is needed than that provided by Illich. It is not an objectionable vision, but it emanates from a reality in which the concept of community is changing and, to a certain extent, radically so, to the point of total disintegration.

Illich's starting point is that children's education is a unifying force, which should provide a basis for optimism and community renewal, but he does not delineate the process by which this renewal can take place. In any event, this sort of vision will not be an answer for the lower classes, as the communities in which there could be such organization and where resources for structuring education outside of school could be found (in other words, not funded by the state) are those of the middle to upper classes.[15]

Another line of criticism, which is my starting point for this book, rejects the basic description of the school as an institution constructed and operating for the benefit of the individual. This critique is based on the assumption that schools, like any other social institution, are part of the superstructure of society that is intended to ensure the preservation of society's production relations. School is a segregative institution directed at the academic and, consequently, the social and economic success of a privileged minority of pupils, generally from the upper social classes, while allowing the lower classes a certain margin of mobility (for reasons of public relations and/or out of socio-economic necessity). A school's operational modes are clearly derived from this goal and, accordingly, are based on discrimination, preference for the strong, employment of institutional violence against minorities, women, and the poor and, in short, anyone who does not belong to the bourgeois success model.

This criticism opposes the humanistic image of the school, for two reasons: first rejecting it as an instance of hypocrisy and pretense, a pathetic attempt to rationalize the mechanisms of discrimination and repression in the guise of equal opportunity; second, because in many cases, it is precisely in subscribing to a humanistic perspective that a school is led to being violent. Indeed, modernistic thinking is based *a priori* on clear assumptions about nature, culture, science, and thought; it differentiates sharply between correct and incorrect, between good and bad, and between a savant and an ignoramus. This is a chauvinistic,

---

[15] In the U.S. in particular, we are witnessing the expanding home-schooling movement, which, in certain places, involves a number of families organizing themselves to provide education services for their children. This movement is generally the realm of the middle-class to upper-class.

paternalistic way of thinking that accentuates European values and both overtly and covertly suppresses any attempt at different thinking, creativity, values, and cognitive and cultural preferences that deviate from the mainstream of the dominant culture. This critique portrays schools as repressive, discriminatory, and violent institutions vis-à-vis some of the children, usually from the lower social classes. Schools are indeed built to foster, to train, and, to some extent, even to respond to the emotional and intellectual needs of middle- and upper-class children (generally male); but as such, not only are they not striving for equality, they are systematically thwarting the possibility of ever achieving it.

At this juncture, I want to take a critical line and argue that the myth that distinguishes between schools and the creation of distress is itself a mechanism of repression in the sense that it directly threatens the possibility of some of the children surviving school in a useful way. The starting point for this argument is the assumption that the school staff and the parents adopt the myth that views school as protection against child-to-child violence. It is reasonable to assume that this is a natural process of rationalization, since no teacher or any other educator has an interest in seeing himself or herself as repressive, discriminating, or violent. The majority of teachers enter education out of either idealism or else the ease of acceptance and availability, but it seems to me that there are precious few teachers who have chosen teaching out of revenge or sadism (despite the fact that from a child's point of view, it appears this way); at least these motivations are not present at the outset of their careers. Parents are hardly in a better position. There is no worse feeling for a parent than knowing each morning that you are sending your child right into a lion's den, where he or she is bound to undergo a process of repression, humiliation, terror, and arbitrariness. It is better to assume that the school is a place with good intentions, and even if it encounters difficulties, it is not to blame either for children's distress or for the school reality. The blame lies with the overall social reality, with those few children who come from violent homes, or, in extreme cases, with an unfit teacher.

The distinction made between school practice and distress is part of the professional self-image of teachers, principals, and educators in general, and it forms the basis of the rationalization process represented by the myth of distress and the school as a whole.

However, the moment that the distinction becomes part of the myth, it "gains" an active status. In addition to the fact that it represents the psychological needs of teachers and perhaps of parents, it is also significant in the creation of children's distress. Teachers' inner belief that all their activities are done "for the children" places the children in a strange position, where any feeling of distress, frustration, or anger stemming from arbitrariness, obtuseness, or humiliation from the teachers is automatically handed back to the children, since the teachers are working for the children and know better than the children themselves what is good for them. Thus, the moment a child feels that a teacher's action is harming him, it is clear that something is wrong with *him, the child*. Teachers can be nothing other than "good", and what place do children have if they do not feel comfortable in the place allocated to them by the "good, all-knowing" teacher? After all, the internal logic of the way in which adults perceive themselves decrees that a child attending school has no chance of opposing the teacher's dictates without automatically being classified as a "bad" or "stupid" as not knowing what is good for him. This is an obvious example of the way in which the myth that attempts to dissociate the relationships between adults and children in schools from distress becomes an instrument for creating the very distress it is keen to deny.

In critical research on schools, a distinction is normally made between personal violence (including verbal and physical violence mainly between children and sometimes between teacher and pupil) and what is called systemic, or institutional, violence, which refers to the way in which the institution imposes its procedures and policies on the individual by discriminating against, repressing, and acting arbitrarily toward some of the children. An acceptable definition of systemic violence is the following:

Systemic violence is any institutionalized practice or procedure that adversely impacts on disadvantaged individuals or groups. The adverse effects can be seen in psychological, mental, cultural, spiritual, economic, or physical burdens ... . Systemic violence in schools includes those practices and procedures that prevent students from learning.[16]

This definition is affirmed by a series of analyses of administration, procedures, and pedagogy, which demonstrate how hiding behind innocent-looking, so-called objective school procedures are structured sets of expectations that represent the norms of the powerful people in control of society, which are foisted on anyone who does not meet the official narrative's linguistic, cultural, and behavioral standards.

Among the various examples presented in the literature for this type of violence is the claim that the organizational structure of the school is hierarchical and formalistic, measures the staff in careerist terms, and quickly adjusts to organizational models from the business world, which are characterized by a striving for efficiency and output, aggressive marketing, and achieving results.[17] Since it is bureaucratic, the school is characterized by the depersonalization of the people operating in it, which suits some of the teachers and pupils but impairs the ability of others to learn. And because it is hierarchic, it *a priori* produces scales that grade some of the participants (teachers and pupils) permanently in inferior positions. Here, again, it is clear who is situated at the top of the scale.

Another claim relates to the world of concepts—the school's administrative language, which dictates a reality and a world of images that constitute instruments of repression. One of the best examples of this type of violence is the reference to school man-

---

[16] J.R. Epp & A.M. Watkinson, eds., *Systemic Violence in Education*, Suny, Albany, 1997, p. xiv. This is in fact a definition that appears in Canadian legislation to which Epp and Watkinson added the feature once suggested by Freire, namely, institutional violence as a type of learning prevention.

[17] C. Hodgkinson, *Educational Leadership: The Moral Art*, Suny, Albany, 1991.

agement in terms of military organization. In fact, the domi-
nance of military language and the masculine world of images
appear in the context of almost every management theory. This
is translated into operations of the strategic-planning type; de-
voting a comprehensive discussion to the school principal's con-
siderations of the "human factor", it includes various types of
tactical instructions and integrates well with expressions employed by teachers such as "controlling the class" and "setting
boundaries". But what are military language and this type of
thinking doing in a school? As Watkinson asks, "Who is the enemy here? What exactly is the objective that has to be captured?
Is the school at war? Or, perhaps the language and the imagery
connected to it 'manufacture' the enemy, or more precisely, the
pupil as an enemy of the school?"[18]

Other examples of institutional violence emerge from the
systematic exposure to the continued presence of prejudice, hidden racism and sexism, and discrimination based thereon, even
in schools that are convinced they are irreproachable and among
teachers who consider themselves liberal and open-minded. One
of the most interesting findings appears in research conducted by
Tite,[19] who examined the different ways in which teachers reported child abuse after they were required to do so as part of a
broader public-legislative effort in Canada. The teachers were
required to report on suspicion of abuse, symptoms of abuse,
and its characteristics (physical, psychological, sexual). Two
findings came to light: The one was the fact that the male teachers reported on child abuse differently from the female teachers.
The difference was in the reporting of the actual occurrence of
the abuse (for instance, in the case of sexual abuse, which tended
not to be noticed by the men) and with regard to reporting of the
severity of the abuse (which also tended to be noted as negligible or pardonable when the reporter was male). The other finding was that the teachers in general (men and women) displayed

---

[18]A.M.Watkinson, "Administrative Complicity and Systemic Violence", in Epp, 1997, p. 9.
[19] R. Tite, "Who Knows? Who Cares? Schools and Coordinated Action on Child Abuse", in Epp, 1997, pp. 37-55.

a strange tendency to distance themselves from the report and to ignore abuse of children. According to Tite,

> We need to focus our attention on the institutional context of systemic violence which gives shape to teachers' reactions to children and to suspicions of child abuse. ...There is a kind of ponderous veil of caution at the agency level which guards against bringing teachers into the heart of the matter. For all the policy and research and talk about involving the schools in the problem, getting people to listen and talk to teachers about child abuse remains mysteriously elusive.[20]

What emerges from Tite's claim is that institutional violence is already present in the manner in which adults view children, in their reading of reality. What also emerges is that the ability of teachers to see child abuse, much less respond or act, is extremely limited. This limitation means ignoring distress, which, in turn, means that the institutional reality allows, and possibly even causes, adults to neglect the most fundamental human obligation inherent in the educational endeavor and, perhaps, in simple humanity generally: awareness of the distress of the helpless and, in the context of the school, distress of the child.

The distinction between institutional violence and personal violence is important. First, because the dissociation of school and violence, as described above, does not apply to systemic violence: even if schools can claim that personal violence is not within their realm of responsibility, they cannot ignore the criticism regarding systemic violence. Second, because the distinction draws attention away from the overt, vocalized, symptomatic aspect of the violence phenomenon to hidden processes that are felt less and linked to apparently neutral or taken-for-granted activities and procedures, despite their not being anything of the sort. Third, the distinction assumes a direct and indirect causal link between personal violence and institutional violence, and that part of the physical violence that children display toward their friends and teachers originates in the school's insti-

---

[20] Ibid. p. 53.

tutional violence, which creates an atmosphere of alienation and discrimination.

However, the importance of the critical claim actually lies in reversing the link between distress and violent behavior. Under this claim, children's distress at school could appear to be a *result* of the operation of the school apparatus itself, which is a fundamentally violent activity and not the *cause* of the child's future violent behavior. The importance of these distinctions aside, my approach to the children's distress in schools and the link between it and violence on the part of the school is slightly different, and in order to explain it, I will return to Epp and Watkinson's definition presented above. Under this definition, the principal difficulty inherent to systemic violence manifests itself in the prevention of learning. This argument is completely understandable against the background of the research convention that links the possibility for social mobility with education: as a member of a minority or immigrant, to succeed in extricating oneself from poverty, improving one's economic and social standing, and integrating into society, one must acquire a formal education. Hence, it is the role of social criticism to identify the school mechanisms that prevent learning, thereby preventing access to formal education, pushing certain children out of the system, and, in any event, precluding any possibility of social mobility.

Yet despite its clarity, this definition, in my view, is too narrow. First, I am not certain of the validity of the research convention that links learning with social mobility, particularly in the present era in which the link between the acquisition of relevant knowledge and formal education is tenuous. Second, even if preventing learning is, indeed, a result of institutional violence, it is certainly not the only one. This violence has far-reaching effects on the mental, intellectual, and social life of every individual who is affected by it, far beyond merely impeding learning. Third, the definition emphasizes the institutional aspect of the coercion and obscures the fact that school regulations and procedures are planned and executed by people. In many senses, the potency of school abuse of children is derived from the sad fact that it is perpetrated by adults who are trusted by the children and with whom they expect to have decent human contact. The school myth is intended to deny the violence employed against some of the children in public schools. The denial process occurs by means of severing the link between the violence and school practice, on the one hand, and locating and identifying distress factors responsible for children's violence outside of school, on the other. This process means avoidance, denial, or, at best, impotence with regard to the children's distress; since the distress is caused by factors outside the school, the school bears no responsibility for it and is not relevant in terms of contending with it. Thus, the school must, in fact, relinquish its awareness of the emotional, social, and individual needs of those pupils in distress, particularly those children whose distress is the direct result of the violent practices of the school itself, which it denies by means of the myth. The pinnacle of the process is expressed as the severance of the connection between the school and the welfare of the children. The school redefines itself as a "learning factory", its only concern being teaching, through a mistaken identification of learning with teaching.[21] The role of teachers is to teach, just teach, which becomes a synonym for education. Teachers are not trained to deal with (nor are they interested in dealing with) children's welfare. That is the role of social workers and psychologists, and generally, education has nothing whatsoever to contribute to children's emotional worlds. (It could be argued that one of the important factors bringing the process to a peak is the liberal critique that seeks to dispel any pretense by adults that schools "educate", thereby providing the rationalization for being content with "just teaching".)

My claim regarding this point is an essentially simple one: The school is the manufacturer of institutional and personal violence; it is a direct cause of distress for some children, mainly

---

[21] It is completely clear that there is no significant connection between what is learnt and what is taught. But the concept of the "learning factory" creates such a connection by means of the image of a production line where there is a causal-logical relationship between product and yield and process and means of production.

those most in need of protection, nurturing, and academic achievement. Given this reality and in light of the underlying promise of educational ideology, which is the domain of the adults, the school has a moral and professional responsibility to ensure the welfare of these same children.

However, if the way in which school staff view themselves and their activity as good people acting honestly and devotedly for all (or at least most) of the children stands in such great contrast to the repressive reality of school as a discriminating, violent institution, how can one explain the simultaneous existence of such different views of reality? After all, the staff are not blind, and it is reasonable to assume that were they to get up in the morning and go to work intending to arrive at a learning paradise, but in practice get to a hell that resembles a penal colony, they would soon come to their senses and either abandon the good, beneficent image and try to change the reality or, alternatively, beat a hasty retreat from there while they still could.

But the situation is more complex; the human, liberal image of schools is quite realistic. There are schools where life for children and adults is tolerable, even pleasant. Indeed, in schools where the reality is harsher, there are many classes and lessons in which a humane, learning interaction takes place that feeds the positive image teachers have of themselves. Also, the personal experiences of teachers who have survived the absorption process in the school include significant events interpreted by them as positive. The teachers managed to give interesting lessons, succeeded in getting pupils through examinations in which they displayed knowledge they did not have beforehand, managed to explain some materials to pupils who understood virtually nothing, and so forth.

To a certain extent, even in terms of the personal experiences of the majority of pupils, school is not a black-and-white reality: "Even if the teacher does not understand me, even if I feel estranged and alienated, and I have been a victim of violence here and there, there were also pleasant moments—sometimes with friends, sometimes also with teachers."

But if we were to examine, as a crude generalization, all those wonderful schools, those successful lessons, positive learning experiences, we would quickly discover that they are schools operating in well-established neighborhoods, that the classes comprise children who excel, and that positive experiences are generally the prerogative of children with high self-esteem. We would also discover that the pleasant school moments, when joy and creativity appeared, are the moments when childhood *joie de vivre* is discovered, which originates in the children themselves and in their amazing life force and not necessarily in activities performed by teachers.

The existence of "good" schools, the presence of children who excel and the ability of teachers to give some of the children the feedback that builds for them a self-image of being of value all permit the simultaneous existence of school as a nurturing and growth framework for some of the children and its existence as an institution that discriminates and is violent and neglectful of other children. "Failure" is a state essential to the education system, as it enables relative excellence to exist. It is the air that the school breathes; it is a gift to and gives meaning to the professional lives of people involved in teaching and the public lives of education leaders. It also ensures the continued budgetary and political existence of the national education system as a whole.

Paradoxically, schools accomplish their social purpose precisely with those children who do not succeed in meeting the achievement criteria they set. An accepted premise is that the average school is suitable only for the top 30% of its pupils and that it is not built to serve the 70% who are not destined for further academic education.

A more critical look shows that the main significance of the process of public school apprenticeship is the creation of a low social image for the majority of pupils in a manner that makes them come to terms with a future life suited to the social division of labor: "Since I was not outstanding in class, it seems I am not sufficiently talented, and anyway it is clear that I am not worthy of significant social roles, of an influential position, or a high-income profession." Underlying the competitive-segregative method of the school curriculum is the hidden goal of psychologically training most of the pupils for non-influential social positions. This curriculum is constructed on the measurement of output according to the relative performances of pupils. In other words, it always defines half of the pupils as below average and, from among the other half, differentiates between those who are outstanding and those who are only "okay"; it can never rest on a definite measure that enables all pupils to succeed to the same extent, for instance.

The competitive structure determines that each time a majority of pupils or, to be precise, "too many" pupils manage a learning task, the crossbar has to be raised so that the percentage of those who succeed corresponds with a certain distribution of success in a competitive society. Not surprisingly, despite the fact that the language in which the curriculum is formulated is taken from a series of objective output descriptions (like, for instance, "to get the child to master the four arithmetic operations"), in practice a completely different process has to take place to preclude a large proportion of the children from achieving that mastery. If the goal of the curriculum were, indeed, to get all the children to a certain level of performance, irrespective of what it is, we would witness situations in which most of the children, or all of them, were getting full marks or, alternatively, where there were no marks at all.

What emerges from this analysis is that this is not a case of disparity between a humanistic image and a repressive reality. The image itself is part of the school reality in practice; it exists tangibly, because, in the nature of images, it does not only describe a desirable imaginary reality, but also affects and creates realities in practice. But the nature of the realities that materialize in the wake of the presence of a school's humanistic self-image is not uniform. It is subject to the logic of the social disparity as presented in the critical analysis; namely, from the perspective of some of the "good" pupils and the majority of teachers, they experience what could be interpreted as learning. This experience reinforces and legitimizes persistence of the beneficent image, while another, very great part of the children, who did not have the privilege of participating in the realization of the school image, have a totally different and depressing experience.

The repression is threefold: the first time, it is the repression of children by means of institutional violence; it represses them a second time by branding the teachers as "good" and the children as "bad"; and it represses them a third time by defining them as failures, as "knowing nothing", as opposed to those who succeed and "know" and, therefore, realize the school's self-image.

Chapter 2

The Problematics of Education's Objectives

The school's mythological life is not embodied only in the professional self-image of the teaching personnel. It encompasses a whole world of debate, images, and theories that describe desired school practice. These are theories that lend meaning to children's being together with groups of strange adults in public buildings during the course of most of the day for long, tiring years. These are theories based on which educational theorists and thinkers present objectives for school curricula and desirable modes of behavior and on which the school institution is evaluated, judged, and financed.

All educational theories are agreed that their successful translation into the school's humanitarian activity is achieved through the transmission of knowledge or, in today's more acceptable formulation (after much criticism of the modern school), giving the pupils the possibility to acquire knowledge for themselves. A school is a place for acquiring knowledge, and this acquisition is the basis for and principal definer of educational activity. There is consensus with regard to this across virtually all people working in the field of education, including the various critics of schools from the different streams.

The big debate in educational thinking is not focused on the question of whether "Knowledge" is the goal of schools, but on two other questions. The one is: What is the intended purpose of knowledge acquired in school? And the other, whose answer is derived from the first question, is: What is the knowledge that the school is supposed to instill, enable, or even create for its pupils? A number of contradicting answers have been given to these questions over the history of educational thought, each in accordance with the ideological-educational perceptions of those replying to these two questions.

Continuing the classification suggested by Lamm,[1] I will mention three of the classical answers that still seem relevant, because they appear in one form or another and time and again in educational theory and criticism of it.

The first answer of the three is based on the operational definition of knowledge: knowledge means an array of information, contexts, skills, and behaviors that enable the child approaching maturity to function as a useful member of society. Knowledge is a means of socializing the individual for society. It is the manner in which society imposes its values and norms on the individual, on the one hand, and on the other hand, the way in which individuals acquire the information and skills that will enable them to conduct productive lives in their social environments, a life of freedom and choice, with a degree of autonomy, by means of the social legitimacy they will acquire through their possession of knowledge.

In accordance with this definition, the school curriculum is the essential element of an educational institution, and its contents are defined by the society-state, which is supposed to channel and supervise the instilling of the knowledge that is relevant and effective for its members. Thus, for instance, the state can decide that more engineers, doctors, or railway workers are required or will be required in a few years time and set the desired school curriculum accordingly, since acquiring knowledge as socialization means disciplinary adaptation of the information and the manner in which it is activated to the social division of labor.

A curriculum as a disciplinary program is also an exercise program: it is designed such that it can constitute a framework

---

[1] Z. Lamm, *Contradictory Logics of Teaching*, Sifriat-Poalim, Tel-Aviv, 1974 (Hebrew); Z. Lamm, Ideologies: Educational Factors Affecting Curriculum, *International Encyclopedia of Education*, 1985, pp. 2388-2390.

for actual "training" for social roles. It contains elements of imparting habits, discipline, acceptance of authority, of restraint and controlling impulses, physical and intellectual practice, and so forth. The definition of knowledge as a means of socialization has constituted one of the pillars of educational practice since antiquity. It has been one of the cornerstones in the establishment of scholastic education; it served as a guiding light to the founders of public education in the nineteenth century, and it forms the strongest justification for the continued financing of education systems by the state.

This approach is generally criticized in two ways. The one prong of criticism is "internal" criticism, which stresses the disparity between the goal of training so-called experts and school practice based on uniformity. This latter practice does not recognize children's varying talents enough, does not permit them enough choice, and does not channel children sufficiently. It is based on a curriculum comprising a number of disciplines that frequently contradict one another, and the attempt to teach many different subjects simultaneously is doomed since it does not create expertise and the training in the various disciplines is insufficient. The necessary reform, according to critics following this line of argument, is to make all schools disciplinary-orientated, with each school placing greater and wider focus on one area of specialization.

The second prong of criticism is external: the liberal critics of education, from Rousseau, to the progressive school movement, to Maslow and Rogers, focused their criticism mainly on the aspect of education that seeks to shape the individual, repress his uniqueness, and alienate him from his "real nature", by setting external goals that are not connected in any way to his inclinations. Some of these critics have stressed the demand to remove socialization from the list of educational goals and to place the child at the center of the educational endeavor. This form of criticism implies redefining the term knowledge, expressed in the claim that an individual possesses knowledge only on the condition that it has meaning in his or her life in practice. In other words, knowledge has subjective meaning that logically and morally precedes all social, scientific, and objective meaning[2].

It should be recalled, however, that even among the radical thinkers in education, there were many who viewed knowledge and its imparting as a discipline through practice and training as a legitimate and desired goal of education, particularly with regard to the education of the lower class.

Antonio Gramsci,[3] for instance, who attacked the capitalist society and sought to lay the foundations for a socialist revolution, thought the revolution feasible only through the use of the measures that capitalist education itself provides for the working class.

In accordance with the directive that was in vogue amongst conservative Marxists, that is, to search for the destruction of capitalism in the social forces operating within it, Gramsci proposed educating the intellectuals amongst the proletariat by exploiting the possibilities for public education provided by industrial democracy. The acquisition of knowledge by members of the oppressed class would, in Gramsci's view, lead to a change in society's power structure and allow the proletariat to take control over the means of production, which, in turn, would make a social revolution possible. Attitudes of this kind were and still are fairly common among thinkers who were disillusioned with the poor results of the liberal education, in terms of the lack of success in ameliorating the circumstances of the impoverished and lower classes. Perhaps it is precisely the "good old" education that originally was constructed to mold the image of the scientist, the engineer, and the doctor from the middle and upper classes that could be an appropriate answer to the social mobility necessary to the members of the lower class.

Jonathan Kozol, a foremost radical educator who devoted his life to working in poverty-stricken neighborhoods in the United

---

[2] M. Van Cleve, *Existentialism in Education*, Harper & Row Pub. N.Y., 1969; H. Read, *The Education of Free Men*, Freedom Press, London, 1944.

[3] A. Gramsci, *Selections from the Prison Notebooks*, Laurence & Wishart, London, 1971.

States, argued forcefully that it was not possible to learn mathematics, biochemistry, physics, Latin grammar, logic, law, or hydraulic engineering in the natural way people learn to walk and talk, breathe, and make love. The spontaneity and organic approach advocated by the advocates of open education (amongst whom he had once numbered) are not suited to the learning required for acquiring expertise in one unit of a complex achievement. Learning of this sort entails hours, months, and even years of prolonged and directed work that is not pleasurable and without which, Kozol argued, African-Americans, the poor, the disadvantaged, and society's outcasts have no chance of enduring the technological nightmare expected in the near future.[4]

The second answer to our two questions is that knowledge is the inalienable property of culture and the goal of imparting it is to transform the person into a cultured human being. This answer is similar to the first one, but with a different significance both in the definition of the desirable type of knowledge and in the implications this definition has in practice and in terms of the individual's experience. Under this definition, the goal of school education is to familiarize the child with humankind's cultural heritage and with the intellectual, emotional, and social significance of being a human being (as distinct from animal or plant life). The type of information imparted here concentrates principally on the contents that constitute an example of the sublime, creative, esthetic power of people when they are at their peak— the great works of literature, art, and science, for example. This knowledge might also include humankind's less flattering moments, through the study of human and national history, its heroism and its horrors. This knowledge serves three main needs: One is the need to create in the pupil a sort of "warning sign" with respect to the terrible possibilities existing in culture, thus compelling him or her to trust in law and order and conformist behavior. The second need is to emphasize the liberating power of progress, achieved through science and rational thought, in

---

[4] J. Kozol, *Free Schools,* Houghton, Miffilin Com., Boston, 1972, p. 60.

the struggle against the "forces of darkness" of religion and base impulses, thus instilling in the individual an appreciation of rationality in any form (personified at its best in capitalism). Third is the need to create an identity and a sense of belonging, generally national, in the pupil.

Under this approach, knowledge itself has value. It enables the individual's self-identification as "human"; it enables her to transcend her biological existence, and it functions as a social definer, bestowing a self-identity on the child in the sense of belonging to society. The procedure for transferring this knowledge is different from the previous one: here, again, there is no practice or training, but, rather, the assimilation of values and behaviors. Knowledge in the sense of aculturalization is not intended to achieve specific social functioning or acceptance of authority, but instead the creation of a sense of identity, of loyalty. Knowledge of this sort involves a different progress-evaluation scale, different from disciplinary knowledge that is aimed at expertise or specialization and whose evaluation scale is set by the disciplinary rules themselves. Knowledge in the sense of aculturalization refers to the idea of culture, of humanity or, alternatively, of nationality and national identity. The pupil is tested by the extent to which he approaches the idea and its actualization, since the method has an overall assumption that some people are more "cultured" than others, more "humane", and so forth. It is important to recall that this approach to knowledge formed and still forms an integral part of the curriculum in most schools in the modern Nation-State. It in fact supplements the school's socialization "program", grounded in the psychological convention that there is a human need for a sense of belonging and pride, and fed by the great promise it holds (from the viewpoint of decision-makers) of loyalty.

The criticism of this approach has many aspects to it. To begin with, it is important to note that a considerable amount of the criticism of "knowledge as socialization" also applies to the criticism of "knowledge as aculturalization". This is particularly important with respect to the possibility of indoctrination embodied in the creation of a sense of identification and loyalty and the imposing on the child of values and norms that are presented as objective and scientific and as logically and morally overriding his subjective desires.[5] But there are other lines of criticism, three of which I will note in brief.

The one critique is that of pragmatic criticism, which claims that it is impossible to reach an agreed definition of inalienable property of culture. As a controversial concept, it cannot be used to construct a curriculum in a democratic state, since it would be necessary to alter the curriculum every time the Minister of Education changes or a new party elected to government. This critique does not offer an alternative, but instead seeks to remain within the bounds of scientific and technical knowledge, about which consensus does still exist because it is effective and because it is still convenient to argue that it is objective and not the product of vagaries or fashion.

The second line of criticism is the Euro-American culture critique. When we talk about a "cultured" person, we are in fact referring to the Western cultural model, which defines both the image of the desired person and the way in which members of other cultures need to be educated, that is, in accordance with and subject to Euro-American values. The acculturalization approach is bourgeois, arrogant, chauvinistic, and racist, with colonialist overtones that accentuate the supposed superiority of Western culture over the cultures of other nations by defining Western tradition as inalienable, universal, and human property. In practice, even in Western European and North American countries, this approach creates a sense of belonging for the locals, but discriminates against immigrants, women, and children from the lower classes, who live in a sub-culture that is not subject to the accepted bourgeois standards. Knowledge dispersed by the advocates of the Euro-American approach is partial, censored, and biased, including only what has been canonized over the course of Euro-American history, but which is presented in universal packaging as "world" knowledge, accompanied by a narrative of technological superiority, which lends it the appearance of being scientific and objective. Knowledge includes only

---

[5] Jules Henry, *Culture Against Man*, Random House, 1963; D. Cooper, *The Dialectics of Liberation*, Penguin Books, 1968.

what promotes Western achievement and excludes Chinese po-
etry, African narratives, South American art, and feminine
thought. However, this line of criticism is not anti-culture; rather
it suggests another, multicultural definition of knowledge and,
accordingly, an educational outlook that stresses the acceptance
of "the other", the legitimacy of variance, and the real possibility
of possessing knowledge that is not hierarchical and does not
contest the rights of others to think and understand things differently.

The third critique is ecologist in nature. It asserts that
"knowledge as culture" is simply a modernistic fiction originating in the Judeo-Christian religious tradition. This tradition created an artificial distinction between the mind and body, between the earthly and divine, and between man and nature. It is a
mistaken approach that distances the individual from herself as a
biological organism that interrelates with its environment and
gives the false sense that humans are superior to beasts. This
sense enables us to continue to exploit and destroy the environment and to distance ourselves from nature, our principal source
of vitality. Placing culture at the top of our learning scale of priorities and its presentation as fundamentally different from the
honey produced by the bee or the music produced by the whale
are not only a falsehood, but could turn out to have both me-
dium-term and long-term disastrous ramifications.

All three of the above critiques have a substantial presence in
the European and American education systems, particularly in
middle- and upper-class schools. The first critique is manifested
in the abandonment of the attempt for value-oriented or national
education and the attempt to create social affiliation in many of
the schools, with focus instead on objective technological-
scientific education. The second critique has been well received
in some schools, especially in those areas of Europe and the
United States that take in Third-World immigrants. The multicultural trend seems to offer a real possibility for providing answers to instances of overt and covert racism, and it carries a lot
of weight in the redefinition of "knowledge" in education. The
third critique has garnered support from two sources. The one is
science, which, in recent years, has undergone a remarkable

changeover from the traditional accent on physics to an emphasis on biology and understanding ecological systems. The other source of support is the world of politics, which is reacting to public anxiety about the destruction of the environment, by allocating resources to schools so they can study ecology. The result is that in many schools, we are more likely to find river-cleaning activities or activities assisting turtles to return to the sea than outings to museums or a Shakespearean production (though, of course, many schools do try to do both).

The *third answer* to our two questions about knowledge (What is the intended purpose of knowledge acquired in school? and What is the knowledge that the school is supposed to instill, enable, or create?) is that knowledge is a form of self-discovery. This answer has become part of educators' standard stock of responses when they are required to define for themselves and for outsiders the meaning of their educational endeavor. Its origins are ancient, and it is evident in various cultures (Indian, Chinese), but its entry into the store of educational rhetoric of European culture can be ascribed to Socrates, who proposed the aphorism of "know thyself" as an educational ideal.

The idea of "knowledge as self-discovery" has appeared in modern educational history in various forms, for instance, in nineteenth-century German humanism. Under the approach that guided some of the intellectuals involved in the constructing of the education system in nineteenth-century Prussia (mainly the Berlin University), the most important knowledge a person can acquire is the knowledge of himself as a subject. The role of education, of *bildung*, under the original humanist conception, is to create a process of self-education, in the framework of which the individual molds himself so that she may realize her unique potential.[6]

---

[6] A. Aviram, "The Humanist Conception of the University—A Framework for Postmodern Higher Education", *European Journal of Education*, 27(4), 1992a, pp. 397-414. Later analyses of the concept show that it underwent a process of change. Under the influence of German ideology, it acquired the meaning of realizing the

However, in the spirit of German idealism of that period, the individual's "unique potential" was regarded as simply her ability to identify herself as the subject, and this ability is contingent on her ability to identify the general, universal aspect she embodies and not necessarily her uniqueness as an individual (as Hegel contended). Thus, self-knowledge means a process that begins with self-identification as a unique individual and goes on to recognition of the manner in which that uniqueness is merely an expression of general social and universal awareness.[7] This approach to education did not draw much attention in the nineteenth century. With the departure of German idealism from the European intellectual arena, it was shelved, but aspects of it were resuscitated in the second half of the twentieth century in humanistic psychology and in the critical discussion of education as socialization.

Other examples of the perception of knowledge as self-discovery can be found in liberal and progressive ideologies. According to Aviram,[8] it was John Stuart Mill who laid the theoretical basis for the highly influential liberal definition of an autonomous person as the proper objective of education. The necessary conditions of a conscious activity of identifying wishes and its rational definition for the individual's ability to be autonomous can be derived from the liberal definition of the autonomous person as a person who identifies his wishes, defines them rationally and strives to realize them. The type of

---

universal in every individual. Later, toward the end of the nineteenth century, it already became very similar to the English concept of apprenticeship of molding the enlightened person (the English gentleman). Aviram draws the reader's attention to the fact that in practice, the university did not institute any self-molding program, which he ascribes to the tendency of Von Humboldt and his associates to use Greek culture as a model for imitation.

[7] H.G. Gadamar, *Truth and Method*, Crossroad, N.Y., 1985, pp. 11-17.

[8] A. Aviram, "Personal Autonomy and the Flexible School", *International Review of Education*, 39(5), pp. 419-433, 1993; A. Aviram, "The Justification of Compulsory Education", *Journal of Philosophy of Education*, 20(1), pp. 51-58, 1986.

knowledge that education is supposed to provide also stems from this definition: knowledge that stems from a process of reflection, of discovering the individual's unique drives and tendencies; knowledge that entails the translation of those same drives and tendencies and their definition as "will"; knowledge that enables the individual to act to realize that will. In other words, this is an overall process of apprenticeship that includes self-contemplation and self-reflection, the development of linguistic, conceptual, and rational skills, and familiarization with the environment, society, and the world as places for realizing the will.

The outstanding formulations of the approach that views knowledge as self-knowledge appeared in the humanist and radical educational thought mainly in the 1950s and thereafter. Maslow, for instance, claimed the existence of a basic human and individual essence to all people that is not conditional on culture or society and whose development, identification, and realization are the only goal worthy of the educational endeavor.[9] Existentialists and Freudians (Weiskopf, Fromm, Rogers) have suggested different formulations of education as the development of self-awareness in the individual as a barrier against the dangers of the enslavement of the individual's soul and of accumulated social knowledge dominating him. The role of self-awareness is to act as a kind of guardian of individuals, to assist them in avoiding the excess suppression forced on them by the materialistic, consumerist culture (as analyzed by Marcuse, for instance). At the same time, self-awareness enables people to identify their individual talents and to express their creativity and their unique potential—to feel they exist as subjects (Freire) and not as consumers, worthless objects.

What is interesting about this approach is that it is does not merge into the regular work of the school. Despite the fact that some of its adherents were teachers who even tried to apply it, the approach was generally employed in the framework of therapy or in the margins of a regular school.

---

[9] A. Maslow & P.A. Sorokin (eds.), *New Knowledge in Human Values*, Harper & Row Pub., 1959, p. 130.

Criticism of this approach usually rests on three assertions. One is the claim of "non-applicability" and the difficulty of introducing individuation processes of the type mentioned into a public framework. The second assertion is made against individuation itself. Under this assertion, people who adopt this approach of identifying knowledge with self-discovery are harming the pupils, who, it is claimed, are directed toward too much self-indulgence. Fear of indoctrination and loss of freedom will, in the end, lead to obviating the possibility of education, expanding horizons, and coping with real life.

The third assertion is essentially anthropological in nature and disputes the individualistic verdict. Man and woman are social animals and do not have an *a priori* tendency toward self-actualization; hence, there is no such thing as "self-knowledge". The only knowledge that exists is social knowledge, including the knowledge relating to the individual. Children are unable to examine themselves, indeed are not interested in doing so. Quite the contrary: faith in the "child's world" would lead to fundamentally different conclusions with regard to "imparting knowledge": children do not like dealing with themselves; they like playing and competing with others, and they have a great natural curiosity about world knowledge.

My contention is that the three answers together are simply all part of the myth: schools do not concern themselves with socialization, in the sense of teaching skills or of training to express personal talents through skills and practice. They perform socialization mainly in the sense of reproducing the existing social classes. They do not perform acculturalization in the sense of revelation of or familiarity with culture, but, rather, almost always in the sense of indoctrination toward preference, toward the hegemony of one culture over others, while denying and delegitimizing the latter. The school does not deal with individuation in the sense of revealing the individual's special biological or mental drives, which are suppressed by culture. It certainly does not deal with self-discovery, reflection, or the translation of inclinations into rational concepts such as will or personal ambition. The school has never been prepared or organized to deal with these matters and, in most cases, has not the faintest idea of what they mean or what they entail.

Moreover, the manner in which socialization and acculturalization processes are conducted in the school is totally unconnected to knowledge. Although for the majority of children, knowledge is acquired at school in the framework of activities learnt and of the attempt to meet the requirements of the syllabus,[10] it is not relevant to the structuring of their self-images, their social identities, or social functioning. These latter three are all determined in advance *and* simultaneously with the acquisition of knowledge and are a condition for their generation in the individual's cognitive field. They enable learning and create its contents and the specific manner of its operative translation. This "learning" also takes place in school, for instance, in the sphere of the hidden curriculum,[11] which trains the children to

---

[10] Note that I am not claiming that knowledge and skills are not acquired in schools. Most children learn to read in school, and most also learn to perform the four basic functions of arithmetic. My contention is that the knowledge acquired does not meet the definition of what schools define as the objectives of education.

[11] The concept of the "hidden curriculum" was common in the educational debate of the 1970s and 1980s, particularly in the critical sociology of education. Many researchers were disappointed with the meager results of the steps taken to provide equal opportunity to members of the weaker social classes and the poor output of integration (particularly in places where integration was embraced with great expectations, like in England and Israel). As part of the explanation for the poor achievement of the members of the lower classes in school, mainly in the area of "knowledge acquisition", a number of critiques emerged that analyzed the official curriculum and demonstrated its hidden messages, which are characterized by discrimination and repression of some of the children. See, for example, M. Young & G. Witty (eds.), *Society, State and Schooling*, Falmer Press, 1977; R. Sharp, *Knowledge, Ideology and the Politics of Schooling*, Routledge & Kegan, London, 1978. These researchers stressed the social character of knowledge and the fact that "school knowledge" becomes an insurmountable barrier because it does not touch on the lives, experience, and the expressive possibilities of lower class children. It is static knowledge that has

obey instructions, to ignore their friends and worry only about themselves, to compete for grades, to adapt to selection processes, judgments, and divisions of people, to accept hierarchy as something natural, and to demand immediate reward for certain performances—in short, to adapt to and internalize capitalist values and ideology.[12]

The reality is that schools make different attempts to impart knowledge, including the sincere and genuine desire to improve and refine the accessibility of knowledge to the pupil. The knowledge imparted by teachers is external and objective and is subject to two principal adaptations, which are the bases of the curriculum. The first adaptation is to science. Despite lagging behind technological and theoretical developments in the sciences by a good number of years and despite the fact that much of the reading and study materials are antiquated and academically irrelevant, the curriculum nevertheless undergoes a continual process of renewal. The second adaptation is to the pupils. This adaptation is grounded in various critical claims made in relation to the lack of interest, the lack of relevance, and the arbitrariness of the mode of learning. However, the key to the adaptation to the pupils lies in the political emphasis on the failure of pupils to meet external criteria. The press is constantly publishing articles and commentary on pupils' paucity of "knowledge", on the paucity of the education of college students, on the inability of many pupils to pass final examinations or university entrance examinations.

This exertion of pressure on the education system ostensibly leads to educators listening to the advice of reformers. The type of advice that is generally meted out calls for creating greater interest amongst the pupils by making the learning material

---

undergone a process of reification (Sharp) and needs to be replaced by another type—experiential, creative, and equal—of knowledge as well as of process of acquisition of knowledge. Schools need to be transformed into a place that creates knowledge rather than remaining a place of social reproduction by means of given, static knowledge.

[12] Sharp, 1978.

more relevant to the children's lives. Thus, for example, the reformers argue, it is difficult, even impossible, to teach children citizenship. It would be more effective if we were to begin by teaching them about their neighborhood and community and only then, once we have created initial interest, we could go on to broader and more general studies. It is hard to teach children arithmetic, but if it were done by using calculation examples from football, for instance, they would view it more positively. In short, this adaptation is based on making the curriculum more effective in terms of the student's ability to demonstrate its contents.

This experience of updating and modification and of trying to reach a larger portion of the pupils is not a learning experience, however: it is a teacher's experience, a teaching experience! From the perspective of the pupils, no change has been effected, since they do not know the curriculum studied the previous year. From their point of view, "scientific" updating is not relevant, as by the time they are required to make use of that scientific knowledge, it will be irrelevant. For the pupils, there is nothing more boring than having to learn about "my neighborhood" or listening to a teacher awkwardly trying to impart knowledge using concepts from the children's world—Pokemon, dinosaurs, and Harry Potter are not and never have been teachers of arithmetic, citizenship, or geography.

From the children's point of view, what is learnt best is the link between a compliment and the teacher's game, the link between the ability to follow rules and do homework and smiley yellow stickers and "Very Good" in their notebooks. Children also learn in school that their way of being good, i.e., of being of value in the eyes of adults (teachers and also parents), is to play the game and to do so consistently. However, most of the children learn that they are not the best players, of whom there are only a few—perhaps only five out of thirty. They also learn that those who are not among the leading five are worth less and may even have no real value for the adults. They learn that anyone who does not play the game very quickly becomes valueless and, in certain cases, disappears from the class never to be seen again. And then they learn other reasons for continuing to play the game, despite it not being interesting nor producing stickers and grades, despite the fact that it does not transform them into having value. These reasons are linked to fear and anxiety about the dual threat (both of being valueless and of disappearing). They are connected to the desire not to disappoint parents and to the children's community that exists outside the teacher's reach. They are connected to inertia. They are socialization.

Most children learn how essential the lie is: the school game is based totally on saying what "they" want to hear and not on the truth, which could prove costly. It is always preferable to say that your mother spilt coffee on your notebook than that you could not be bothered to do the homework. The children learn about double standards: adults are allowed to break promises, to ignore what they do not want to hear, and to play the game in an unfair way. None of these are permissible for children; all of these are socialization.

Some children learn to practice at school. In most schools, the practice is unconnected with anything the teachers do. In the majority of schools, there is insufficient continuity in the teacher-pupil relationship, since teachers generally are changed and the curriculum is not overly consistent from year to year. Children learn to practice in extra-curricular ways: in football games, during recess, on the school sports' teams, in the choir, when working on the computer, or when reading at home or in the library. Children also get practice at sitting for hours on end in one place. They practice intellectual detachment and restraint in the world of imagination; they practice maintaining a naïve façade. That is socialization.

With regard to mediating culture, things are not very different. Children acquire knowledge of historical heroes and the masters in art; they hear stories about renewal, heroism, struggles for freedom, and important historical events. If the story is good they like it. If the teacher can breathe life into the stories, the children are spellbound. But to what extent are they aware of the moral of the story, of the irritating didactic aspect that accompanies every educational story that seeks to supposedly instill culture? The answer seems to be obvious and particularly acute in light of the discrepancy between the story and the storyteller. Every child understands instantly that the teacher before her is not a historical hero. She does not delude herself that the art teacher is Van Gogh, and she fully understands that the struggle for "rights", "freedom", and "democracy" is the realm of the stories and that its ontological status is similar, perhaps equal, to that of dwarves and witches and fairies. As a child at school, she does not, and never will, have rights (certainly not in the sense of power[13]). At the same time, we must not detract from the importance of stories. A good story is pure nourishment for the soul; a good story is an indirect teaching of actuality; a good story is the most important basis for the child when one day she comes to tell her own story, her biography.

A number of distinctions can be added to this brief description:
(1) There is no connection whatsoever between the learning material and socialization processes. These processes occur anyway, simply from adults being with children in a framework in which the latter set the rules of the game. There is absolutely no difference between the socialization children undergo with an updated curriculum in the sciences and those who undergo socialization with an outdated arithmetic curriculum.
(2) Children learn from adults, but only for a few does a link exist between what the adults are interested in teaching and what the children learn in practice. This is a structural matter stemming from both the overall competitive/excelling structure of the method and from the teachers' total dependence on the children's performance. Whether they try to disguise it or not, this leads the adults to work with the least number of children, thus protecting their professional self-images.
(3) The likelihood of a child developing a self-image of "I am a learner" (in the sense suggested by Erikson) is extremely low. In fact, this likelihood is related to the percentage of children expected to complete twelve years of school education in a way that will offer them the possibility of continuing their studies— about 20% to 30% on average. The likelihood is higher in

---

[13] This is according to Hobbes' and, in some sense, Spinoza's well-known analogy between "right" and "power".

schools located in well-off neighborhoods, where it can reach
the level of 70%, as opposed to the likelihood of this happening
in schools at the lowest end of the social scale, averaging less
than 10% [14].

*(4) There is an intimate link between the possibility of acquiring
knowledge of the sort teachers seek to impart, irrespective of
what it is, and the self-image of the child as being of value.* In
fact, even if teachers were to come to class with an alternative
curriculum, even if they were to teach about football and to
leave the children to deal with physics by themselves, the learning experience would still be similar to what it is today. A large
proportion of the children would not manage to learn about football (let alone physics).

(5) Mediating culture is a type of socialization. Knowledge imparted through mediating culture is not relevant, but the framework is important: it teaches the use of language (including the
non-verbal languages of the arts); it stimulates the imagination;
and it teaches children that different people have different places
in culture. In fact, the most important learning it contains for
some of the children is an intensification of the feeling that although there is a lot of culture, it does not seem to offer them

---

[14] Erikson proposed a developmental theory according to which children's developmental stages can be characterized in accordance
with the various manners in which they try to shape a personal
identity for themselves. Below, in Chapter 3, I will suggest another
definition for the process of mental construction of identity and
self-image. Under my definition, a distinction must be made between the formation of a self-image and personal identity. These
are two fundamentally different things, and Erikson, who suggested
many excellent perspectives on child development, confuses the
two. According to Erikson, the identity the child tries to form at
elementary school age is of "Myself as a learner." According to my
definition, this is not the formation of an identity, but, in fact, the
construction of self-image, because "to be a learner" is the way in
which the child, upon entry into school, attempts to attribute social
value to himself. See Chapter 3, Section D. E.H. Erikson, *Childhood and Society*, W.W. Norton & Co., N.Y., 1950.

anything, because what is important in culture studies is not "What can I learn about culture?" but "What can it give me?"

What emerges from the above analysis is that there is another aspect to the school myth, namely, that schools always strive for the pupil's best interests. This alleged intention renders it impossible for a school to be an institution that oppresses some of the children. Yet in addition to the fact of these supposed intentions, schools have impressive means for realizing their ideological objectives: the practices for imparting knowledge (putting aside at this point the details of the manner in which it is imparted or created).

The myth compels schools to differentiate between knowledge and teaching and then again between the latter two and learning, despite the fact that this is clearly a very problematic differentiation at best and very deceptive in the case of the child who is not succeeding academically. Since knowledge is supposedly an objective thing, it can be found "out there" and because the school makes the object called knowledge accessible to all the children within its confines, the school is, indeed, realizing its humanist vision. Hence, if there are children who fail "to learn", the school is obviously not to blame. Failure does not appear in the official curriculum; it is not part of the school's objectives; it is not translated into any of the practices appearing in educational theory. It is simply something "imported" from the parental home, which creates a lack of motivation in children—from the substandard daycare for children from deprived neighborhoods, to the "otherness" mentality of immigrant children, to the biological inferiority of girls in relation to boys—but the source is never the school. Even the most vehement critics of the school, including those who point to the problematic nature of its purposes and the gap between those purposes and reality, are agreed that the goals of the school are, in themselves, worthy and that the way to achieve them is via the school curriculum.

To my view, the school curriculum, which is generally perceived as the core of the school's existence and into which is invested the greater part of public, intellectual, and theoretical energy, is of minor importance in terms of its contribution to achieving the objectives of education. Moreover, as I will argue further on, the school's objectives, as formulated in educational theory, are no longer relevant today. We do not have a definitive model of a "proper" society, according to which we can base socialization, nor can we justify cultural preferences in a hierarchical and "objective" way. Furthermore, we do not understand the meaning of individuation, let alone are prepared to pay the price of extreme individualism as an objective of public funding.

Even if we look at the reality in practice, we will see that for most of the public whose children attend school, for the majority of parents and teachers, the school is supposed to enable the child to compete for a good place in a prestigious institution of higher learning, which will allow those who are successful to secure the good, well-paid jobs or, alternatively, social prestige. This is the real meaning of both socialization and of individuation, which really cannot be separated, let alone experienced as contradictory, mutually exclusive processes. In practice, the overlap between socialization and individuation as social characteristics of the postmodern state of being of social fragmentation highlights the tenuousness of the stated purposes of education and the importance of the hidden curriculum in the shaping of children's personal and social images, including with regard to their possibilities for learning.

Nonetheless, it is important to remember that knowledge, inasmuch as it can be defined or touched upon in the postmodern era, has tremendous importance in terms of the individual's independence and striving for social equality. To my view, it seems appropriate to redefine the objectives of schools as educational institutions aspiring for freedom and equality. This redefinition can then be used to test the approach to knowledge, both in the overt, formal ways in which it is treated and in the teaching methods in the hidden, "automatic" behavior that critically affect the possibility of generating knowledge.

This criticism notwithstanding, it is apparent that the modern school holds great promise. It is still the most protective environment for children. It is a viable option even for children in Third World countries, in the slums, and in immigrant societies.

In Bombay it protects children from being sold into slavery; in Sao Paulo, from death in the streets; and in the slums of the giant metropolises, from the only other alternative—a live of drugs, crime, and poverty[15]. Despite the fact that modern schools are built to perpetuate social disparities, their margins enable mobility; and these margins are of great importance, particularly for the people occupying them, and cannot be ignored. They include people born into the lower classes who today work in industry, in commerce, in the liberal professions, and in politics. They include large numbers of enlightened individuals from immigrant groups, minorities, and women, some of whom succeeded despite school, while for others school was the place where they got their first real opportunity.

One interesting context is academia, where in recent years, the teaching staff has included, in growing number, lecturers and researchers from the traditionally disadvantaged sectors of ethnic minority groups and immigrants. Many of these lecturers regard their personal histories, particularly at school, as the key to their present success. Ironically, many of the lecturers from more established backgrounds claim that for them, school was a total failure as an experience and that they reached academia "despite" school.

What emerges from the criticism is that schools, in being subject to social processes and the dynamics of social struggle, cannot change. Since we live in a world where the socio-economic gap seems forever expanding and since capitalist economic forces are the controlling forces in that world, it is absolutely clear that a change toward openness, equal opportunity, personal autonomy, and so on, is not possible. School, as part of the social superstructure, is an institution that represents conservatism, stasis, and perpetuation of the prevailing social state. In fact, many radical Marxist critics of schools have always

---

[15] Even Hyman & Snook stress the fact that as compared to any other framework, from the street to community centers, the school is the safest place in the violent American cities. Hyman & Snook, 1999, p. 8.

claimed the impossibility of schools' changing, maintaining the necessity for overall social change.

The various critics of schools since the 1960s have claimed that schools in Western countries do not change their ways at the proper rate and that in all the most essential components of the educational process, they are similar to schools designed in the nineteenth century (with some even claiming that there has been no change since the Middle Ages). These claims are generally made against what is known as the school pedagogy, in other words, the manner in which the school performs the process with which it is most closely identified: the process of imparting knowledge.

But if we put aside for the moment the idea of imparting knowledge, it is possible to discern processes of dramatic change in schools: the elementary school in Liverpool in the second half of the twentieth century is a totally different institution from the kindergartens of nineteenth-century Dickensian England; a school in Harlem in the 1970s was completely different from any framework available to African-American children at any time previously in American history; a modern school in New Delhi is radically different from Muslim and Hindu religious schools and from the pre-independence schools during the time of the British Empire in India.

In industrialized countries, the influence of the social revolution in the 1960s was felt in modern schools with the introduction of new ideas, the change in atmosphere, the legitimization of individualism, and in a series of aesthetic, technical, and methodological changes. However, the principal changes have actually taken place in the postmodern period of the past thirty years. The school my children attend is different from the school I attended in my youth. The change is substantial, and it can be felt in almost all the parameters that constitute the school reality: teacher-pupil relations, the make-up of the school population (both pupils and teachers), teaching methods, the organizational structure, the curriculum, and even the hidden curriculum. The change has not necessarily been for the better. Sometimes it is manifested in growth and expansion of possibilities (i.e., a change toward freedom, autonomy, and flexibility); often it is a change that distances children from learning, teachers, friends, and themselves, a change that exacerbates economic, academic, and cultural disparities and creates new types of alienation and anonymity. But the central point is that significant change is occurring.

The change in the school reality at the outset of the third millennium is part of the social reality taking shape in the era of rampant, boundless capitalism and in the nihilist and anti-intellectual atmosphere suggested by atmosphere of postmodernism. In order to evaluate the ways in which this critical social situation affects schools—both as a problematic situation that exacerbates and intensifies processes of social alienation already evident in modernity and as a situation of hope in which constant change represents new potential for freedom—I will briefly present the crisis. I will argue that the way in which the crisis is generally translated into the school reality (confusion, despair, and submission to market forces) is by no means a necessary reality. An alternative translation can be suggested, another way of confronting the problem, which will place schools in a new position, one of renewal and hope.

Part II

The Postmodern Challenge

Chapter 3

Postmodernism and Neomodernism

The application of postmodernism as a concept ranges from a critical-intellectual stance to an analysis of socio-economic reality at the closing of the twentieth century. As an intellectual stance, postmodernism is a cultural critique that casts doubt on the validity, necessity, and morality of all the epistemological foundations that underlie the thought, ideology, and reality-perception of modernity. These foundations do not represent all-embracing meta-narratives (theories) that are detached from daily reality, real life, which are nothing more than a justification of the power structures and for the white European male to manipulate anybody different from him, by means of concepts such as rationality, progress, and enlightenment.[1] Postmodernism signifies the demise of the meta-narrative, whose function, under the criticism, was to establish and legitimize supposedly universal human history. The rejection of the meta-narratives is important because it enables the replacement of modernist logic (regarded by postmodernism as manipulative and fetishist) by postmodernist pluralism, by a heterogeneous variety of lifestyles and language games.[2]

As a social analysis, postmodernism addresses the radical changes in the second half of the twentieth century in production

---

[1] H. Giroux, "Postmodernism and the Discourse of Educational Criticism", *Journal of Education*, 170(3), 1988, pp. 5-30.

[2] D. Harvey, *The Condition of Postmodernity*, Oxford, Blackwell, 1989.

relations and social frameworks and patterns, with the development of new technologies that have fundamentally changed communication between people and the process of economic, political, and cultural globalization. According to Lyotard, the demise of the great beliefs and theories of modernism (socialism, communism, liberalism, etc.) is closely linked to our constant bombardment with images, news reports, and advertisements via the new technologies. This bombardment undermines the sense of continuity of reality and transports the person to worlds of fantasy and imagination, the world of television, the shopping mall, video games, and Disneyland, all of which are simply a gigantic production, marketing, and consumption mechanism. In fact, claims Lyotard, politics has ended, and people have become uninformed consumers with the dominant language of packaging and advertisement.[3]

We find in the research literature innumerable descriptions and analyses of the condition of Western man at the end of the second millennium, as a person in a new historical period that is different in every aspect of human existence from the periods that preceded it. This period is called the postmodern era, with the accent on the ideas: cultural aspects that differentiate between it and the period prior thereto—modernism. This period is also called the post-industrial era when considered from the economic perspective, in light of the shift from a state economy of capital and industry to a global economy of information and technology.

Aviram[4] dwells on a number of familiar examples representing the new and different nature of the postmodern era, as compared to the period preceding it, and attempts to demonstrate the significance of the change for education. According to Aviram, the essential characteristic of the new era is the loss of the absoluteness of the coordinates that have guided the history of Western culture since its birth.

---

[3] *The Hutchinson Dictionary of Ideas,* Helicon, Oxford, 1994, p. 420.
[4] A. Aviram, "Non-Lococentric Education", *Educational Review,* 44(1), 1992b, pp. 3-17; Aviram, 1993; Aviram, 1992a.

At the ideological level, postmodernism is characterized by an epistemological revolution whose chief feature is the transition from an objective world-picture, which dominated Western thinking for thousands of years, to relativist views. This transition includes the erosion of the decisiveness of dichotomous distinctions between "reality" and "imagination", between "truth" and "falsehood", between "good" and "bad". Alongside this transition, there is a discernible renouncement of modern ideological methods (socialism, communism, fascism, etc.), replaced by pragmatic, utilitarian attitudes, and a shrinking in the status of social ideologies in favor of individualist attitudes.

At the social level, postmodern society is characterized by the erosion of social definitions and the loss of meaning of social frameworks. This erosion is evident in a number of spheres: in the disappearance of the division of traditional social roles (such as the traditional male and female social functions, generational social functions); in the inability to characterize social frameworks, even the simplest ones like the nuclear family; and in the loss of meaning of these frameworks as a super-framework that imbues the life of the individual with meaning.[5]

In the economic sphere, the postmodern era is characterized by an acceleration and intensification of economic competition. This sphere is distinct from others in that there has been an expansion of the modern capitalist economy to the point of global control over the means of production, over information, and over capital. This is the economy of compulsive production, turning everything into a consumer product (and the person into a com-

---

[5] In the past, social frameworks served as the basis for creating meaning: a person would form his identity by identifying with an external idea, a "grand" idea presented in the social framework ("I belong to the church", "I am a member of a social movement", "I am a soldier protecting the homeland", etc.). The power of grand ideas was lost with the death of meta-narratives. In the past, Kennedy's dictum, "Ask what you can do for the country!" was very meaningful. Today it would sound ridiculous because the attitude to the social framework is only of the type "What can the framework contribute to me? How does it benefit me?"

pulsive consumer), while shortening the shelf-life of its products. Where the lifespan of a product thirty years ago was a few decades (and in ancient times, hundreds or even thousands of years), today it is scarcely a few years, sometimes even months (electronic goods, for example).

In the technological sphere, the post-industrial society is undergoing developments with far-reaching ramifications for many areas of human life. These developments range from the communications and computer revolution, which, like all technological revolutions, has changed the people who brought about the revolution, to genetic engineering, which has given people historically unprecedented power—the power to intervene in the act of "creation", indeed, the very power to produce and change life itself.

In the organizational sphere, postmodernism is characterized by a transition from centralization, hierarchy, and organizational rigidity to flexible, versatile, more democratic and decentralized structures. This transition, which is characteristic primarily of technological societies and of economies that have shifted from heavy industry as their basis to information, affects also other organization and, to a lesser extent, even public institutions that are undergoing leveling, democratization, and privatization.

The job market of the postmodern society is characterized by an excess of education, unemployed university graduates, and career shifts. Whereas in the industrial era, the average career was linear and stable and generally people had one job for most of their adult lives, in today's reality, people often have two or more careers. They switch professions, sometimes a number of times over the course of their lives, frequently moving to totally new and different fields.

In the psychological sphere, the postmodern state is characterized by an increase in psychological pressure and tension to which the individual is subject, deriving from two simultaneous processes. The one process is the increase in the pressure to make choices that has resulted from the abundance of possibilities presented by the technological, economic, and employment changes. More and more, people are living in a reality of an endless choice of stimuli and possibilities—cognitive, consumer, employment, etc. Yet all the parameters according to which people make choices, which were previously based on a system of social, value-oriented, and conceptual coordinates, have eroded following the epistemological and social revolution. Consequently, people are faced with a multiplicity of choices and with no way of implementing them all.[6]

Constituting a continuation of the brief presentation given above, Aviram refers to the fact that the modern education system, as it developed in Europe and North America, is inappropriate for the postmodern reality, for it is a system that was designed in the modern era, the second half of the nineteenth century, and, naturally, has features of modern institutions—in other words, defunct features that are no longer relevant to the new reality. This unsuitability manifests itself in all the components defining the school organization. The goals of the organization, which were universal goals (shaping the person according to a model), lost their meaning as a result of the relativistic epistemological revolution, which rejected the continued justification of definitive goals with universal validity (there is no longer an agreed model). The organizational structure of the school is lococentric, hierarchic, and dependent on government bodies. Thus, it is unsuited to the post-industrial reality, which requires a transition to flat, democratic organizations. The school curriculum, which is based on an objectivist perception of knowledge and holds scientific knowledge as absolute truth, does not take into account the complete change in the status of knowledge stemming from the relativistic revolution.

---

[6] The question of the psychological and conscious significance of the postmodern situation on the personal level is a broad subject, which I will consider in part in the discussion below. Engaging analyses of the effect of the present era on the formation of the self in light of the loss of the subject can be found in K.J. Gergen, *The Saturated Self*, Basic Books, USA, 1991; E.D. Ermath, *Sequel to History: Postmodernism and the Crisis of Time*, Princeton, 1992, pp. 106-124.

Aviram adds Postman's assertion regarding the disappearance of childhood, from which it can be inferred that the target population of schools, i.e., children, is no longer definable in terms of a social, psychological (and, later, also legal) justification. Hence, schools in fact do not have a target population.

These insights lie at the heart of Aviram's call for radical change in the structure of schools, in their most basic definitions, and in their mode of operation, in order to adapt themselves to the new reality in which they operate. Today's schools need a paradigm shift from the outmoded paradigm of modernity, to enable them to redefine themselves in the chaotic reality in which they are attempting to function.

Against the background of this description I propose a slightly different understanding of the postmodern situation and its implications for education. Although I agree with Aviram and other authors about the postmodern state as constituting a type of crisis, I take issue with the contention that this is a unique and unprecedented social situation, differing in all social, epistemological, and psychological features from the social circumstances that have preceded it. My argument is that what is referred to as the postmodern crisis is simply a landmark in the "natural"—historic—development of world capitalism. Furthermore, I argue that it would be erroneous to assume that the school, or any other social institution, has been in a state of unsuitability. If schools operate according to an outmoded paradigm of modernity, it means that there is a real social need for this sort of existence, in other words, that it serves the socio-economic interest of those wielding power in society. Under my stance, which I will present below, it is precisely in the weakness of the school, its irrelevance, and its pathetic functioning where hope for change should be sought. Public schools are, indeed, in need of change, but this change is necessary not to adapt them to postmodern reality, but to enable them to struggle against some of its costs.

For the purposes of clarifying these claims, I will distinguish postmodernism as an intellectual stance, and in the next Chapter, I will consider the social challenge represented by neocapitalism. I will then examine their significance in the school context.

As an intellectual stance, postmodernism has three significant features that relate to education in general. The first is apparent in its tendency toward skepticism and relativism, which undermine the very possibility of identifying, in principle, definitive "knowledge" and "values". This tendency at least seemingly constitutes a genuine threat to the possibility of education per se, since "education" is defined and justified as a process of imparting, bequeathing, or at least creating knowledge and values. How can a curriculum be planned in a world with no agreed definition of knowledge? How can children be socialized or indoctrinated in a reality in which there are no values toward which we educate? Postmodernism represents a stance that asserts that not only can knowledge and values not be identified as definitive, but any attempt to do so is an exercise in power-mongering and an attempt to take control by means of certain types of definitions of knowledge and values, which represent the interests of those wielding power in society.

This position, however, is unfounded for a number of reasons. First, the school curriculum has never required philosophical justification: there was never any justification for learning mathematics as an absolute science, as Plato, Keppler, and Descartes all called for. The absence of this sort of justification was apparent before the designing of the current curriculum of most schools, beginning with the empiricist skepticism of the eighteenth century, to the "new" possibilities of nineteenth-century geometry, and ending with the instrumentalism of the twentieth-century Copenhagen school. But the lack of such justification is a far cry from employing a central curriculum in mathematics presented as God's law to the pupils. The ability to present things that are relative as absolute, without batting an eyelid, is one of the wonderful talents of an educational institution, which can simultaneously teach about the "truth" revealed to Moses on Mount Sinai, the "truth" contained in refuted Newtonian physics, and the "truth" of Darwinist theory—all by the same teacher, on the same day.

Second, the postmodern criticism contains an internal contradiction. On the one hand, it proclaims that "objective" criteria and definitiveness are absent; on the other hand, it claims that any attempt to identify criteria like these is *a priori* subject to power struggles and manipulation mechanisms. Yet this latter claim is itself a timeless, *a priori* truth. There is one truth to which even the most radical postmodernism is bound: behind every attempt to create an understanding or to define truth lies a textual structure that is fundamentally manipulative and driven by power struggles[7]. Is this not sufficient to define truth? Is this not a "truth" that it is important and appropriate to reveal? Is it not appropriate to discern that "reality is but a text" and the personal and social implications of this insight?

Third, it is easy to claim that values have a relative basis and vary with time and place. They also are designed in different ways by means of hermeneutic social processes that change the procedure for realizing them, and there is some point to the Nietzschean tendency toward an existential situation that is "beyond good and evil". At the same time, postmodernists would also agree that there is a difference between values that have become part of historical reality (like values of nationality, of economic freedom in capitalism, globalization, etc.) and values such as equality and freedom in their critical sense, whose realization has proved to be very problematic (assuming that a genuine attempt was made to realize them). There would also be agreement that fallacious history has been written in the name of and light of values, which has served as a basis for repression and manipulation. Values, by virtue of being relative—that is, because they could appear to oppose a specific repressive reality—have different epistemological statuses.

Two important assertions frequently advocated by the most ardent opponents of postmodernism must be added to the critique of its stance. One assertion is made against the postmod-

---

[7] Habermas raised this type of claim against postmodernism in his famous argument with Lyotard. It seemed inappropriate to present it in full in the current framework, but it is clear that Habermas is right—at least on this patter. J. Habermas, *The Philosophical Discourse of Modernity*, Cambridge, Mass., 1987.

ernist link between relativism and nihilism; in other words, the inability to determine definitive "truth" or "good" forms the basis for the creation of a nihilistic posture for the postmodernist, in which he is not committed to anything and in fact collaborates with the ruling social forces. This assertion stresses the rapid shift from "there is no absolute truth" to "there is no truth at all" or the shift from "anything is possible" to "anything goes", which is characteristic of the postmodern nihilism that appears as submission to—even embracing and admiration of—the consumer culture.

The second criticism is connected to the scope of the postmodern intellectual phenomenon: Is this a view of the intellectual elite in the First World, over-contented American and European society, the 2% of the world's population that can afford nihilism and the Roman stoicism of skeptical philosophy, or is this a wider phenomenon?[8] Indeed, what is the meaning of "loss of truth" or, in the postmodernist terminology, "loss of the real" in a world in which most people have never reached that "real", that the postmodernists lose with such abandon?

The second feature of postmodernism as an intellectual stance is its critique of modernism. This critique is built on a series of "isms", traditionally identified with the period of enlightenment, whose deconstruction reveals their power-oriented, Eurocentric, and chauvinistic foundations. It is an exposure of all the "isms" that lie at the foundation of public education—"liberalism", "nationalism", and, particularly, "modernism"—as a lie by consensus. It is also a representation of narrow, pro-rational, pro-Western, colonial, and racist views that justify the use of the technological superiority of the rich world under the guise of science, enlightenment, and progress to establish global control over the Second, Third, and Fourth worlds by exploiting their human and natural resources and turning them into the cultural

---

[8] See, for example, an interview with Stuart Hall, in D. Morley & K.H. Chen (eds.), *Stuart Hall: Critical Dialogues in Cultural Studies*, Routledge, 1996, p. 133.

metastasis of America and Europe. What is interesting about this critique is the fact that it is not "post" by any manner or means. It is a development of modern critiques, chiefly Marxist and neo-Marxist, that were appropriated by scholar who identify themselves as postmodernists, to support ideological relativism or nihilism. Since the views represented by modernism are simply mechanisms for power and control, they are not justified according to the rationalist and humanist criteria of modernism itself. Therefore, we cannot hold them as "truth" or as an aspiration, and rationality itself is falls into doubt. As many of the enlightenment "isms" are identified with public education's goals and modes of operation in industrialized democracies, this very education cannot be justified.

Without delving too deeply into this critique (a very important one, in my view), I will make two comments. The first is that the postmodernist critique relates to modernism in too general a way, thus throwing the baby out with the bathwater. Many of the "isms" of modernism stand in total contradiction to one another, for instance nationalism versus individualism, socialism versus fascism. Modernism is a long, complicated series of intellectual trends and projects, of which only a small part has found expression in political, economic, and social history. The interesting projects are precisely those that have never come to fruition, such equality and freedom for all and pluralism. The claim that the time has come to try and realize these projects, precisely with the exposure of the power structures preventing their realization (regardless whether this can be done), is itself a modern argument or, more precisely, neomodern and not "post" anything. My second comment is that schools built on the basis of modernism have never been capable of realizing most of the educational conceptions designed under modernism. After all, modernism is a hierarchic, segregationist structure that was never intended for developing the autonomous individual or equal opportunity. Its ability to support scientific research, creativity, democracy, and liberal values was always extremely limited and, at best, impacted only the narrow, privileged sector of pupils who, in any event, did not need school to achieve this.[9]

In certain important respects, a school is, indeed, a modernist institution, particularly in its fortifying of the division of social labor and in socialization, where it provides national and nationalist values. It prepares the majority of its students for a meaningless life, for having no social value, for being unable to influence, and to come to terms with all this by presenting an "objective" reality of exams and scientific criteria that explain to them for years that they are "below average" or not outstanding enough to have social value. At the same time, with regard to the modernist, humanist image of schools mentioned above, it is clearly evident that schools were never designed to promote a considerable part of the values it preaches, particularly equality and freedom.

The third feature of the postmodern intellectual stance is, in fact, its optimistic feature. This feature manifests itself in claims that it is precisely the postmodern critique that reveals the internal contradiction in modernism and it is its historical inability to realize its liberal and humanist values that has facilitated the transparency necessary for realizing those values today. With the exposure of hidden racism, chauvinism, capitalist cynicism, and the ecological destructiveness of the process of social production, it is possible to instigate new types of solidarity and resistance that will redesign abandoned ideals. It is a sort of optimis-

---

[9] One need only examine the ideal of Kantian education in order to detect that schools were never prepared to realize this. According to Kant, education is intended to enable the person to realize his potential as a human-cultured creature. This realization requires that the child's physical and psychological needs be taken care of; the refinement of thoughts, feelings, and artistic taste; the strengthening of character and self-discipline, while withstanding irrational temptations; and the development of moral thinking and behavior derived from categorical prescriptions. I. Kant, *Education*, trans. A. Churton, Ann Arbor, 1966.

tic neomodernism that rejects the postmodernist nihilism and forms the background for the current debate.

The most common example of this type of outlook is the multicultural approach prevalent in certain industrial democracies. The uniqueness of this approach lies in its proposed revival of the unfulfilled modern ideals of pluralism and equality. The approach represents a value-oriented militancy against all types of racism and discrimination, suggesting interesting models of life in a multifarious, multi-possibility, open, tolerant society where all have the option to be different or at least unique, as well as enjoying equal rights. Because this approach is generally advocated and advanced by clever intellectuals, it recognizes the identity between rights and power revealed in the postmodernist critique: for people to have equal rights, they must have equal political power, in other words, shared control of the social means of production. In many cases, this includes a practical demonstration of how to overcome prejudices, how to educate toward tolerance, and how to devise school procedures that will enable the reconstruction of the school as an institution so that it becomes a more open, pleasant, and equal place.

At the same time, it must be remembered that there are appreciable drawbacks to the multicultural approach, and I will mention two. One is the relationship between the individual and her culture of origin as her ultimate definer. Every person has a cultural history, ethic origin, and family, national, and sectarian affiliations. These are her personal identity-definers. A person's "education" is directed at legitimizing that identity and allowing it to crystallize, as opposed to modernist education, which denies cultural identities, gender affiliation, and nationality and attempts to shape the cosmopolitan person according to the European-American model.

Despite the great value of this approach, it is difficult to ignore the fact that it fixes in advance every ethnic group and every individual to a specific cultural narrative external to them and that they have not chosen. It restricts the individual's possibility to choose to be a "world citizen" or simply a "person". Under the multicultural approach, we have to be either European, African, men, women, etc., as the overall approach accepts the postmodern critique that decrees that there is no super-framework, but, rather, only specific cultural structures within which meaning is determined.

The second notable drawback of the multicultural approach is its compliance with value-oriented relativism: every ethnic group, every culture, has its own set of values that is inherently justified, without any external criteria for judgment (since these criteria, as we have learnt from history, are simply the conde-scension of and control by the dominant culture). What emerges from this contention is that there is no justification for acting against racism and inequality within ethno-cultural groups, but only externally to them. The oppression of women is justified in certain cultures but not in others; individual freedom is impor-tant to one culture, but trivial to another. Since we are not pre-pared to determine in principle that one culture has a preference over another, we are caught in a structural contradiction between the desire for equality and freedom between the various groups and the inability to advance those values within the culture. My argument on this point is simple: the mere striving toward a mul-ticultural society entails a liberal-modernist commitment to plu-ralism, freedom, and equality. This is a supra-commitment that is external to the postmodernist critique not because it has theo-retical justification, but because it has no material refutation: it has never been realized in history. It is precisely its non-realization that constitutes the justification for it being adequate for social action and education, and there is no need at all to make apologies for the obligatory or paternalistic nature of these values. They are values that have existed forever in the thoughts and feelings of a large portion of humankind in all cultures, where the socio-economic reality, at all times and in all places and including the school reality, opposed them and did not per-mit their realization.

In sum, it is my view that postmodernism is intellectual "pos-turing" that cleverly proposes consistent doubting that does not include any commitment to any particular stance and, in most cases, ends in relativist, superficial, and familiar idealism[10] so very familiar throughout the entire course of the history of ideas. However, it does also offer a systematic philosophical critique—namely, the exposure of hidden mechanisms and of contradictions and injustice—that is itself a rational method that immediately raises the question of alternatives. Postmodernism, portraying itself as nihilistic critique, avoids suggesting an alternative, thereby returning to classical modern values. In this way it presents an important challenge with respect to social criticism, particularly to the exposure of hidden mechanisms for repression of women, ethnic minorities, sexual minorities, etc. It also bears with it the experience to test the possibility of a multicultural and pluralistic reality, which today constitutes the most important battlefront against racism, chauvinism, cultural repression, and exploitation. However, it is important to remember that this important process, when it is adopted by the opponents of postmodern nihilism, has a price. The critique of the repressive elements of Euro-American modernism presents other modern values as an alternative, such as equal rights and pluralism. The effort to realize the pluralist, liberal ideology (based on modernism, of course) stresses the importance of the unique personal (and equal) identity of the "Other" and in some sense ties the person to her external social-ethnic-sexual definition. In a multicultural society, a person is deprived of the possibility of being simply a "person" (which she might never have had). She is forced to become attached to history and to the customs, tastes, and preferences of her culture; she is forced to define herself in a specific social fashion, and this, too, is a modernist, even conservative, stance.[11]

---

[10] See, for example, Ellen Meiksins Wood's Introduction in E.M. Wood & J.B. Foster (eds.), *In Defense of History*, Monthly Review Press, N.Y., 1997, in which she criticizes postmodernistic solipsism.

[11] It should be mentioned that the claim in favor of multiculturalism actually presents cosmopolitanism, the absence of a unique cultural identity, as a capitalist interest, thus marking itself as a radical

As an intellectual stance, postmodernism constitutes an important challenge to education: it rightly makes it more difficult to define specific knowledge as objective, thus confronting schools with the need to redefine themselves as frameworks working with knowledge. There are many diverse ideas for how to contend with this challenge: adopting, as proposed by Freire and his followers, a critical pedagogy constructed on the joint systematic, dialogic entry of adults and children into the world of knowledge, while deconstructing the codes in which they appear by revealing their power-hungry, subjective nature; or turning schools into learning frameworks, research frameworks, that create knowledge through collaboration between adults and children.[12] This latter idea accepts the postmodern critique with regard to the relativity of knowledge and attempts to suggest frameworks in which creativity and, hence, control of knowledge are removed from the sphere of external social mechanisms and transferred to small, local, and more democratic forms of organization.[13]

On the other hand, postmodernism connects between epistemological relativism, which is the inability to offer certainty or objectivity, with ontological relativism, which has no concreteness and contains only texts and, according to which, reality is a collection of signs and possibilities for their decoding. Philosophically speaking, this is a reasonable stance, but as a position

---

stance confronting processes of globalization and anonymity being imposed on people in the commercial reality of a world economy.

[12] Habermas makes the well-known optimistic proposal about the type of activity that could guide collaborative structuring of knowledge by means of a communicative action. The concept of communicative action is defined by Habermas as "the type of interaction in which all participants harmonize their individual plans of action with one another and thus pursue their illocutionary aims without reservation." J. Habermas, *The Theory of Communicative Action*, trans. T. McCarthy, Boston, 1984 ,Vol. 1, p. 294. Further consideration of Habermas' proposals is given in Ch. 7..

[13] S. Aronowitz & H. Giroux, *Postmodern Education: Politics, Culture and Social Criticism*, Minneapolis, 1991.

vis-à-vis education, it is untenable, since it means that the very existence of learning as an intentional activity is placed in doubt. Education can withstand the fact that we find it difficult to create objective knowledge, but it does not have to accept the so-called conclusion that there is no objective reality. The political and power-oriented use made of scientific knowledge and the inability to get to know the laws of nature does not mean that there are no laws in nature and that it is not important to continue searching for them. It is important to remember that one can still attribute to epistemological critique the striving for knowledge, the attempt to decipher the material foundations of reality, which is perceived by us as external, as a reasonable purpose, and as an educational imperative.

In my opinion, the most important educational challenge set forth by the postmodernist position is *not* the question of knowledge. Despite the fact that schools define themselves as institutions whose purpose is imparting knowledge and despite the fact that postmodernist criticism casts doubt on the possibility of justifying knowledge as objective, it is quite clear, from the perspective of basic common sense, that we know much more about the world than our predecessors knew. The procedures and the technology at humanity's disposal to become familiar with reality and to decode its overt and covert mechanisms are more sophisticated and reliable than they have ever been in human history. The fact that they frequently indicate contradictions, inconsistencies, and the need for new, alternative kinds of understanding is not necessarily a weakness, but perhaps an advantage. The distance between scientific research and nature and people is revealed in the reality of the "knowledge explosion", pointing to both the complexity of and the need for other ways of thinking, for creativity, and for humanity, and not necessarily to the "loss of the real".

If we add to this position the critique of modernity and social criticism as formulated in the politics of identity (particularly in feminism and multiculturalism), we can begin to discern the possibility of the neomodernist position constituting an answer to the postmodernist trend. A position of this sort accepts the criticism and attempts to formulate answers by means of new and different types of equal, level, pluralistic, and critical dialogue. In my view, this type of position rests mainly on those very values of modernity that were rejected by the impressive history of capitalism and that can form the basis for determining educational purposes. Some of these purposes have already appeared in modernity and, in a certain way, still exist in the self-images of those dealing with education, but it has never been possible to achieve them. A nihilistic atmosphere, intellectual submission, and the claim about the inability to justify anything could all turn out to be the appropriate background for new attempts, for the creation of new commitments. In my opinion, the real challenge in education lies in the sphere of the self-image of the individual as being of value, which I will consider in the next chapter. The starting point for my discussion of self-image in the school context is the assumption that school is the social forum that shapes the way the individual perceives herself as having social value. I also assume that this shaping, translated into school language as the image of "myself as a pupil" or "myself as a learner", logically and epistemologically precedes the possibility of the individual undergoing a positive experience of learning and performance that adheres to external rules.

Chapter 4

Schooling in Neocapitalism

The social analysis of capitalism, of the total commercialization mechanisms, of the terrible alienation of people from their natural and human environments, of people from themselves, of poverty, repression, and anonymity as part of the overall process of objectification in capitalism, have already been presented in detail convincingly by Marx and Engels and their followers. This is not to say that capitalism has not changed since Marx and Engels. On the contrary, it developed and expanded throughout the twentieth century in ways and on a scale that even its most perceptive nineteenth-century critics could not have predicted. The most striking, major developments were: the changes in the means of production and in automation; improvements in the standard of living in developed countries; the growth of the middle class, which has proved to be an important new social presence (both as a new type of producer of services and as the ultimate consumer who forms the basis of the power of capital); the collapse of the classical dichotomy between the proletariat and the bourgeoisies; the preeminence of services as opposed to production; the widening of economic disparities; globalization; and the new divisions of capital.

This series of changes is so extensive that is raises the question of whether, in fact, we are dealing with a new socioeconomic reality. Is quantity in fact becoming quality? In my view, most of the basic components of capitalism have not changed, and we still cannot contend that it has exhausted itself or is even close to doing so. Indeed, the very opposite is true: the social reality at the onset of the third millennium, with its blatant, detached materialism, reveals the force of the Marxist perspective and the fact that we are not in "post" anything, but actually in a state of neocapitalism.

I use the expression neocapitalism in arguing that on the one hand, we are still in the yet prevailing era of global capitalism as per the basic definition "A system is capitalist if the primary dynamic of social activity is the endless accumulation of capital."[1] On the other hand, we must note the new forms that capitalism has taken on, to the point of a change in elements that, in the past, seemed fundamentally definitive (like the social significance of the proletariat, for instance). On this matter, I agree with Peter Burger's observation that the capitalist mode of production has endured, in the sense of the "private appropriation of collectively produced surplus value."[2] The sociological concept of postmodernism does, however, represent far-reaching changes on the social level, but is still an immature concept historically, because "the maximization of profit remains the driving force of social reproduction."[3]

The sphere of technology and communications, particularly mass communications, has been filled with drama, especially in the second half of the twentieth century, and has led postmodernists to think about a new era, a new reality. This new form of communications is breeding a change in people's consciousness,

---

[1] I. Wallerstein, *The End of the World as We Know It*, Univ. Minnesota Press, Minneapolis, 1999, p. 57.

[2] Burger quoted in M. Peters & C. Lankshear, "Postmodern Counter-narratives", in H. Giroux et al., *Counter-narratives*, Routledge, N.Y., 1996, p. 7. In the same place, the writers refer the reader to Ernest Mandel (1975) and an article by Frederick Jameson, who argued in the 1980s that postmodernism represents the last appearance of capitalism. What Jameson calls "late capitalism", following Mandel's famous definition, is, in many senses, similar to what I call neocapitalism here. E. Mandel, *Late Capitalism,* trans. J. de-Bres, Humanities Press, London, 1975; F. Jameson, "Postmodernism or the Cultural Logic of Late Capitalism", *New Left Review*, 146, pp. 53-93, 1983.

[3] Burger, 1996.

in their private zone. It is rubbing out the distinction between private space and public space, engendering a new sense of time, space, and movement; it is a medium that makes people passive, impoverishes their language, and moves them away from human contact. It enables new modes of marketing, sales, and political manipulation. The world of technology and mass communications is a world of mass tourism and mass consumption. It produces a global expansion of mass culture and standardization of goods; it is characterized by the domination of consumer patterns of behavior, of television programs, pop-culture symbols, clothing, cars, and films. It is also characterized by the domination of English as the language of global commerce, and even in culture generally, as the anthropologists have shown, it is the language that mediates between the different languages of faraway cultures, while becoming immersed in the local dialect and speech.

This "uniqueness" of reality and the processes of commercial globalization that characterize it demonstrate the totality of that reality and to what extent the essence of the reality becomes transparent and cynical in neocapitalism based on manipulation by means of advertising symbols and images. This form of capitalism both produces and mediates between experiences in ways that no longer allow a distinction between the private and commercial realms, subject the most intimate aspects of our lives to a consumerist language and logic, under which what appears on the screen is more real than our lives. This is an exposed capitalism that has "taken off its gloves" and no longer requires rationalization in the form of morality or self-righteous preaching about the Free World (not that such rationalizations hurt, of course), in which the economic reasoning that drives society, culture, and the individual is transparent and exposed in full force. Here, in the clearest and most direct way, capital determines the objectives and applications of political power and public debate. This is a world in which familiarity with it leads to despair and fatalism or, alternatively, to a real need to attempt alternative ways of living.

If we examine the series of changes in the nature of social frameworks and the new ways in which people relate to these frameworks (as presented above), we can discern a direct link between neocapitalism and the change processes. In purely commercial terms, there is no difference between Black and White, Muslim and Christian, homosexual and heterosexual, man and woman: so long as they are buying and consuming goods and thereby justifying the continuation of production, they are legitimate. The old social frameworks (the Nation-State, the school, the family), which preserved the social structures that assisted the establishment of capitalism in the twentieth century, are no longer necessary. Neocapitalism no longer requires an ideological veil, nor does it have any need for institutional mechanisms, since it is, in any event, democratic, open, and more tolerant. It has at its disposal the technological means for performing reproduction, managing global consumerism, educating the masses through television and advertising, creating the "correct" public opinion, and even for creating a sense of satisfaction, authenticity, and self-realization directly and obviously linked to consumption.

Neocapitalism collapses the traditional dichotomy between the bourgeoisie and the proletariat. The principal social rank on which it bases itself is the middle class in the wealthy countries and in some of the developing countries that are adjusting to the American way of life, primarily where there is a combination of production workers and service personnel. The members of the middle class are the largest consumer force, brought up on obsessive, addictive consumerism of goods devoid of all value or utility, on destroying the earth's resources and exploiting the resources of poor countries that do not participate in the circus of purchasing, marketing, and endless gluttony. However, with the middle class constituting the central pillar of neocapitalism along with the changes in the means of production, which are becoming more automated and require less working hands, ever-increasing sections of the population are either unemployed, dependent on welfare mechanisms, or simply impoverished.

The option of being proletarian, in the sense of the poor, oppressed social class, but also productive and at work has almost completely disappeared in the reality of the industrialized countries in Europe and North America. Production workers belong to the middle class (although generally at the bottom rung), and they are beckoned to invest their lives and earnings in the consumer circus. But their jobs are also very much in danger, for it will quickly become apparent that they are too costly; while they are useful as consumers, there is no need for them as costly workers with costly rights and no reason not to move their work to machines or, alternatively, to cheaper workers. Production workers are voluntary or involuntary immigrants from the Third World to whom the historical achievements of the First-World and Second-World labor unions do not apply. Alternatively, the production plants themselves might be transferred to places where the workforce is cheap and available, since globalization makes it possible for a certain part of the production process to be transferred to such places.

Indeed, a new social reality has been created with a broad middle class, some of whose members earn a living under duress (generally production workers and minor service workers) and are in fact poor, alongside a social stratum of unemployed; casual laborers; transients; immigrants who have finished their stints as foreign laborers and have been granted citizenship in one of the rich countries; and foreign laborers who were imported by industrialists with the support of their governments and who attempt to exist under great duress in a way that is supposed to allow them to send money to their families in the poor world.[4] These workers are due either to return to their countries or else to change their status from immigrants with no rights to legal immigrants. In the latter case, since they will be entitled to the rights of citizens, their wages will rise and it will be necessary to fire them, thus sending them to join the ranks of the unemployed; at the same time, it will be necessary to import new cheap foreign laborers from poor countries. This class division blurs the historical class war in two important respects: first, with the lower and middle classes *as* two strata existing *alongside* each other with no zone of friction between them, the blatant, direct exploitation that existed in the past has disappeared;

---

[4] ˙Saskia Sassen, *Globalization*, The New Press, N.Y., 1998.

and second, the lower class includes more and more people who are not involved in productive work, i.e., they do not produce the surplus capital of the bourgeoisie. Putting aside the matter of the impact of this change on the overall social level, it is important to stress that for the purpose of the present discussion, the members of the poor lower and lower-middle classes have children and these children enter the public education system and constitute a significant part of that system, far exceeding the proportion of poor to the general population.[5]

Moreover, neocapitalism has released itself from some of the myths attached to the old form of capitalism, particularly the myth of self-destruction (for which the Marxists are responsible) and the myth of the need for stability (for which the capitalist economists are responsible). The first myth stated that the internal contradictions of capitalism, particularly that between the need to increase production logarithmically and the need to sell those goods (namely, to give buying power to people), would lead to a reduction in profitability and decrease in capitalism's exploitative capability, to the point of destruction of goods. In other words, it would lead to a war between the capitalist forces and, ultimately, to the collapse of capitalism from within.

The second myth stated that capitalism operates best, most efficiently, in conditions of political stability. Trade is the enemy of war, and capitalism means universal peace. Today it is clear that neocapitalism is not a time-bomb about to self-explode due to its contradictions (which are well tended to) unless we are

---

[5] The reason why the proportion of poverty among children in public education exceeds the proportion of poverty in the overall population is related to two factors: first, the birthrate among poor families is relatively higher than the upper classes; second, the fact that a considerable proportion of upper-middle-class families and, certainly, of upper-bourgeois class families do not use the public education system, as they have private frameworks at their disposal. Hence, if the rate of unemployment is, for instance, 10% in a certain country, it is very likely that the percentage of children of unemployed people in the education system of that country could reach 15% or more.

talking about the likely process of the overall destruction of the world, which is liable to result from external resistance to capitalism and not from any internal contradiction thereof. It also appears that capitalism does not require political stability, for it also flourishes in turbulent environments. It has no problem at all with a reality in a constant state of flux—indeed, quite the opposite might be true. One of the best solutions to the need for destroying goods is shortening the shelf life of merchandise. This process is the change dictated by fashion, the shifting rhythm of life, the subtle directive to "get bored" quickly with everything. Neocapitalism is nourished by and nourishes a rapidly changing reality, and chaos provides it with congenial lodgings, exactly like nihilism.

This last point is interesting because it links the sense of postmodernist chaos to neocapitalist logic. On the one hand, this sense stems from the rate and intensity of change, and, on the other, from the inability to base self-identity on a reality in which all the social parameters that served in the past to define that identity (gender, ethnic origin, family, nationality, etc.) are disappearing. This sense impels many people to seek stability, to cling to the past, to return to religion, to yearn for strong "leadership", family values, and any framework that gives the illusion of permanence and transcendentalism.

However, these structures and conservative tendencies are merely part of the consumer game itself. The economic dynamic that dictates the return to religion is easily discernible; you do not have to be an anthropologist to recognize the ridiculous ways in which a "new", recently-discovered authenticity appears out of the blue, in the shape of a so-called culture or in-depth philosophical insight, supposedly emanating from the "good old days", the pre-capitalist days or perhaps the ancient and wise Eastern cultures. Clearly, the neocapitalist totality leaves no stone unturned, and the various conservative fashions offer no opposition whatsoever to that totality. On the contrary, they are sold to the highest bidder and instantly become the basis for establishing powerful economic entities that market the (religious, medical, psychological, educational, etc.) new "alternative" with all the aggressiveness of moneychangers.

One of the social frameworks that at least apparently could be relinquished in the neocapitalist reality is the public school. This, after all, is an antiquated institution whose indoctrination processes are slow and certainly not as dramatic as those of television, for instance. It is an institution that is not suited to the fast neocapitalist rate of technological growth, whose teachers are not computer-literate and are untrained in mass communications. The economic potential of its "customers", i.e., the children, is very limited—in short, not interesting. It also seems that the public financing of educational systems, particularly in industrialized European countries, is becoming an intolerable burden on the free economy. It creates gigantic deficits in the public purse and encumbers the activities of market forces, for instance, hampering the unavoidable competition with the Asian Tiger, which does not invest even half the amount in its schools.[6] The relative advantage of modernist schools, namely, the social segregation that established the ranking of the moneyed elite, on the one hand, and the production workers, on the other, no longer seems to be required: first, because this is guaranteed by the private apprenticeship systems of the upper social classes; second, because fewer production workers are needed—in the era of globalization, they come from Third- and Fourth-World countries at a negligible cost and the moribund Nation-State does not need to invest any resources in them.

There is another reason for the redundancy of the modernist school's process of segregation; namely, the neocapitalist era has far more successful ways of achieving social reproduction

---

[6] One of the suggestions made by Naisbitt to explain the superiority of the Asian economies, particularly Southeast Asia, over European economies is the claim that in the former, the public investment in education and health is extremely low. The output of the public systems is not lower as a result of this low investment, since it relies on the successful functioning of the traditional, extended family as a complement to the state-provided education and health services. J. Naisbitt, *Megatrends in Asia*, Simon & Schuster, N.Y., 1996.

than schooling, particularly by means of the "culture industry".

The concept of culture industry was devised by the Frankfurt School to describe the effect of advertising, entertainment, and mass communication on the loss of personal autonomy, the loss of the autonomous subject, which was a pivotal modern ideal. Under the conceptions of Adorno, Horkheimer, and Marcuse,[7] the culture industry creates various types of entertainment (including news and information entertainment) for purposes of profit derived from the culture industry's symbiotic contacts with mass consumption's demands and possibilities. It is a kind of mass culture in which people appear not as subjects but as "objects of manipulation", as Adorno phrased it. Under this conception, a social reality determined to a considerable extent by the culture industry suppresses personal freedom, individualism, and the pursuit of authenticity in sophisticated, dramatic, and hidden ways, much more quickly and effectively than the exertion of overt force, as in intentional indoctrination or education. The guaranteed, seemingly willing identity of the individual with consumerism and communication, the internalization of their values and acceptance of the oppression they represent, turn the individual into Marcuse's *One-Dimensional Man*, but render almost all the old tools for shaping the individual (such as schools) fundamentally superfluous.

The portrayal of the culture industry as the bankruptcy of culture in general and of the arts in particular distinguishes between the postmodernist position and that of the Frankfurt School.[8] Under the postmodernist position, the distinction between "high culture" or "smart culture" and popular culture is anachronistic, no longer justified, and simply a manifestation of the cultural hierarchy's attempt to seize control and put the artistic tastes and tendencies of the social elites above the ordinary

---

[7] M. Horkheimer & T. Adorno, *Dialektik der Aufklarang*, Frankfurt a M, rep. 1988; H. Marcuse, *One-Dimensional Man*, Beacon Press, Boston, rep. 1988.

[8] Z. Lavi, *Is Education Possible in Times of Postmodernism?*, Sifriat Poalim, Tel-Aviv, 2000, p. 21 (Hebrew).

person, while intentionally blocking access to the inalienable products of Western culture and the so-called elegant, genuine, desirable arts. In contrast, among the members of the Frankfurt School, whose thinking preceded the postmodernist position, are discernible both a romantic streak that distinguishes between kinds of culture as well as an aversion to mass culture, which they did not adopt with the same ease and delight as the postmodernists do.

My position on this matter is closer to that of the Frankfurt School thinkers, particularly to that taken by Marcuse. In my view, the problem with the culture industry is not the abolishment of the culture hierarchy, which has forever been an expression of power and manipulation and even today remains unscarred, despite being unjustified. Van Gogh's paintings have never fetched better prices than they do today, although they appear on cheap posters at the same price for all. The chances of being accepted to art school in New York are no greater than they were twenty or thirty years ago—indeed, quite to the contrary.

The problem with the culture industry lies in the subordination of culture to industry, namely, in the creation of production mechanisms, in outputs known in advance, that stem from a logic that allows the existence of only what can be marketed and sold. Neocapitalism proves that marketing in large quantities and at low prices is preferable to the opposite situation, thus creating gigantic consumption mechanisms and constant competition for efficiency, price reductions, and increased quantities. Of course, this process has considerable advantages, as it enables many people to own consumer goods and, in many cases, turns art, for instance, into a commodity, making it accessible to people who previously had no chance of reaching it. But, at the same time, it obviates the existence of a personal, creative, unique sphere in which the artist (for example) felt free and expressed her freedom and illusion of autonomy. This reduction in existential options, or, in Marcuse's parlance, "consciousness reduction", is not unique to art. It is part of neocapitalist life, seemingly able only to bypass the industrial producers themselves and entrepreneurs who are required to show greater creativity in relation to the new and sophisticated ways in which they accustom us to need what we need.

Here we can see a clear similarity between the culture industry and the education industry, which is part of the former. The debate surrounding education is, itself, peppered with industrial-marketing terminology; schools are required to subject themselves to output and efficiency indices, becoming an arena in which commercial companies look for clients to expand their marketing options. However, the high price that education pays appears in the form of reductions: school life is reduced to a cluster of activities intended to achieve directly outputs, which no longer include the simple conduct of communication between people in a neutral environment, who are just "chatting", taking an interest in one another, exchanging stories. This is now all considered idle, purposeless activity. School life is limited to purposeful, disciplinary learning, with the gradual diminishing of the legitimacy of any activity not measurable directly in terms of output. There has also been a critical reduction in the range of responsibility of the adults toward the children, in the sense of commitment to the overall well-being of the children. This reduction is most acutely felt in the consciousness of teachers, who today perceive themselves as knowledge technocrats, as instruments of teaching, and not as educators.

One possible place for education is the place that, in many cases, the people who turned to teaching sought—namely, love for children, the desire to know them, nurture them, protect them, and live with them. The existence of such a place is denied by the neocapitalist reality of the school and has become abstract and restricted, not only as a physical place, but also as a place in the consciousness of teachers. It has disappeared in the morass of the feverish, paranoid, and violent activity of daily life and has been pushed away into its "proper" place in the depths of the subconscious.

At the same time, it is important to recognize that the school is in a different place from commercial forms of life. It does not produce capital, rather, spends it. The traditional role of the school as a training institution for the needs of industry (i.e., as an institution that trains production workers, work managers, housewives, etc.) seems no longer necessary. The world of high-tech and communications, which currently is the principal tool for raising, manipulating, and producing surplus value, is barely assisted by the old-fashioned school education, which cannot keep pace with the development of the world of computers, for example. The neocapitalist world no longer has any need for antiquated school hierarchies, since it has been found that work in flat, more democratic organizations reaps higher outputs. Even the so-called education of members of the lower class to help them to come to terms with a social destiny as production workers is not necessary: there are fewer such workers needed, and it is not difficult to import them from poor countries. In any case, members of the lower class are destined for a life of unemployment and unproductive social rejection, so there is absolutely no point in investing the taxpayers' money in them.

However, public education in industrialized countries has not disappeared and, in my opinion, is not likely to disappear in the near future. Schools will continue to exist in a format similar to the present one, with a number of changes, which I will consider below. There are three bases to this claim. First, as I have already pointed out, many people, particularly the middle class in industrialized countries, have a tendency to cling to and reinforce frameworks that seem to them to be traditional and protection against chaos.

One of such institution is the public school, along with the myths associated with it and its narrative as a bastion of values, continuity, and stability as well as progress and success. This is an attractive package that is hard to reject in a seemingly chaotic reality. Second, schools will not disappear, because they provide a place to leave children when the parents go to work. The school is the ultimate babysitter and, as such, cannot be relinquished. Even the postmodern predictions of a shift toward working at home with the development of computer technology and new methods of communication have proved completely groundless. People have not left their workplaces, despite the absence of any technical barrier to doing so. They prefer human contact and sociability to sitting at home. It is also unclear how many middle-class parents in the big cities of affluent countries

are capable and willing to remain at home with their children—
most of them would probably be climbing the walls within a
week.[9] Third, even the tendency that was prevalent in the past
among upper-middle-class parents to open private schools in
which their children could be protected against the supposedly
harmful influence of poverty-stricken children and in which they
could realize for their children the liberal educational fantasy of
freedom seems to have come to an end. The public school system has wisely organized itself quickly to meet some of the parental demands, and parents themselves have reached the conclusion that it is preferable to cooperate with the educational
establishment and enjoy government funding.

The great social challenge for schools in the present era is
linked to three parallel features: one, the significant decrease in
the social importance of the school; two, the schools being regarded as a refuge and babysitter; and three, the real option
available to the majority of schools to carry out reform, which
stems from the two other features. Interestingly enough, establishment pressure on schools has diminished of late, as part of
the general weakening of the Nation-State and the decentraliza-
tion processes it is undergoing. At the same time, parental, particularly middle-class, pressure is increasing in the determination
of the educational policy of the local community level.

Unlike in the past, today's school has the actual possibility of
implementing an educational concept, proposing organizational
structures, and designing curricula in a much freer way. In fact,
schools can do virtually anything they want, provided they can
enlist parental support and backing. The question is really, what

---

[9] I mentioned above in Ch.1, that in the U.S., home schooling is
prevalent. A closer inspection of the phenomenon reveals that
most of the parents involved in home schooling are from the mid-
dle- and upper-middle classes and they do not sit at home teaching their children. Rather, they generally find creative solutions
through the community center, private tutors, working in turns,
etc. In short, they create the structure of a private school, if they
have the means.

do they want? And, not surprisingly, the answer is that in most cases, schools adjust to the evolving neocapitalist reality, although this in not imperative by any means. This adjustment manifests itself in a series of changes that characterize many schools in the public sector. My argument is that these changes widen social disparities and exacerbate the already-existing grim situation of lower-class children:

(1) Practical reinforcement of the social disparities at the systemic level. This process is manifested at the state, regional, or municipal levels and expressed in the clear distinction between "good" schools, in which life and studies are certainly tolerable for the majority of pupils (generally in areas inhabited by middle- and upper-middle-class populations), and schools "for the poor", in which the academic level and motivation level are particularly low. In the latter, institutional violence and personal violence reach a peak and repression and paranoia prevail. The schools are ruled by teachers and either municipal or private security firms that send guards and install surveillance equipment to watch the children. This phenomenon is most acute in inner-city schools in the United States, where electronic surveillance equipment and "legions" of municipal guards who are not subject to the authority of the school management are common in schools plagued by violence. These are the places where the teachers unions have instructed their members to distance themselves from children and avoid any physical contact with them as a self-protection tactic.[10] Phenomena like these are justified against the background of a cultural reality

---

[10] Devine presents a grim picture of inner-city schools in the U.S. as violent places, where the corridors, changing rooms, and places of pupil circulation are loaded with anger, aggression, and delinquency. According to Devine, the security systems, with their electronic surveillance equipment, security personnel, and violent, paranoid logic, undermine the violence prevention programs in schools and bear authority over the pupils' behavior, something that stands in contradiction to the traditional roles of teachers as guardians and agents of moral behavioral. The teachers, Devine claims, become information bureaucrats, while the pupils' welfare is handed over to electronic instrumentation and to people without

against the background of a cultural reality that identifies youth with monstrosity and psychopathy, in which the television programs and films it produces cultivate the demonization of children and portray adults as the innocent victims of impulsivity, selfishness, and the lack of values of postmodern children. The economic analysis indicates the sad fact that in most places, middle- and upper-class schools forever find ways to enjoy large chunks of the public educational funding and that the many important disparity-reduction projects pale in comparison to the force of the discriminatory mechanisms, which rely on their very existence as the basis for egalitarian demagogy.

(2) Massive presence and greater parental involvement in schools. A series of supposedly ideological proclamations on collaboration, communality, the responsibility of parents for their children's education, etc., as well as a series of practical observations regarding the importance of parents in reducing tension and violence in schools, improving the level of learning, and so forth, usually accompany this phenomenon, which originates in broader social processes (some of which I have mentioned above). The truth is that in most cases, there is not much connection between the perceived presence of parents in schools and their actual involvement in the educational processes. This is essentially consumer involvement based on relating to the school as a service provider and to the parent as a customer. This relationship stresses primarily the public school's interest in raising additional financial resources from the parents (both through direct collection and by enlisting them to work and provide services) and the desire of certain parents to advance what they see as their children's individual interests. Thus, in many schools

---

educational training and no desire at all to educate. Devine quotes from various recommendations that appear in publications of the American Teachers' Organization, according to which teachers are required to distance themselves from pupils and avoid any physical contact with them, even in the event of a need arising to protect them. J. Devine, *Maximum Security*, Univ. Chicago Press, Chicago, 1996, pp. 82-83.

there is an active parents committee, which initiates the collection of money from parents, organizes extracurricular activities, and brings pressure to bear on the school with respect to the functioning of certain teachers or the desired contents of the curriculum.

In any case, it is clear that parents who fully utilize this new-found opportunity are those who are well versed in consumer language and behavior patterns, those who have the free time, the energy, and the verbal skills to bargain and conduct negotiations. They know how to stand up for their rights, as it were, as customers. They have the confidence to demand and be assertive and, in short, are parents from the middle and upper-middle classes of consumers who are promoting their children's interests. Lower-class parents, in any event not used to consumer life as assertive customers, generally find themselves outside this sphere of involvement.

(3) Obvious change in the sphere of teaching methods, particularly in middle-class schools. Without going into a detailed analysis of this sphere of change, I will mention two changes that, to me, seem to represent a general trend. The one change, which has been taking place systematically for years, is the shift from frontal teaching to alternative teaching; the second change, related to the first, is the shift of the classroom arrangement to that of group work.

The basic idea is that frontal teaching is rejected as a technique because it perpetuates "banking education", in Freire's terminology: the arrogant all-knowing position of the teacher vis-à-vis the pupils, the teacher's arbitrary power, and the supposed fact that the teacher holds all the answers, contradicted by the fact that he or she demands of the pupils to answer all of his or her questions. To counter this teaching technique, educational technocrats have attempted to install a teacher who is closer to the children, to construct a different setting in the classroom space, made up of centers, in which every pupil has easy access to the teacher and his or her friends. Generally, this change is accompanied by a series of recommendations regarding "working on your own" (namely, filling in notebooks) or "the pupil's responsibility for the learning process" (autonomy!) and a series of rationalizations regarding the importance of teamwork. In practice, in most cases, it appears that the pupils have lost out on those teachers who were excellent, interesting lecturers, but quite abysmal tutors. The rejection of the legitimacy of frontal teaching has turned teachers into prisoners of a method for which only some of them are trained or interested in and which surely does not suit them all. The various new methods have created a situation in which the pupils sit in groups, but the practical sense of group work is not expressed in their activities. A learning group in a class is generally a collection of children who are working on their own or, rather, one child who is working while the others are bored. There is an enormous gap between sitting around a table together and teamwork, which, in most cases, is quite unbridgeable in a system where the adult tutors do not know how to work as a team and where the work roster almost always places the teacher alone in the classroom with the students and the door closed.

(4) The change in the organizational form of the learning contents. There are two obvious features involved in this sphere: one, adoption of the developmental argument, which posits that the development of children's intelligence from sensor-motor activity to abstract thinking is a deterministic, unidirectional process (a sort of simplistic version of Piaget); and two, acceptance of an assumption that children are incapable of understanding things removed from them and that they have to learn through things "close" or familiar to them. The manifestation of the first parameter is the collection of curricula, particularly in the first years of school, that are built on children's sensor-motoric activities. During these years, children spend most of their time cutting, pasting, and drawing. They do not conduct discussions, and adults avoid talking to them; they have to operate on the sensory level, since it is "appropriate" for their developmental stage.

Any attempt at intellectual discussion or to meet children's intellectual needs is absent from the curriculum, as the children supposedly do not have this need in any event. This anti-intellectual, anti-communicative situation is accompanied by the structuring of a curriculum from the immediate environment.

The most notable examples I found of this in all the schools I have observed are the curriculum of the type of "my neighborhood", "my home", "my family", etc. This type of curriculum is marvelously tailored for children from the middle and upper classes, for what could be nicer than showing familial and neighborhood affiliations? What could be more instructive than looking at a manicured living environment as the microcosm of the world? The problem is that in most classes, particularly in the slums, there are children who do not wish to import their impoverished family life and its daily hardships into the classroom. The neighborhoods they live in are not exactly a place from which they draw strength or to which they want to belong. If they are children of immigrants or minority groups who do not really feel they belong or are worthy, this type of curriculum exacerbates (sometimes unintentionally) the lack of belonging. It is perhaps worth mentioning that in my view, these two assumptions are groundless, and for two reasons. First, many children have intellectual needs, and some even have difficulty with cutting and pasting; second, I do not accept the proposition that children learn better through what is familiar to them.

(5) The reduction in adults' scope of responsibility for what happens to children in the postmodern school. The logic of capitalism mandates that although the supplier is responsible for marketing good merchandise, it bears no responsibility for the way in which the customer consumes that merchandise. This reduction in responsibility appears in a number of forms. One way is the reduction of the hearing and seeing skills of adults in schools, particularly with regard to children's distress. This loss, which originates in anxiety over the inability to respond to the distress when it is either heard or seen, has a long-term effect on the relationship between adults and children and on the way the school operates. Thus, for example, teachers avoid private encounters with children, and when they are forced to meet with them, they make sure to talk, reprimand, or prove so that they will not be forced to listen and see. This avoidance has a great impact on the pace of school life, which has become feverish and urgent, where there is never "any time", where the adult never stops to look into the eyes of the children or listen to them.

Another way that responsibility has been diminished is through the systematic transferal of responsibility for what happens in school to the children. Current school language is loaded with expressions like "It is your responsibility," "You choose," "It's your decision." This trend is supported by the ideology of personal autonomy, which advocates developing the responsibility of the learner for the learning process (i.e., it is the customer's responsibility for how she or he consumes the product) and is by the transferal of some of the responsibility for what to children in schools to the parents, supposedly by means of an understanding of their responsibility for their children's education. In fact, this trend stems from a desire to put all the genies that threaten the teachers back into their bottles, i.e., the parental home.

Another sphere in which the school's responsibility is being reduced is, ironically, the sphere of its own activities, which, according to school logic, have their status as voluntary activities exchanged for a status of arbitrary "law of nature", supposedly imposed on the school by nature. A prominent example is the competition and pursuit of excellence that are dictated by the school and whose destructive results for some of the children (those who finish after third place in every race) are always presented as a necessity stemming from the supposedly competitive nature of children, the world, reality, nature, and so on, although there is no necessity in practice for schools to run a race track. Another example is the creation of peer groups, which become a driving, formative, activating, conservative, and sometimes very destructive social force. Schools today refrain from taking responsibility for the operation of the children's peer community, although they are its direct and indirect creators. A large part of the social life in school—the effect of the school's organizational structure (in itself not at all necessary!)—is conducted outside the field of vision and range of hearing of the adults and, consequently, outside of their sphere of responsibility.

These processes are not imperative, and there are some wonderful schools that show that it is possible to fight against them, that resources can be used more wisely, and that teaching techniques can be selected in more suitable and flexible ways. Children and adults can be allowed broad self-expression; joy and optimism can be preserved in a chaotic reality; the general tendency toward excellence can be countered, as can commercialization and competition. There can be greater sensitivity to children's distress, out of compassion and a willingness to take responsibility. There is a real possibility of countering the above-mentioned developments that prevented schools in previous eras from acting differently.

Schools can refuse to conform with the capitalist processes and can stop the commercialization of education by not to allowing those working in education to turn into traders of goods; they can refuse to condone the avoidance of observing children's distress and can cease to demonize children. They can take practical steps to put a stop to the overall social trend-taking place outside the school walls. Paradoxically, the relative weakness of schools is also the secret of their strength, because it enables them to make smart and genuine use of parents' anxieties and because it enables the community to back schools in a reality in which public opinion is becoming more and more a medium of change. This means that there is a possibility for a radical return to the psychological origins of education, as a medium that enables those involved to be focused on the children, to have empathy and compassion for their distress, and to struggle to shape a better reality for them.

It is important to remember that social chaos generates the option of fulfillment and activism, and not only despair and gloom. This chaos is characterized primarily by the absence of a guiding hand, by the fading away of all the hierarchic administrative procedures that characterized the realization of old capitalism, the very thing that defined them as rational. This chaos also holds hope for new kinds of organizations, social solidarity, egalitarian multiculturalism, and for a new type of humanism. One way of achieving this is by insisting on the actualization of the other, by recognizing his or her pain and distress, and by embarking on an uncompromising struggle to change reality.

Part III

Generative Mentoring

Chapter 5

Mentoring: The Generation of Self-Image

The word 'mentoring' has its origins in Greek mythology. The goddess Athena decided to appoint an adult chaperone for Odysseus' son, Telemachus, of whom she was known to be particularly fond. When Telemachus reached marriageable age, he requested to go to sea to search for his father who had not yet returned to Ithaca. He was accompanied by a mentor, an adult chaperone who was none other than Athena in disguise. Her duty was to mentor the young man, to serve as a guide to him in the wide world.

The idea of adults mentoring youth was not unique to Greek culture. It was an integral part of the educational process, particularly for the children of the ruling classes, in various cultures in the ancient world and continued to be the preferred way of educating until public education systems were set up, about two-thousand years ago in China and 150 years ago in Europe.

The concept of mentoring in its various historical and cultural incarnations is fed by three different images, each of which plays an important role in shaping the image of education in general.

The first image is that of the revered mentor. This is the type of mentoring that was (and, to some extent, still is) common in Indian culture and in the traditions of various religions. It is associated with the figure of the guru as a person who, through his personality, represents contact with the sublime. This image has the adult teacher taking charge of his young trainee following the youngster's referral to him from the outside: the pupil or his family approaches the teacher and asks him to be his mentor. The teacher is a person with superior knowledge who holds the keys to the secrets of the universe and is supposed to lead the young man down the right path, the path to release from the cycle of rebirth, to enlightenment. But this learning is not theoretical in nature; rather, it is embodied in the "study" of the personality, behavior, and lifestyle of the revered teacher who has achieved unmediated contact with the most important idea in the culture (God, Brahman, absolute truth, integrity, the virtues, etc.). This contact, which is basically transformative, puts the teacher on an ontological platform that is above ordinary people, thus turning him into a courted object, into an ideal to be strived for, and against which the various criteria for personal progress must be assessed.

The relationship built around this image is based primarily on the unceasing attempts by the trainee to come to grips with the mentor's knowledge. These attempts include verbal interplay, in the form of repeated questions, the answers to which are delayed by the mentor until the trainee is "ready" for the knowledge. This readiness is usually achieved after many years of maintenance and service work by the trainee for the convenience of the teacher, the purpose being to achieve the required virtues, usually presented as moral virtues, such as modesty, purging of desire, and following society's codes of conduct, which are the essential conditions for recognizing the truth as it were. The mentor is the hard rock of knowledge against which the trainee's questions, curiosity, and struggles shatter, and he is supposed to determine whether an optimal level of hardship has been reached, whether the belief is sufficiently strong in order to progress to the next stage, and whether the trainee's morality is sufficiently well-forged to permit him to grasp the secrets of learning.

Mentoring of this sort has never been part of the teaching methodology in modern public education, although its reverberations were strongly felt in parochial education (Jewish, Christian, Indian, Chinese, etc.). In fact, the only manifestations of mentoring in schools today are in the isolated appearances of particularly charismatic figures whose charisma is more threatening than constructive.

The second image of the mentor is that of the expert. This image, which was prevalent mainly in the Ancient Greek and Roman cultures and among the nobility of most of the world's cultures, attributes to the mentor mastery in all transferable skills and knowledge. This image severs the necessary link between the mentor's personality and his knowledge and turns the knowledge itself into the purpose of the mentoring relationship. This type of mentoring generally has three types of manifestations: one, in the form of the artisan-apprentice relationship, which characterizes the guild-like division of labor; the second, in the form of the personal tutors (in mathematics, science, arts, manners, etc.) hired by wealthy families to educate their children; and the third, in the form of the freelance expert who sells his merchandise, his "knowledge", and convinces people to entrust their children's education to him (along the lines of the Sophists in Ancient Greece).

In all three of these forms, the mentor is not necessarily a member of the upper class (in Rome, he was often a Greek slave) or with a charismatic personality or supreme virtues; he is required to have nothing beyond professional mastery of the discipline he is supposed to teach (although having these virtues never harms his popularity). All that is required of him is ordinary teaching skills and effective didactics that are regulated and measurable.[1]

This type of mentoring is still common today (for instance, in the field of the arts, which preserves the guild model) and exists

---

[1] We can learn from the history of monitoring that the measurement of outputs in education is not necessarily an upshot of the capitalist situation. In certain senses, it has always been practiced. On the other hand, it is possible to interpret this differently—the relationship with the mentor as expert was from the outset an economic relationship aimed at the product. In other words, already in the ancient world, it existed as a type of trade relationship connected to the division of labor and control over the means of production; hence, its capitalist character.

alongside the public school, mainly as academic mentoring of students having difficulty with their studies or of teachers of such students. Academic mentoring suits the presumptions of educational theory, such as that different children require different amounts of time to learn; that extra lessons are a good medium for cognitive support; and that individual practice can improve children's mastery of the learning material. Without contesting these presumptions, my argument will be that academic mentoring is only effective if it enables the child experiencing difficulty to create a self-image of being of value and that, in fact, there is no connection whatsoever between the extent of the mentoring's effect on the child and the mentor's pedagogic skill or the child's cognitive ability.

The third image of the mentor is that of advisor and counselor. This is mentoring that is based on the contact between the adult and child being built completely on the child's needs, wishes, and abilities. The goal of this type of mentoring is to further the full realization of the child's potential and not to impart external knowledge or values. This image existed in the ancient world in Judaism ("Educate the child in his own way"), Greece (Socrates), and India (the *Bhagavad-Gita*), but it has drawn most of it force from modern liberal humanist attitudes. The most complete manifestation of this image in the twentieth century appeared in psychoanalysis, particularly in its humanistic version. In education, it is embodied in the form of the phaedocentric approach. Psychoanalysis reduced the mentor-trainee relationship to a therapist-client relationship by constructing a relationship with the client at the center.[2] The purpose of the psychotherapy process is the personal happiness and welfare of the client, which is achieved by developing her ability to achieve personal insight. But this ability is only attainable by means of the professional skill of the therapist to contain, process, and reflect the client's feelings toward him or her. The content of the ther-

---

[2] This reduction is part of the image and not part of the history of the theory of psychoanalysis. Freud was influenced far more by the Hegelian model of master-slave than by educational ideas.

apy content is determined solely by what the client brings to the session with the therapist; however, a considerable part of that is related to the relationship with the therapist, which serves as a kind of laboratory in which the client learns to cope with her fears and anxieties.

The child-centered approach in education, which was greatly influenced by psychology and a considerable number of whose founders and champions were psychoanalysts, offers a model of the teacher-pupil relationship that is not based on the transferal of dry, external knowledge from the teacher to the pupil or on indoctrinating binding values. Instead, it advocates, as the legitimate and effective basis of the relationship, cultivating relationships, interests, creativity, curiosity, and personal knowledge in the child. This model of education, which has never been suited to the institutional structure of schools, remains in the margins of the educational endeavor, but has influenced its imagery and concepts through accepted images of the teacher as the midwife (returning to Socrates) whose job is to "deliver" what already exists in the child and as the gardener (Maslow) who enables the seed to develop toward its preordained destiny as a mature tree.

This third type of mentoring is different from the previous two types in two senses. One, it gives the mentor presence in the trainee's intimate psychological life, emotions, and impulses. Two, the mentor's specialization, knowledge, and professionalism are not transferred to the trainee; in fact, they remain hidden from the trainee, and it is the mentor's job to use them as tools to allow the trainee to progress toward her own goals.

Against the background of these three images of mentors, I will suggest another, slightly different possibility for mentoring, which, in my view, is desirable, legitimate, and possible. I refer to the generative mentoring model that propounds a self-image of being of value to others and is intended to promote the individual's freedom and happiness, whilst recognizing the necessity for social change. Three basic assumptions of this type of mentoring are: that freedom and happiness are both a personal and a social matter; that the individual's ability to imbue his or her life with meaning (namely, to keep sight of its purpose and act accordingly) is a function of his or her social existence; that individuation, in the sense of self-realization, is not a matter to be settled within the person, but between her and other people. A further assumption is that people, and children in particular, need other people—to acknowledge them, love them, and respond to them. They need other people as objects of intent, as a purpose, as a possibility for expressing their ability to love. They need others in order to create themselves, so that they have substance, exist.

A fourth assumption of the generative mentoring model is that the encounter between the adult and child is a generative encounter—in other words, it generates a concept that did not exist prior to the encounter, namely, the child's self-image as being of value (positive or negative) to others, which I call the child's "actualization" below.

The fifth assumption is that the social and personal reality of neocapitalism is a repressive class reality that does not permit people to recognize others as subjects, instead restricts them to a view of others as objects. It is a reality that distances and alienates people from one another and, consequently, from themselves. It is a reality in which the only mechanisms for creating meaning are objectification, consumption, and acquisition, not humanization and the common pursuit of ideas.

What emerges from these assumptions is that the way to create a reality that is more humane, more tolerable, more just and free, and more worthy of life is to nurture individuals by bringing about their complete actualization. Simply put, this type of nurturing means creating meaningful human relationships and interpersonal solidarity that will enable people to accept one another. Acceptance means allowing others the possibility of existing, of recognizing themselves as being of value, of forming insight into themselves, of giving meaning to their lives, of realizing themselves as free individuals. What also emerges is that the apparently simple act of interpersonal communication, of mutual recognition, is a freedom-granting gesture with broad social significance that moves from the individual sphere to the social reality. The problem is that the human contact that is anchored in the basic need of every person for the other, which is the only real and concrete possibility for existing and being free, virtually does not occur. We must invest effort, energy, and dedication in order to create merely the possibility of it occurring. It would appear that the proper forum for this contact is the place that children go when they leave their parental home (where they generally experience warm, loving contact, albeit problematic) and where they encounter an entirely unfamiliar social world— in other words, in the child's encounter with the educational framework.

Generative mentoring is based on the unmediated encounter between adult and child, but does not culminate in the act of meeting or through dialogue between the two. Rather, it requires also a genuine world-altering activity. The need for this activity derives both from the social reality that mandates change and from the encounter between the adult and child, which creates the mentor's devotion and commitment to the child's happiness. Together, these two factors will necessarily be expressed as a series of actions aimed at allowing the child greater freedom, opening up opportunities where he or she lives, and waging an uncompromising war against the restrictions, alienation, repression, and avoidance that threaten children's ability to develop a self-image of being of value. Since these are all external factors, generally social and institutional, the adult is required to take real, practical action. This sort of action can be in mediating between the child and the various institutions he encounters, between the child and other adults. It can manifest itself in work with children toward achieving academic or other goals, which will expand their range of options for the future. It can also express itself in the creation of a variegated, private environment in which the child can be with herself, rest, or escape the pressures she bears. But what is important is that the activity is not set in advance and is determined solely by the dynamics of the interpersonal encounter and the reality of the child's life.

Generative mentoring, therefore, is a humane meeting between adult and child. From the child's perspective, it is intended to familiarize her with a person who may constitute a significant adult for him, in other words, an adult, who, by virtue of the manner in which he or she relates to the child, gives that child a sense of space, presence, substance, and being of value to others. Acquiring this sense is a basic human need that exists, *a priori,* in all of us, and being aware of it is a condition for actualization, for the generation of a self-image of being of value in the child. Having a self-image of being of value means being able to identify and recognize others as subjects and oneself as being a significant entity for others.

But the mentoring process is more than this; it is not exhausted merely in the acquisition of a "feeling". Rather, it is a generative encounter that produces a new attitude, knowledge, interest, and concepts and a significant expansion of the world. It is an encounter that enables the expression of a range of feelings, serves as a place for their conceptualization, which extends beyond the realm of the applicability of those feelings, and induces new, unfamiliar feelings. It is an encounter of physical experience, of activation of the senses and body—it activates an array of psychological-physical faculties in a person and is based on relating to the person as a whole, on seeing the child as a totality. The adult's significance for the child manifests itself also in the manner in which the encounter changes reality.

Since generative mentoring requires action and because it seeks to change the objective reality of the child's life, it is a process of creating value and substance. Through mentoring, children experience being of importance, the fact that someone is willing to act on their behalf and to try to change the material, real world for them, that someone is prepared to take action and not just speak to them about responsibility or accuse them of making bad choices.

For the adult, an encounter of this sort can constitute the realization of the idea, of the recognition of the human relationship as a vital condition for creating a new reality. It is an expression of the practical realization of the possibility and need to transcend herself, to go beyond herself to something that can be served, to a person who must be loved, directly and without any self-interest—that is, another who is a part of the meaning of her life. In this encounter, the mentor's awareness may be expanded through the meeting with the world of the child and with the ways in which the child experiences, contemplates, and learns, for this meeting is likely to allow the adult to contemplate her memories and to become reacquainted with herself as a child, perhaps only because the age gap between the adult and child entails different rhythms of learning for them, different extents of wonder and curiosity, and different understandings of experiences.[3]

For the mentor, the encounter with the children enables her to love to the extent that she is searching for meaning, accompanied by a feeling of helplessness and social pangs of conscience. For the mentor, this encounter can constitute therapy of the most meaningful sort, since the mutual dialectical process built into the relationship allows the mentor to feel that she is of value to others.

A. The Generation of Self-Image

Mentoring means being a significant person for another. The assumption is that having a significant person in one's life is the (perhaps key) condition to people's ability to perceive themselves as being of value for others. Being of value to others means having a positive self-image (which gives rise to self-esteem, and so forth). But there are two aspects to having a positive self-image. First, it is a conscious emotional state that is a condition for the person's ability to create, to operate in a fashion that seems free to him or her, and to change the world by shaping it: in other words, *to work and to create*. Second, it is a condition of a person's ability to see, feel, and think about others fully and in an unmediated fashion; that is, it is a condition for her ability *to love and be loved*.

In his book *Childhood and Society*, Erikson relates that Freud, in the twilight of his life, was asked what a person needs in order to be normal. The old mentor thought for a moment and replied, "To work and to love." If we accept Erikson's evidence and Freud's definition of who is a normal person (which was so rare in Freud's writings and research), mentoring is the human

---

[3] V. Frankl, *Man's Search for Meaning*, Washington Square Press, rev. & updated 1998.

contact that enables a person to feel he or she is of value to others, enables one to work, create, and love, and enables one to be normal, to be a person. The problem is that value-creating processes in the neocapitalist reality nearly always and for almost all of us tend to exchange the human value for commercial value, to create a self-image of object and goods, the value of which is always determined by market forces. Already from childhood, people learn that their value is determined according to their ability to participate in the buying frenzy of labels advertised on television, that the childhood screen-heroes are stickers, posters, and expensive pieces of plastic. They are supposed to feel of value only when the television advertisement is directed at them personally and defines them as consumers. They learn that for other people they are nothing but objects; and they learn to relate to others as objects to be used, competed against, frightened of, and never seen in their entirety as subjects, people.

The goal of mentoring is to unravel reality, to enable the generation of a humane self-image and actualization, based on the conscious-psychological possibilities that are repressed in the existing reality by a multiplicity of its mechanisms, including school. In this sense, generative mentoring is radical, because it strives to reach the basic human element that is in everyone's grasp and because it functions in a reality whose components all move in the opposite direction and do not enable creation and love.

At this point I will expand briefly on the meaning I give to the term "self-image", by contrasting it with the common expression "personal identity".

Self-Image: The term "self-image" refers to the manner in which a person imagines herself to be perceived by others. It is a mental construct based on other people's gaze, and it develops and changes over the course of our lives depending on the way in which we imagine we are seen by people around us (this does not refer to the way people perceive us, but the way we imagine they see us). Underlying this definition is the assumption that a person who has hatched out of an egg on a deserted island has no self-image and that this image is the outcome of the interaction with other people. Under this assumption, all our "self" concepts, all of one's perceptions of one's self, are merely the outcome of a dialectical process that evolves through contact with others. In different terminology, we can say that our self-image is simply the sum of all our social ties and that these ties are constitutive of us.[4]

The interpersonal contact that constitutes one's self-image is not total. First, not every other person can serve as the generator of another person's self-image. In the course of our lives, we identify "significant others", whose gazes are taken as the building blocks of our self-image. Second, not every gaze is a generative gaze. We conduct a dialectical process of mutual constructing with other people, which includes negotiating the disparity between the way in which we imagine ourselves to be perceived and the way in which we would like to be perceived by every one of the significant figures in our lives. This process is dialectical also in the sense that it relies on the ability to recognize other people's gazes.

The underlying assumption of this ability is that we have the tendency to look at reality through the eyes of others and the more we succeed in imagining others looking at us (that is, the more we develop a self-image), the more we succeed in identifying the other in a more sophisticated way: to see through his or her eyes, feel his or her feelings, think his or her thoughts. In my opinion, this process is universal. It is the basis for creating the mental construct *on behalf of others*, and it enables us to distinguish between various gazes of different people, as we encounter different people during the course of our lives and our self-images are constantly being shaped. In other words, the way in which we interpret those gazes can change at any time, meaning that self-image is a dynamic construct that can change endlessly.

---

[4] The most interesting analysis in this context was, of course, offered by Hegel in the chapter on "Master and Slave" in the *Phenomenology*, although self-image as I use the term was for Hegel only the beginning of the road of building self-consciousness—which enables the subject to identify himself as the deviser of reality as a whole.

From the moment we imagine that we have noticed another person's gaze, we ask for the answer to one, and only one, question: Do I have value for him or her? The answer to this question is not simple. Already in childhood it is complicated, in the encounter with the parent as a significant other (some say the most significant other in our lives), which involves a built-in tension between the way in which the parent sees us and the idea the parent had before we ever saw the light of day. It remains complicated for as long as we uncover the various meanings of being of value, meanings that vary with different people, and becomes more complicated as we get to know others and the concept of our value changes as a result.

However, despite all the complexities entailed, there are still two eternal parameters that qualify our ability to be of value. One is our ability to change the world, in other words, to operate physically in a material world. The other is our ability to give and receive love and compassion.

These two motifs appear repeatedly throughout our lives, at different levels of complexity but as the ultimate basis for our ability to feel of value for others. In fact, the most significant difference between having a self-image of value and of lacking in value, between positive self-image and negative self-image, is that between someone who feels potent and capable, who influences reality by shaping it, and someone who feels incapable of changing anything, impotent. It is the difference between someone who feels she arouses sympathetic feelings of love and compassion in others and, consequently, can sense those feelings when directed at her and someone who thinks the only feelings she can evoke in others, if any, are anger, contempt, rejection, and loathing. No less important is the difference between the adult who is aware of the value of her work, of creativity, and of others (and who may struggle to increase social recognition of this values, who will develop awareness of the power of solidarity, who will know how to translate her demands into a value, into social terms), and someone who accepts the social verdict that defines her as less valuable to society, her class destitution, and her alienation from herself and others. It is important to remember that self-image, to the extent that it is dependent on others, does not remain in the actual interactive sphere throughout our lives. For the majority of people, due to their evolving ability to form images of others, there is the very real possibility of conducting interactive dialogues with imaginary figures (or "internalized" figures as Freud called them)—what we might call "ghosts" that exist in our consciousness, sometimes throughout our entire lives. They do not necessarily represent real people, rather, the manner in which they "gaze" at us. This option is important because it seemingly has the potential to reduce our dependence on people who appear arbitrarily in our lives and permits a choice of imaginary others who are more sympathetic.

Ironically, however, this option can only form the basis for actualization if a self-image of being of value preexists, i.e., for those who least need this option. Sadly, in many cases, it is precisely those people who desperately need sympathetic figures, even if imaginary, who have no way of creating and holding onto them. Since their self-images are poor, they do not enable them even to consider being of value to someone. The nineteenth-century romantic fantasy of the rejected, humiliated child who imagines she has a loving parent "somewhere" out there, who yearns for the day when the curse is lifted and she is recognized for her real worth, is no more than a romantic fantasy. In reality, rejected children believe those who reject them. Their belief is so strong that they are incapable of imagining themselves as having value, and as a result, they cannot imagine themselves in an alternative reality. Often, the situation is even more problematic when the only imaginary figures with whom they can conduct a dialogue are stricter, more frightening, and more emasculating than the real figures in their lives. This obviates any theoretical possibility of hope and opens the way for depression and anxiety.

Personal Identity: The expression "personal identity" refers to the way in which a person defines himself or herself in relation to society. This is based on a series of factors that express the person's belonging to social categories and frameworks, and from the moment it is defined, the sense of belonging becomes a permanent mental presence that accompanies the person throughout his or her change-filled life, giving him or her a sense of stability, belonging, and continuity. The factors that have featured over the course of human history as the forming personal identity have generally been: gender (the way a person identifies himself or herself as male or female); work (profession); family; age; ethnic affiliation; nationality; religion; and membership in a social framework. Determining the self in relation to and by means of each of these parameters means having a sense of belonging (for better or for worse) and creating meaning that emanates from that belonging. Added to this are the normative patterns of behavior expected of people who define themselves according to any of the parameters (a man is supposed to behave like a man, and so forth).

Historically speaking, personal identity has served as a framework for creating self-image. The ability to define oneself by means of external parameters can, in certain social conditions, be perceived as a way of creating one's self-image. Indeed, over the course of a history comprised of class, gender, and economic and national struggles, all the characteristics of personal identity have appeared as possessing value (positive or negative). Even today, a person who is struggling in creating her self-image—in other words, is not getting feedback at the interpersonal level—can use the external definition of her personal identity to perceive herself as having value or lacking value for others. In Europe and North America, if I am a rich, white, European male, I am of value for society. By contrast, if I am a poor, non-Caucasian woman, chances are that I lack value. In fact, the social significance of personal identity constitutes a kind of substitute for generative interpersonal relations, and in my view, there is bound to be a connection between people who cling to external definitions of their identity and the difficulty those people experience in interpersonal relations, which are the primary basis for creating an image of being of value.

The importance of personal identity is heavily stressed by psychologists, who generally view it as the basis of mental stability (from the Freudian super-ego theory to the theory of the self); by the sociologists who regard it as a condition for social cohesion (Durkheim and his followers); and by political theorists who view it as a necessity, but do not agree on its status (from Marxists, who see personal identity as an expression of production relations and social control, to liberals like Berlin, who saw it as a condition for personal autonomy).[5] But the most significant contribution to the importance of personal identity has been made by various ideological movements seeking to eliminate social repression in what is known as the politics of identity. These movements, like the feminist movement and various rights movements (African-American, Native American, and Asian minorities), have operated and continue to operate steadfastly against the historical colonial-chauvinistic-capitalist attempt to deny and quash the self-identity of women, African-Americans, national and ethnic minorities, and the disadvantaged.

The basic line of argument common to these important struggles is the claim that the reality we live in nullifies the identities of some people, by denying their histories, ways of thinking, nationalities, and cultures, while attempting to subject them and shape their identities according to modern European male parameters. The destructive force of this class-economic-political repression manifests itself in ideological indoctrination that maligns the self-identities and authenticity of these people and replaces it with an external, counterfeit identity that is to the liking of those yielding power and control.

Without disputing the enormous importance of the struggles being waged by the champions of political identity, I would like to draw attention to the problematic nature of its fundamental assumption as a starting point for a slightly different perception of social struggle. My argument is that the importance attributed to self-identity is greatly exaggerated and is, to some extent,

---

[5] The psychological approach deals more with self-identity, and not necessarily with personal identity, linked to the social aspect, and, hence, also the person's exterior (the persona, the social mask). Self-identity, as it is considered by some of the psychology literature (Lacan, Winnicott, and, in particular, Kohut), is more closely connected to what I have defined as self-image, rather than personal identity.

misleading because it needlessly associates personal identity with self-image.

Personal identity as both an individual and social problem appears, in full force, against a background of the postmodern reality, presented in the previous chapter. In this reality, people experience difficulty defining themselves in relation to each of the parameters that, historically, have served as the basis for determining identity: the distinction between man and woman, the definition of the family, national, and professional identities—all of which are undergoing a process of accelerated erosion. Even having recognized the importance of the distinction between femininity and masculinity, for instance, how exactly are we going to apply it? After all, the changing, semi-chaotic reality in which we live offers no clear point for this sort of distinction, certainly not in the simple manner in which it was accomplished in the past (hair length, jewelry, clothing, traditional roles, etc.). Even if we were convinced of the importance of national affiliation, reality teaches us that the importance of the Nation-State is fading fast in favor of large corporations, and even if we were to want to belong to a family, to what family are we supposed to aspire? The nuclear family we learnt about from sociology textbooks was perhaps suited to a certain type of American image from the 1950s (father, mother, two children, and a dog, small house in the suburbs with a white picket fence), but today this image has virtually no significance in the reality of single-parent and single-sex families, high divorce rates, communal life, and so forth.

In fact, one of the important factors contributing to the inability to comply with the defining parameters is the politics of identity itself, which, by questioning historical chauvinism, the superiority of the white race, and the soundness of modernistic thinking, created the basis for epistemological and cultural relativism. This justified relativism is accompanied by a leveling of the hierarchy that prevailed among cultural frameworks and categories in modernity. In the past, it was clear that it was preferable to be a man rather than a woman; it was clear that it was better to belong to a Western Nation-State rather than to an Eastern one; it was clear that it was preferable to be a Protestant rather than a

Muslim and hold scientific beliefs rather than pagan ones. In the past, all this order of preferences (which underwent a powerful shake-up in the postmodern era) gave personal identity the power to serve as the alternative basis for creating a self-image in the sense of being of value. However, their enfeeblement raises a complex methodological and existential problem: on the one hand, we believe that people need a personal identity in order to fight for their freedom; on the other hand, we are fighting to blur the hierarchies that have given identity its formative power.

B. *Identity versus Image*
Two central approaches can be discerned in the literature dealing with the politics of identity: one is the "essentialist" approach, which propounds that a person has an intrinsic, "authentic" personal identity that is determined historically, genetically, or by his or her latent "inner being" (real "self"). Under this approach, modern life distances people from their authentic being and creates sort of counterfeit identity cards for them that are prescribed by coercive social interests. Take, for instance, the claim of American feminists that the woman, whose body is intended biologically for pregnancy, breastfeeding, and orgasms, has been cruelly repressed throughout history and prevented from really getting to know her body and abilities. Another formulation of the same contention would be that women have a way of thinking that is unique to them, an understanding and analysis of reality that has been repressed over the course of masculine history. The essentialist feminist approach demands the revival of repressed and lost femininity and the granting of legitimacy to the feminine voice, and in its radical incarnation, it seeks to create a feminine society, separate from men.[6]

Similarly, a process of the revival of ethnicity is taking place in the name of multiculturalism. Artists, liberals, and fundamentalists join together with postmodernists who recoil from the unifying yet crushing global power of neocapitalism and confront

---

[6] C. Gilligan et al., *Mapping the Moral Domain*, Harvard Univ. Press, Cambridge, M.A., 1988.

what seems to be a trend toward white Euro-American hegemony, neo-Fascist movements, anti-immigration policies, and manifestations of ethnic cleansing. Behind this trend, liberal ideology appears in full force, seeking to revitalize supposedly lost cultures, return to the fount of an original state of greater harmony with the environment and nature, and identify the repressed and denied wisdom attributed to those cultures. This revival is a revival of the personal identity of the immigrant, minorities, and the oppressed, who, by returning to their roots, may rediscover their original identities and authenticity.

What lies behind these contentions is an assumption concerning the significance of personal identity for self-image. The assumption is that acquisition of a defined personal identity that will necessarily engender a feeling of belonging and of creating a "place" or presence will later lead to the revitalization of all the unique ethnic, cultural, intellectual, and emotional motifs that are the individual's personal and social legacy and of which he or she was systematically dispossessed by the ruling society. When this revitalization is achieved through a persistent struggle against repression, it will, in the end, lead to a sense of self-esteem, to the formation of a potent, positive self-image.

In contrast to the essentialist tendency, postmodernist thinkers, particularly in their Neo-Marxist manifestation, advocate the "constructivist" approach. Under this approach, a person does not have an authentic internal being. All our symbols, our desires, and our most intimate inner sense of self are no more than mental constructs formed on the basis of our material experiences and social relationships in the world or, alternatively, on the basis of the language and culture in which we grow up. Under his position, as presented by Weedon, for example, there is no such thing as a "feminine nature".[7] Women are the prisoners of the culture they grow up in, and if that culture assumes either overtly or covertly that women are inferior, women's experience in practice will be of being of inferior nature. The same applies

---

[7] C. Weedon, *Feminist Practice and Poststructuralist Theory*, Basil Blackwell, Oxford, 1987.

to ethnicity. There is no such thing as "original" ethnicity or nationalism. Indeed, they are inventions by people in an historical context, within a specific "language game", as researchers from Gellner, through Anderson, to Sollors have demonstrated.[8] This line of argument, common to thinkers such as Derrida, Lacan, Foucault, and Altusher, amongst many, stresses the critical importance of language in shaping reality, while relinquishing it as a descriptive medium.

According to this line of thought, social structuring is total and leaves no real room for searching for authentic identity. Identity is a mere social construct behind which lie interests. The veneration of motherhood, for instance, is not the outcome of biological or survival imperatives, but, rather, part of the power structure of a given society whose language creates an ideology that supports the enslavement of women to do housework and raise children without being paid and, incidentally, creates the appropriate imagery of femininity and feminine mystique.[9]

Similarly, the critical analysis reveals how national identities have actually been shaped and determined from the outside. When the British conquered India, for example, the Indians were defined as the ultimate "Other" in relation to the European, which enabled the British to forge their sense of independent-nation identity and the Indians to define themselves ethnically. This is a fascinating line of criticism that exposes the completely modern, non-traditional origins of fundamentalist movements, the high commercial value that dictates the awakening of a particular ethnic consciousness, the invention of national affiliation where it never existed before,[10] and the construction of the self in ways suited to a life of obsessive consumption, while palliating them and creating a spiritual dimension to accompany them.

---

[8] W. Sollors, "The Idea of Ethnicity", in Anderson, 1995, p. 61.

[9] This sort of contention is made by Maureen O'Hara, who mentions Betty Friedan's well-known terminology, O'Hara, 1970, p. 153.

[10] Compare W. Sollors, "The Idea of Ethnicity", in Abderson, 1995, p. 61, with B. Anderson, *Imagined Communities; Reflections of the Origins and the Spread of Nationalism*, London, Verso, 1985, p. 62.

Adhering to constructivism means assuming that all the contents of our minds, conscious and unconscious, the entire array of our experiences in the world, including the experience of a sense of personal identity or of self, are no more than a construction of signs, of symbols with logical-grammatical links. It also means accepting the fact that this world of signs was forced upon us, given to us arbitrarily, and the ways in which we can make interpretations and attach meaning to these signs are also predetermined.

This sort of belief can lead to pessimism, nihilism, and despair as far as creating an authentic, extra-systemic identity is concerned, and indeed, constructivist thinkers are known to be dejected (Derrida, for example). At the same time, however, it is difficult to avoid the liberating force of this approach: it frees its adherents from the need to find an authentic identity tied to nationality, to religion, or to family as categories determinative of identity; free from eloquent contentions regarding biological fate or "Blood is thicker than water." It is an approach that permits a person greater movement around dynamic, changing identities, by recognizing interpersonal interaction as a symbolic medium constantly and endlessly shaping reality in a variety of ways.

The radical starting point for the creation of a linguistic and psychological platform for new types of personal and social fashioning can, in my opinion, be found in the term "actualization" as presented above. Actualization, as a process of generation of a self-image of value, is the clearest challenge to all the processes of determining value prevalent in neocapitalist society. It rejects viewing people as goods; it rejects relating to people in a fragmentary manner; it does not regard people as instruments for realizing interests or personal goals. Its entire objective is to accept each person as a complete entity, unique and valuable in his or her own right. Just looking at others or the willingness to accept the different ways he or she feels or thinks about reality is the creation of a new value.

It seems to me that it is not by chance that there are powerful forces at work in the neocapitalist world that limit our ability to actualize and be present in the full sense. Evidently, the human encounter, which is, apparently, taken for granted and might even seem banal, is the most rare event in our lives. How many times have we really met other people, in the generative sense discussed above? And even if we have had encounters like these, how quickly did we translate them into "professional" terms? To what extent did we agree to leave the other person whole, without pigeonholing, judging, or reducing her to familiar categories? To what extent is this at all possible?

In order to conduct a generative meeting of actualization, we have to recognize that self-image bears epistemological and social priority over personal identity. In order to perceive themselves as free, to struggle against injustice, to even realize that injustice has been done, people need positive self-images; in other words, they need to perceive themselves as being of value for others. This image cannot be built by means of self-identity, both because this sort of identity no longer exists (i.e., for practical reasons) and because this type of identity is merely a pale substitute for the constituent power of generative interpersonal interaction that can only be built by means of a significant other. My contention is that even if we examine those cases in which people have taken up the cause of social change, recognizing the social and personal injustice done to them, they did so not because they managed to identify their legacy, not because they "learnt" history, and not because their eyes were "opened up" after they acquired "knowledge" (although all these certainly helped); rather, they did so because they were faced by a person who believed in their ability, who gave them a sense of being of value for others (even if the person was imaginary).

Moreover, in my opinion, personal identity is not important, or at least not as important as the essentialists tend to think. It is not a condition for achieving class emancipation as it does not lead to class solidarity, and it is not important for achieving personal freedom.[11] Quite the opposite is true: it is socialization that exploits people's desire to belong and subjects them to a series of terms, categories, and institutions that exist outside of them, as it

---

[11]. What stems from my above contention is that it is precisely self-image that could serve as a basis for the consolidation of class solidarity, and not personal identity.

were, and although they seem to them strange and arbitrary, they are people's most intimate definers.

On the psychological level, a free person is one who can move between personal identities, who can take on various personas, who has an inventory of responses to changing situations. It is a person who has the self-image of being of value, who is free of attachment to external patterns, but is familiar with them and can adapt or reject them at will; a person whose loyalties are based on unmediated consciousness of others as a level for creating values and beliefs, and not based on the social dictates.[12]

With regard to this precise point, feminist literature, particularly of the constructivist variety, has a distinct advantage over other kinds of politics of identity. Since its inception, the feminist struggle has been directed at the creation of a sense of value in repressed women, despite the fact that the definition of feminine identity has remained controversial. In fact, in this struggle, feminist thinkers have established the precedence of self-image over self-identity. They are fighting to change the parameters that define a person's value-creation, which are work and love, and, in a fully conscious way, leave the question of defining identity to a later stage. Hence, with the feminist movement, we are witnessing a struggle for equal wages and equality at the workplace, persistent battling for legislation and equal rights, and insistence on the right to work and to create value and the ability to love and be loved. In short, the struggle is over all the parameters defining the self-image of being of value, by crossing

---

[12] William Tierney proposed building communities on the basis of difference, in a process that would lead, in his view, to overcoming the rigidity of personal identity. According to his version, a state of perfect entropy and endless crossings can be reached in the level of identity and knowledge derived from that identity. My position is totally different from the postmodernist versions of Nietzsche's ideas on self-creation. It requires a seed of self connected from one side to others, by means of the procedure of creating value, and, on the other side, it weakens the status of the social persona as a legitimate basis for the creation of the same value—but in any event, it is not entropic, but stable. W. Tierney, *Building Communities of Difference*, London, 1993.

the entire national, ethnic, cultural, and even gender dichotomies of self-identity.

C. Actualization as Biography

I mentioned above that in part of the postmodern and psychological literature, there is confusion between what I define as self-image and personal identity. Erikson's developmental psychology, a product of the 1950s and 1960s, describes a person's developmental stages from childhood to maturity through a series of conflicts, eight in number, with each appropriate for a different social and biological age.

According to Erikson, the manner in which children manage to resolve the conflicts determines the ways they will approach subsequent conflicts, where the dynamics that dictate the transition between the conflict stages is of consolidating personal identity. With regard to Erikson, there is no difference between what I call self-image and what he calls personal identity. Thus, for instance, a child of elementary school age is in a period of preparation for life, a period of learning and acquiring basic skills. Children learn to be proud of their efforts and seek approval and recognition. Erikson argues that during this period, children identify with the "possessors" of knowledge and learn to obey rules and perform tasks. They develop the belief that "I am what I learn, what I will be able to apply", and this belief relies on social recognition. If a child fails to gain a sense of achievement in learning or creativity, he might become weak, unmotivated, and tortured by feelings of unsuitability and inferiority. The internal conviction created as a result of an inability to handle the task of shaping the self will have a crucial effect on the degree of difficulty in shaping the self encountered at the next developmental stage, adolescence.[13]

According to Erikson, the stage at which the tendency to build a personal identity in its full social sense takes shape (in other words, of defining the relationship between herself and

---

[13] E.H. Erikson, *Identity, Youth and Crisis*, W.W. Norton & Co., 1968, p. 125.

social frameworks and categories) is during adolescence. At this age, Erikson argues, boys and girls are very preoccupied with the questions: Who am I? What will I be when I grow up? How do other people perceive me? What is the right profession for me? And so forth. Per Erikson, the condition for our being able to consolidate our personal identity is the binding together of all the manifestations of the self spread throughout the past, the present, and in a vision of the future, into a meaningful, complete sequence.

Constructivist thinking tends to identify people's personal biographies with their personal identities, since the way in which we perceive ourselves is merely a collection of signs and the manner in which they are connected makes it possible to read our self-perceptions as a kind of text. And what text could be more profound than our personal biographies, than our narratives? By combining the narrative approach with Erikson's contention, we can arrive at an interesting perspective on the subject of image and identity. During childhood, children collect various types of self-images, which are simply "materials"—sentences and paragraphs in which their evolving self features as the subject. This collection of materials should constitute the first section of their future biographies or, more accurately, of one of their possible biographies.

The question is: To what extent does the life experience of various children provide the required materials for building a narrative and what kind of narrative is formed? After all, it is not hard to imagine a situation in which a certain child does not have any positive sentence of which he is the subject. In fact, if we look at the children of the lower class, of immigrants, and from certain societies, we will recognize a strange situation in which the entire lives of children pass without a single situation evolving in which they attribute positive "sentences" to themselves. One of the characteristics of the social rejection of the lower class and, particularly, of poverty is the disregard and denial of their experiences, perceptions, and even the very knowledge of poor children, accomplished by means of the experience, knowledge, and expectations of the official institutions, including schools.

The problem with denial is that it creates a psychological foundation of lack of structured confidence, in which the person (in our case, the child) loses her grip with a familiar world through institutional delegitimization, in exchange for which she does not receive any holding point that can be used to build a self image or even a hackneyed superficial personal identity. Children who live in poverty are not "entitled" to the social subject identity prescribed by neocapitalist reality since they are not consumers, and chances are that they will not become either suppliers or purchasers of goods.

School life is not equal in the manner in which it provides biographic material to children. For some of the children, the moment they begin to attend school, the place of honor of being able to use the *first person* is offered in sentences such as: "I can do arithmetic"; "I am a good student"; "My behavior is exemplary"; and "I am a model pupil." By contrast, there is a different group of children who hear only sentences like "You do not understand"; "You know nothing"; "It doesn't help, even though I try"; and "You cannot control yourself." How can these negative sentences be translated into a positive version? After all, these sentences are empty in terms of their contribution to a future story. They need to be translated into the first person, but a translation of this sort could turn out to be very strange: "I am not somebody who knows, understands, controls, etc. So what am I?" How can one create a story from a collection of sentences all relating to "what I am not"? At this point, our imaginary child may get help from the adults at school. They have at their disposal a sophisticated system for translating negative sentences into positive terms, which always begin in the third person: "This is an emotionally-deprived child"; "This is a case of a child from a neglectful family"; "He has a lot of behavior disturbances"; "She suffers from a learning disability."

This series of diagnoses does not get to the child directly. Its chief purpose is to help the adults formulate their narratives, which provide the reason why a particular child remains devoid of positive statements and the basis is laid for a future prospect where losing the battle for survival and against failure and dropping out of school are perpetuated.

Certain children, generally from the lower classes, have no opportunity of building a personal biography within the school reality. They remain empty, and the collection of sentences with which they leave the school experience is extremely meager. Other children have a story, but it is the adults' story. This is their personal story as they understood it from the body language of teachers and therapists and advisors, from listening to conversations about them through the crack in the door, from the adults' palpable embarrassment when a child enters the room in which the adults have been sitting discussing the "matter" of the child, and from the politically-correct syntax that defines the children according to what they are *not*. This is a pathetic story, with scanty contents, but it does have a dimension of chronology and a clear narrative that points to the parental home as the problematic "past", to the school as a nice and well-meaning midway station, and to the street as the future that someone with this kind of past and this kind of present deserves.

As a process of actualization, mentoring signifies a real possibility being offered to children to collect materials for their future biographies and to tell their stories. It means creating positive statements in which the child features as the subject and the actualization of those statements. It is not enough to say to the child, "I can see you; you are important to me; I believe in your ability," in order to create a real change, to lay down a foundation for a personal biography. The mentor, together with the child, has to reach the point of making a statement like, "I can see you playing the guitar; you teach me something I don't know; I believe you can catch up to the others in arithmetic." However, even a statement like this is not sufficient. The mentor's role is to actualize the linguistic signs and translate them into substance; to demonstrate to children their ability in, for example, playing the guitar; to show them the way the mentor learns from them; to help them catch up academically—in other words, to generate the self-image of being of value, initially for the mentor and, afterward, for other adults.

Chapter 6

Conditions for Actualization

The approach proposed in the present discussion states that the primary, *a priori* objective of education should be the creation for children (and adults) of a self-image of being of value, particularly for those children who are precluded from developing this type of self-image. The correct way to do this, I have suggested, is by means of personal contact between adult and child: through the mentoring encounter.

But how does a person become a mentor of somebody else? What are the necessary and sufficient conditions for a person to become the significant person whose affiliation with the other will motivate and enable the latter to create a self-image of being of value?

The primary condition is the encounter. Namely, a real presence of someone else alongside me, opposite me, with me, must exist in order for me to accept him as a significant person. But what is the meaning of "real presence"? Real presence is a presence that creates in me a feeling that I am facing someone who sees me, who can look at the world through my eyes, who can feel what I feel, think my thoughts, and have my intentions. It means that I am regarded by that person as a person who is worth knowing and important to know, of value according to criteria that are important to the other person and which I meet even though I didn't know what they are. In other words, a significant person is a person who can and wants to identify me as the "Other".

A second condition is that the meeting should be with a person who can be of value for me, namely, that the way in which he looks at me and knows me has meaning that can serve me also externally to the specific meeting. In the past, culture determined precisely who the significant characters were in people's lives: those people whose views were highly esteemed. They were generally the community stalwarts, teachers, or people considered clever, successful, or worthy. When this kind of person noticed me, it meant that I have value. Today, in the neocapitalist era, which is characterized by the enfeeblement of social frameworks and a reduction in their significance for the individual, it is difficult to arrive at an external definition of who is a significant person. Is what the teacher thinks about me significant? After all, my father says the teacher is an absolute idiot. Is what the community leader thinks about me significant? On television I saw that he was caught stealing. The external parameters that determine the significance of the person looking have lost their validity. Yet the child's need, every person's need, to build a self-image by means of the gaze of a significant person has not in the least diminished. It has in fact increased. In the past, it was sufficient to meet the criteria of a social framework—of the church, school, or youth movement, for example—for the individual to gain a sense of being of value, even if there was no specific significant person who looked at her in a focused, personal way. The personal look could also be found by building fantastic, imaginary characters who, if they were to look at me, would smile with pleasure. Today, with the diminution in the formative power of social frameworks, the personal need for real human contact is heightened and the criteria for being of value for me can no longer simply be derived from a given external cultural reality. This strange situation, in which the individual has an ever-increasing need for others while, on the other hand, has fewer and fewer means for defining the Other as having significance, creates a renewed definition of mentoring. It now entails an intentional action on the part of the adult toward the child, without having any certainty as to how this intentionality will be interpreted by the child or if the adult will have any control over the child's ability to be of value.

Hence, in the current era, mentoring is an action that is determined solely on the basis of its internal intentionality and in no way dependent on external factors, and as such, it requires the mentor to be a person with strong personal resolve and belief in his abilities. To this end, the mentor himself must have a strong self-image. He must perceive himself as being of value for others and his actions as a social duty. In fact, this is the most important prerequisite for any person working in education or therapy: the sense of capability and relevance for others that leads to the willingness and decision to accept the type of personal and social undertaking embodied in the educational endeavor.

A third condition is that the mentor is external to the family framework. A parent can be a mentor, but parental mentoring is not sufficient, for two reasons: First, a child's need for a mentor is in addition to his need for parents. Parents do, indeed, meet many complex physical and psychological needs for their children. Despite the fact that insofar as the way they conceive themselves is concerned, they would be interested in being mentoring figures for their children, in my view, significant figures outside the family unit are very important and children look for figures like this. The second reason is that the structure of the family relations includes a strong symbiotic dynamic: from the strong mother-infant bond to the different ways in which parents try to realize their different ideas and fantasies about the child "they want" in the children that are actually born to them. Since the parental viewpoint is *a priori* influenced both by the symbiosis and by the idea, it provides the child with a very specific (and usually also very problematic) reflection of himself as an individual. The power of mentoring, as a conscious act, lies in appropriating the possibility of self-identification and, subsequently, of forming a self-image from the emotionally-charged and fantastic territory and then transferring it to the social-cultural arena, which, to the child seems objective and neutral. In other words, there is a significant difference between what my mother thinks of me and what the teacher thinks of me—and I need both.

A fourth condition is that the meeting between mentor and child should take place on the child's territory. This is based on the assumption that children have their own world, which is categorically different from the world of adults. Indeed, an adult's willingness to make the shift and exist, even for a brief moment, in the world of the child and to this for a specific child means that he accepts the child's existence as a worthwhile existence. This implies the adult's recognition both of the existence of the child's "territory" and of the fact that he can offer the child the real, humane option of removing himself from the limits of that territory through dialogue with an adult.

This point is extremely important because it makes the claim sounded frequently in the education-therapy debate that it is important to meet the child "on equal terms" in a more general, principled context, which has broader implications for the setting of the meeting, its dynamic, and its content. The real meaning of "on equal terms" is likely to emerge as the ability to sit in silence with the child, to play ball with the child, to go for a walk together in neutral, undefined territory, and not as it is usually understood, namely, as a conversation between the adult and child in which the adult tries to pepper his language with expressions used by children or in which he shows polite interest in television cartoon characters, for example.

A fifth condition is related to the intentional aspect of the meeting. For the meeting to form a basis for actualization, it has to be interest-neutral. It has to be based on the direct presence of two people that is not subordinate to any prior intentions, prejudices, or aspirations or to any knowledge or impression that the participants bring with them from outside. The meeting must put the whole world on hold, because it generally takes place in a cultural environment that teaches us to relate to people as objects and not as subjects. It takes place between people who have practiced for years at seeing others as instruments, as a means to an end. As such, the meeting requires a conscious silencing of the external voices and real intentionality toward the other, her eyes, feelings, and thoughts—to her generally as a whole person. This kind of ideal meeting is quite rare, and it is reasonable to assume that it will not exist without conscious intention. This intention is important, particularly for the adult, for two reasons: one, adults have a longer and more critical history of alienation from others and of relating instrumentally to people; two, because mentoring is an educational activity, namely, it is an action by the adult vis-à-vis the child, only the adult bears responsibility for it. At this point the adult may find himself alone, without the child as a partner, although this is rare.

What emerges from this presentation of the concept of mentoring, both its overt and covert connotations, is a paradoxical picture of the reality of adults with children in school. Indeed, it is absolutely clear that generative mentoring is an educational activity *par excellence*, for it conforms with the most profound, important, and critical goals of education. In fact, it seems that a considerable part of the contents of this activity allows us to justify the educational activity in general—as opposed to the activity of teaching, which derives its justification from other sources. My underlying assumption is that at least with regard to a sizeable number of teachers, the ability to meet the need felt by children to form a self-image of being of value, the understanding that children need a significant adult to do so, and the possibility that the adult is "Me, the teacher"—were and still are the *raison d'etre* for their choice of education as a profession.

On the other hand, it seems that the educational endeavor, which, in recent years, has been reduced to the practice of instruction alone, stands in complete contradiction to mentoring. This is because it appears that most teachers cannot meet the most basic criteria that define the activity: teachers seldom meet with children and talk to them individually, especially on the child's territory. Talks like this, if and when they occur at school, almost always take place on the adult's territory. Teachers do not regard themselves as being of value, and the social and personal situation in which they are trapped is harmful to both their self-image and their ability to feel they are charged with a mission for the sake of others. Teachers are systematically removed from addressing children's feelings and are directed toward shifting any attention to these feelings to the home and/or professional therapists and caregivers (psychologists, for instance). Perhaps the most significant point is that the way in which teachers are judged, measured, and evaluated depends not on the manner in which they operate, but solely on the performance of other people: the children. Teachers have a clear personal interest in every meeting of theirs with a child. Therefore their ability to "silence voices" or put reality on hold appears to be, *a priori*, an impossible task.

A. Mentors and Parents

From the standpoint of psychological theory, the beginnings of actualization, in the sense of reflecting the self through the gaze of others, are in the first meeting between a baby and its mother (Winnicott, Lacan, Kohut). The psychological literature provides a collection of images that connect between the ability of an adult to forge an identity for herself and interact with others and the basic, initial relationship she had with her caretakers as a baby, particularly with her mother. These images include: the encounter with the mother as an object for satisfying infant physical impulses, as suggested by Freud and developed by his followers in the theory of object relations; the ability to develop the linguistic format "in the name of the father" as Lacan believed; the ideal of the "good enough mother" and the fear of her abandonment, as was analyzed by Winnicott; and the figure of the mother as the "transforming object", as suggested by Bollas. The basic assumption underlying these images is that the child's parents are the significant figures in her life; it is they who will enable her to have an image of herself as a functioning and creative creature. It is through them that that she will be able to process reality on the normative scale, and they are her conveyors of culture, its values, prohibitions, contents, and norms.

Without casting doubt on the veracity of the above description, our present discussion begins precisely at the place where the child finds herself outside the parental home, in her first significant encounter with a complex "external" world with its own contents and dynamics, a world of strangers (both adults and children) and the entry into which creates in every child the need to renew his self-definition, to find his place, to reorganization his self-image, and to adapt that image to the changing reality. This place is critical because it puts to the test the way in which children have built their self-images in a reality that is not controlled by their parents and that is dictated by what appears in the childlike experience as incomprehensible arbitrariness. It is a place in which children check to what extent the way their parents see them matches the way in which others see them. It is a place where children have the privilege of freedom from their parents' idea of the child they wanted; it is also the place where children try to reach a significant adult who is different in a some way from the parent—an adult who will "choose" them, with whom the contact is not taken for granted, an adult who gives them a sense of having value in their own right and not by virtue of family connection, which is a sort of *force majeure*.

Much of the psychological and sociological literature supports the supposition that for a person to be able to adjust successfully to a new environment, she must have a stable self and a positive self-image, which can serve as the stratum on which to construct new identities and appropriate operational strategies. The starting point of this assumption is the distinction between the structure and its foundations, between the body and its clothing. A child can adjust to a new environment on the condition that she has "good foundations", i.e., self-confidence, a sense of potency, the belief that she has firm backing in the sense that she has somewhere to return to. Under this supposition, children who come from warm, supportive, approving and stable homes that give the child a sense of having a place have the best chances of successfully surviving the transition to new, external social frameworks. In some of the sociological literature the claim is made that the average middle-class and upper-middle class family units are more in line with the description of a supportive home than is the lower-class family unit, which, for reasons beyond the latter's control and for which it is not to blame, has a lower supportive potential. In lower-class families, the exigencies of life leave them with no time or energy to invest in their children, and the culture or sub-culture in which they live does not include (or does not permit, depending on the theoretician) any investment in children as a central objective and as an aspiration close to the top of the family's priorities.

Under this view, which has become a somewhat of a convention that is taken for granted in theory and in the culture in which we live, a poverty-stricken single mother living in an urban slum neighborhood who, herself, has a poor self-image after failing to obtain an education and being deserted by her partner, who is frequently in a state of anxiety, surviving under duress from casual work, has virtually no prospects of becoming a "good enough mother". To do so would require skill, resources, knowledge, and energy that are generally far beyond her reach. A mother capable of breaking her symbiotic bond with her baby and identifying him as an individual in his own right, who is able to reflect his being a separate, complete person, who is capable of softening for him the anxiety of her abandonment of him already from the moment she leaves the room after the first feeding, who can give him the possibility of owning transitional objects, and who has the knowledge, the skill, the patience, the softness, and the mental strength needed to help the baby grow in a stable, protected environment (which generally requires the presence of a father)—can usually be found in a family from the middle-class and higher.

In my estimation, the basis of this convention lies in the need for rationalizing the given social situation, in which a reality of poverty and backwardness seem to be the historical destiny of members of the lower classes, in the sense that they are transmitted from generation to generation and most of their children do not break the cycle of distress, do not succeed in school, and do not advance up the social ladder. There are two possible explanations for this: either the social institutions (specifically schools) do not enable them to do so or they cannot utilize the social resources at their disposal, because their psychological, family, and conscious states are not suited to the intelligent use of those resources.

The first explanation, as I argued above, cannot be accepted by the institutions and stands in total contradiction to the way educators, welfare workers, and therapists tend to imagine themselves and the institutions in which they, and on whose behalf, they operate. Hence, the second explanation is generally more commonly offered and requires only a small theoretical effort to explain the continuity of the distress in terms of the lack of parental functioning in poor families. Given the well-known truism that everything begins in the home, it is obvious that this is a "scientific" causal explanation that releases us—the higher quality, humane, etc., members of the establishment—from direct responsibility for the distress of the members of the lower classes.

There is dispute on this point among welfare and education workers. The conservatives tend to avoid over-investment in the lower classes on various grounds, using claims such as "We provide them with equal opportunity—it's not our fault they come from families like *that* or from a culture with *that kind* of mentality," or "They really are unfortunate, but nothing can be done about it." By contrast, the liberals tend to preach affirmative action for the lower classes, arguing that equal opportunity is conditional upon a uniform starting point and since children from poor families do not enjoy that starting point, it is society's obligation to invest in them to bring them to that point. This claim is based on a utilitarian calculation: it is preferable to invest in children in order to bring them into the realm of normative society rather than get them when they are older as needy or as delinquents.

The truth is that the two arguments are both specious, both the claim that everything begins in the home and the claim that essentially poor homes are not as good as homes from the middle and upper classes. Judith Harris recently launched an attack on the idea that the parental home is the principal determinant of a person's personality and behavior. According to Harris, there is no empirical research basis to the claim that parents, in the way they behave, act, feel, and think, shape their children such that they determine what they will "grow up to be" as adults. Harris, who attacks both the supposedly scientific research, which is tainted by the nurture assumption, and the cultural ethos that attributes everything to the parental home, refers to other, no less dramatic, possible dominant formative factors. Among other things, Harris argues that attention should be paid to the social factor manifested in the peer group and its far-reaching effects on children's behavior patterns, their motivation, and how they make choices that will determine their future. In fact, if we link the influence the peer group has on the child's personality to her unique genetic make-up, we get a model that explains her personality and behavior as she gets older that is far more convincing than obstinately insisting on the home as the only source of explanation.[1]

Harris' arguments seem quite convincing, except for two errors she makes that are related to the present discussion. The one is that according to Harris, the nurture assumption is a Freudian legacy that has taught us about parental pangs of conscience and has made us feel that no matter what we do, we will "screw up" our children. Harris is mistaken. The connection between the activity and family origins of the child, adolescent, and even the adult and the cultural generalizations linking personality, worldview, and the private biography of its owner is a universal ethos that has always existed in the history of the various world cultures. It is not just the province of European-American culture (it is extremely strong in China, for example) and existed long before Freud was born (in the Bible, for example). The great power of the parental image can be derived from the universality and strong cultural presence of that image the basis for determining her personality. This is a central cultural image that cannot be invalidated easily, certainly not by means of any empirical research as Harris, with a certain degree of naiveté, seems to think, even if this image is not grounded in research and is not correct in any scientific sense. The existence of an image that finds parents guilty *a priori* for every future act of their children, even if they have not been born yet, is a cultural act that generates reality rather than describing it. Parents know they bear responsibility and feel guilty even if they have done nothing. Moreover, they are perceived by their environment as having the potential to threaten society.

Recently, while watching the news on television, there was a legal discussion of a murderer who killed a youngster "for fun"

---

[1] R.J. Harris, *The Nurture Assumption*, Touchstone, N.Y., 1999.

in order to see if he were capable of committing murder in total psychopathological cold-blood. At the end of the discussion, the camera focused on the murdered boy's grandfather, who went up to the murderer's mother and said to her, "You raised a monster, a monster. What did he suckle from your breasts? Milk?—No!— He suckled poison! You fed him poison and he turned into a monster!!!" The grandfather was expressing his tremendous pain. He had not read Harris, nor had he taken any interest in the empirical research that confirms or refutes any particular causal theory. He was acting on behalf of the cultural image that identifies the parent with her child, an image that has always existed in human society.[2]

The problem is that the most faithful acolytes of the parental image are the parents themselves. Parents believe they are the principal reason for their child's failures, whether because of what they did or refrained from doing—regardless, they are always guilty. It is important to note, however, that the causal connection only works in the event of tragedy. If a child was born a genius, it is not at all certain that people would place wreaths of glory on the parents' heads. By examining a number of current examples, we can see that generally, when the child turns out "successfully", people tend to explain it as something that happened *despite* the parents, whereas when the child is deemed unsuccessful, the explanation is that this is *because* of the parents.

The generative presence of the parental image has a very powerful effect in lower-class families. In being rejected socially, most of the adults who surround the children in poor families have a self-image of being of no use to others. This self-

---

[2] In the course of writing the book, a few weeks passed, and it turns out that the grandfather, aided by other family members, is suing for damages from the murderer's parents, claiming that they are responsible for his deeds, even if legal responsibility cannot be proved. The court case is due to begin in a few months time, and it will be interesting to follow the various positions taken during the course of the proceedings. In any event, this claim seems to me to be a precedent, although it stands full-square with the social implications of the parental image.

image prevents them from enjoying the luxury of being a significant figure for the children, because they, like every adult in any culture, are familiar with the myth that the parent is the reason for the child's failure. Hence, many children from families where the parents are poor, unemployed, itinerants, immigrants, with a history of failure, lacking belief in themselves, etc., do not benefit from the experience of reflecting and actualizing themselves as being of value simply because their parents, siblings, uncles and aunts, etc., accept the parental image myth and feel they are not worthy of transmitting to the child that she has value for them. There are parents whose misery is so great that they are scared of looking into their child's eyes and transmitting "You have value for me," for fear of infecting the child with the grim fate of the person looking at her. If you have value for me and I am myself of no value, you are also liable to be of no value.

If we add to this description the parental hopes, aspirations, and fantasies directed at children in poor families—namely, hopes that "My child will not be like me," "My child will manage to escape," "I failed but she will succeed," etc.—we will find that children from the lower classes are destined to find themselves in an impossible situation. On the one hand, there is no adult in their immediate environment who transmits genuine belief in their abilities that rests on their being significant and of actual value for the adult. On the other hand, these children carry the whole structure of family fantasy and hopes on their tiny shoulders. For them to fulfill the dreams, they need to be believed in a real way.

I have already mentioned that in my opinion, the claim that poor homes are "less good" is groundless. In fact, research does not support the contention that poor parents do not nurture their children or that they neglect them physically or emotionally in comparison to parents with means.[3] Yet it is important to note that what emerges from the above analysis is that in terms of addressing the distress of a child in her search for an identity through forging her self-image, there is, indeed, a problem that

---

[3] Some of the research appears in Harris, 1999.

characterizes poor families. More established families in which there are children in the company of adults who feel themselves to be of value for society, who work and create, will stand a better chance of being looked at by adults who transmit their actuality to them as well as their being significant. Furthermore, it is reasonable to assume they will tend less to find themselves bearing the family fantasies on their shoulders, and since the adults who surround them feel real and fulfilled, these adults constitute a kind of model or standard against which the children can measure themselves. Hence, a poor home is, indeed, worse-off, but not because the adults there are not good people or do not love their children or lack psychological "knowledge" about the child: they are worse parents because they believe they are bad and the society in which they live confirms this belief (or, more accurately, lack of belief) on a daily basis.

Herein lies the mentoring activity's great advantage. The appearance of an adult, particularly someone who is not part of the family framework, could be the key for certain children to identify themselves as having value, as interesting and capable, while creating a positive self-image of "I am capable" and of "me as a learner", a new and unfamiliar experience to these children. Years of experience show that there is no point in suggesting to a child with a terrible self-image to improve it through studies, without her first experiencing mentoring. In fact, if we examine most of the activities considered successful rehabilitation in education practice and the literature that describes the path of the underprivileged child from darkness to light, we will always be able to identify (if we insist) the shadow of some mentor in the background, through whose presence the child managed to turn herself around, even if the adult himself was not aware of this or did not intend this and deluded himself that this was the result of an innovative teaching or therapy technique. Thus, mentoring is a social action both in the sense that it is the basis for a real educator's response to children's distress generally and in the sense of its being the substance and necessity of his work with a child in poverty-stricken neighborhoods. In this sense, mentoring is a true battle against poverty.

B. Anti-Mentoring

If mentoring means forming real contact with others, and if real contact is the secret desire of all people as part of their self-definition, and if mentoring signifies the radical meaning of educational endeavor, why does it not exist as the principal form of educational endeavor?

One of the saddest phenomena in schools is children's insistence on finding significant figures for themselves, which stems from their need to formulate a self-image. Children seek adults as mentors, but ironically, instead of an empathic, containing, and constructive figure they get—they get a cold and alienated biology teacher. In their plight, they turn to adults who not only have no interest in being mentors, they do not even perceive themselves as being fit to serve as significant figures for children.

My argument is that the real reason for the inability of teachers to be mentors is not something inherent to these adults themselves. Teachers can (and were they given the opportunity would be happy to) function as mentors for children. The problem is that the framework of external, economic, organizational, and professional pressures and the system of internal, psychological, and emotional pressures in which teachers operate systematically distances them from the possibility both of perceiving themselves as mentors and of operating as such. We are currently in the midst of a system of pressures, which is only intensifying as the social environment becomes more chaotic, more capitalist, more competitive, and more cynical. I will consider some of these pressures that constitute an "anti-mentoring" reality in the life of teachers, beginning with the pressure discussed in previous chapters:

Education as Instruction: The term "education" in its general sense is used to denote the attempt to shape a person according to an agreed model. This sense corresponds with modern educational visions that place the individual at the center of the world and attempt to shape him or her according to an image of a desired, future reality that is different from the problematic existing reality. Currently, modern ideologies are being replaced by pragmatic and relativist approaches. The public policy that currently dictates the allocation of resources to education in the majority of industrialized countries is governed by sectarian interests and has to satisfy various national, ethnic, class, and ideological groups, each of which has a different educational perspective. Given this situation, there is very little possibility of reaching agreement on a desired model to serve as a guiding light for educational purposes. The only matter on which there still seems to be agreement is the necessity of learning, usually interpreted as the acquisition of scientific knowledge. Education's added value as an activity directed at children's minds and not necessarily at their cognitive skills has become superfluous, or at least impossible, because there is no agreement about either who the person is or what the desirable person is.

It should be remembered that modern critics are critical of educational activity in the pre-modern era. This criticism has been aimed principally at religious education that sought to familiarize the child with religious dogmas and their unquestionable veracity as part of the process of socialization. However, there also is fundamental criticism of education in general, warning against the dangers of the indoctrination inherent in it, as a process that runs counter to human nature and the individual's right to freedom.

The path chosen by most industrialized societies in the modern era has focused chiefly on the teaching of the sciences, but has also permitted additional so-called educational elements to exist alongside them. The main such educational elements that have survived until today are those that foster nationalism, social values, and law abidance. An interesting aspect of this, which is modernism's "scientific" legacy, is a tendency that was clearly discernible in the twentieth century—namely, to transfer the value-oriented social education, which is based chiefly on personal example and experience, from the interactive, active sphere to the academic sphere. Over the course of the twentieth century, both value-oriented education and love of one's country or of man became areas of learning that had to be taught "scientifically", since they were considered part of learning. Hence, in this process too, it seems that an educational activity that, in the past, was based on the image of the teacher as a charismatic person who embodies in his or her personality and behavior the given culture at its best has become progressively more of a teaching activity subject to prescribed lesson plans—an activity that is essentially teacher-proof and presentable in structured training formats to anyone and not conditional on inclination, talents, belief, etc.

To these processes another factor must be added, one that, in recent decades, has become one of the most influential factors in the educational activity known today as teaching: namely, the massive and steadily growing presence and involvement of parents in schools. The source of legitimacy for parental involvement does not, as communitarian theorists tend to think, lie in a world view that sees parents as partners in the educational endeavor, but in the ever-increasing weakness of the education establishment, which is being subjected to unceasing public pressure, on the one hand, and is in the process of losing its justification, purpose, and direction, on the other. It is, therefore, obliged to accept parents as a fact of life. This weakness manifests itself in the school's inability to justify its claim that the responsibility for the education of children must be given to so-called professionals and is not the exclusive responsibility of parents.

A claim of this sort, which might have found a place in modern ideology, is not relevant in the current era. Parental involvement in schools represents a series of pressures placed on the education establishment that are expressed principally as a demand for realizing the individual interests of the children. As interpreted by the majority of parents and teachers, this realization means offering the child a path to social and economic success by virtue of achieving good grades in high school, attending a prestigious academic institution, and eventually getting a job with a decent salary. In order to achieve this, teachers are required to provide the individual children with maximum access and the chance to contend with learning material that is relevant to their learning, present and future. This process leaves no room for any activity that is not teaching. All educational activity that is directed at shaping or influencing the children's world views, values, and emotions is perceived by most parents as a threat to their status, which is, in any event, precarious. Like the teachers, they too are in an embarrassing situation where, on the one hand, they feel an enormous and ever-increasing responsibility for their children's education (since there is no social agreement outside the home on the possibilities of education) and, on the other hand, they have fewer and fewer purchase points by means of which they can formulate procedures and content for education like this or, in fact, practice their parenting generally.

In Chapters 1 and 2, I argued that if we were to examine the traditional aims of the modern school, as expressed in the humanistic model mentioned above, we would find that they attempt to cling to socialization and self-realization as two aims befitting education. I also argued that these two aims, which appeared to be conflicting in the course of social and educational history, have become the one and same aim in the neocapitalist world: the translation of the good life into having a good job with a respectable income, a large house in the suburbs, and more than "the Jones's" in the material sense is merely the direct and obvious expression of the dominant neocapitalist ideology that shapes all of us as consumers and as "still greater consumers". Thus, there is no longer a contradiction between socialization—i.e., the shaping of people as consumers and as merchandise—and the private interest of self-realization, perceived today to be the realization of the individual's consumerist possibilities.

This merging of contradictory trends in education into a single common aim has implications for educational activity. First, any activity that advances some of the children toward academic excellence inevitably advances the teacher's professional aims as an educator. In other words, the neocapitalist one-dimensionality that identifies the public with the private automatically also creates an identification of teaching with education. Second, since excellence is defined in advance as the domain of the few and not everybody (otherwise it would not be excellence), the educator is relinquishing the notion of equality. Any activity, whether directed at the individual or the group, is *a priori* a segregationist activity in which its segregationist element is totally justified, an activity that excludes the majority of children from its realm, defining in advance the outstanding minority in opposition to the mediocre, failing majority, but not as an acknowledgement of the constraints of an inequitable reality, but as a professional ideology imposed on the teacher.

Another factor that nails shut the option of education as an additional activity or as added value to simple teaching is the removal of the emotional realms from the teacher's sphere of operation. This process, which originated in the compartmentalization of knowledge that began at the height of the modern era (at the end of the nineteenth century) with the emergence of various so-called scientific disciplines, manifests itself in the attempt to professionalize the teaching profession. Teaching has set aims in the cognitive sphere, which is differentiated from the emotional sphere, the domain of the psychologist. Teachers are not psychologists and are prohibited from dealing with children's emotions. They do not have the necessary "scientific" knowledge, and besides, there are other people doing already doing this work. Consequently, if a child in the teacher's class is suffering emotional distress, he or she should be referred to the professional dealing with emotions; otherwise it would be an incorrect, unprofessional, and possibly criminal intervention.

Here we can see two paradoxes. One, precisely when the teacher's educational "living space" is reduced comes the social demand for teachers to take responsibility for providing a broader spectrum in children's lives. Teachers are held responsible for the absence of values in society, social alienation, violence in the streets, loss of parental authority, and misleading children, as well as all sorts of other grave maladies that are simply the epitome of the capitalist social syndrome with which the school collaborates unknowingly and whose victims are the teachers together with most of the children. The second paradox is that the teachers are forced to detach themselves from the lives of their pupils in the name of "professionalism". Yet, at the same time, it is clear to them too that the only way of practicing that professionalism, i.e., to enable children to engage in meaningful learning, must begin with interpersonal contact and concern about the pupils' well-being.

Teaching as Production: The "professional" distinction between emotion and cognition, between learning and overall quality of life, creates a strange situation in which the teacher has nothing to do with children's well-being. Moreover, teachers are not allowed to do otherwise because they have to relate to teaching as a profession with defined outputs and they have to meet the so-called objective criteria that measure output against input (in other words, against the cost of the teacher's work). In my estimation, we are not far off from the day when claims for compensation will be made against teachers whose pupils fail to solve a math problem or do not pass college entrance examinations.

It is interesting that the pressure to produce results is being forcefully directed at the teaching profession, which has never been noted for its connection to causal processes. In fact, if we were to test a child's "knowledge" at the age of ten and then at the age of fourteen, we could never establish an exclusive causal connection between one teacher or another and the change in the scope of the child's knowledge or skills. It is very likely that the change was due to life experience outside of school: at home, in the streets, from television, or as a result of the pupil's own interests and talents.

There is no procedure for verifying whether a particular teaching activity is translated directly into learning in a specific person. In this respect, the teaching profession is different from other social professions, such as medicine, for example, where a direct connection can be made between the taking of medication and the patient's changed health and between a surgical procedure and the doctor's success at improving the patient's situation. Surprisingly, in medicine, the criterion for measuring a doctor's performance is not just the health of the patient, but mainly the professional procedure employed. Did he or she work "according to the book"? Were her actions the professional actions required in the specific case? And so forth. If the answers to these questions are in the affirmative, then even if the patient has died, the professional action was legitimate. By contrast, teachers are not measured according to their actions—their didactic style, the manner in which they teach, and the activities they choose to employ. Rather, they are evaluated according to their success in achieving goals, namely, high marks for at least some of the children. In the event of failure, both that of the teacher and of the children, the teacher cannot hide behind any method or methodology in the face of criticism.

Many teachers function as mentors: some because they like children and they care about them, others not consciously, working under the illusion that they are "just teaching", but the children pick up other things from them. Some teachers become mentors unknowingly: they are adopted by certain children who weave an aura around them, conduct an internal dialogue with them, and turn them into significant imaginary figures that accompany them throughout their lives. Yet, all this occurs "alongside" the teaching activity, external to it as a sort of added value that must not be confused with the "real thing"—producing academic output. Mentoring, however, is a type of activity that is difficult to classify as output: first, because it is performed individually and is therefore "output poor" and "input rich" (as opposed to one lesson performed to thirty or forty children); second, it involves activities that take place in a subjective space and that seem to be hard to teach.

It is important to note that the need for output captures the school's most precious resource: time. In today's schools, there is never enough time. "We have to cover all the materials." "I do not have time to sit with him personally." "If I had time I could achieve great things with her." The constraints placed on time, evidence of the harmonization of schools with a turbulent, technological, producer-capitalist reality, is a further example of how the domain and the manner of teaching are becoming more and more restricted. It is not just that the territory in which teachers operate has been reduced, but the time they have to produce outputs in the pupils is diminishing.

The psychological reduction of time is yet another form of segregation—the distinction between the quick pupils, who manage to cover all the material, and the slow pupils who cannot "keep up". This is segregation according to output level that is totally in keeping with socio-economic developments in a technological reality of information and computers, which accentuates the enormous advantage of people who are quick over people who are slow[4] and one of the heights of capitalist alienation, embodied in the cliché "Time is money".

Two paradoxes appear at this point. The one paradox is that in order to maximize their professional ability, teachers have to achieve an ever-increasing grade output with their pupils, but, at the same time, their professionalism as externally defined requires them to focus on a small section of their pupils, those who are either outstanding or quick learners. The second paradox is that in teaching, the output required is measured solely according to another person's performances. At the same time, there is nothing in the profession that can guarantee that output or clarify the procedure necessary for a specific person to learn a particular thing.

The Reduction of Language: One of the interesting aspects of capitalist reality, particularly in its postmodern version, is the reduction of everyday language into commercial language. This process is one of the most severe expressions of the way in which people get used to relating to themselves as merchandise, i.e., as self-imposed social alienation, and it has been analyzed by thinkers such as Marcuse and Adorno. Today's tragic reality in which we have to sell our work more and more, sell ourselves and our creations, exceeds the bounds of trade and has become an integral part of our intimate lives. We market ourselves to our friends and companions and to ourselves. Without marketing, we have no right to exist since commercial reality is the order of the day: it is the only reality, in which "he who does not sell—does not exist". For our purposes, the important aspect of the process of linguistic reduction is the fact that language not only reflects reality, it also creates it. With regard to children, they are born into a social reality littered with commercial language that

---

[4] On this matter, see, for example, Alvin Toffler, *Power Shift*, Bantam Books, 1990, pp. 389-390.

shapes the way they create their self-images (in a one-dimensional way, as suggested by Marcuse[5]).

For years, schools have been importing organizational "advice", which originates in the commercial world and is basically intended to maximize the possibilities of an economic organization and produce profits. As such, it has many advantages in identifying the link between goals and methods of operation, between inputs and outputs, between expectations and the means of realizing them. It seems that these advantages are also required in fields not traditionally directed toward profit. Since social reality is determined exclusively by capitalist logic, it exerts ever-increasing pressure for the economic rationalization of social services. In other words, it has the expectation that a social institution should function according to the same standards of efficiency as a commercial company does. This applies particularly to those social institutions that cannot easily be converted into economic bodies (i.e., cannot be privatized easily) such as welfare services and education.[6] These institutions have called upon the type of advice that is supposed to help them carry out the transformation from a situation defined as "inefficient" to a situation of so-called economic autonomy—in other words, to function according to market economy standards.

This process is accompanied by a reduction of the original institutional language to a trade-relations language. It began a few decades ago when expressions like "ideals" and "vision" became anachronisms representing fantasies that had departed from this world, and "good riddance" (especially with regard to various socialist concepts and ideals). Accordingly, they were replaced by such operative concepts as "goals" and "objectives";

---

[5] Marcuse, 1988.

[6] This is not to say that education and welfare are not undergoing privatization. They are being privatized, but gradually. The problem with welfare is the low economic potential, whereas in education, there is no economic problem—certainly not with respect to raising money from the middle or upper classes. Rather, the problem is with the authorities' attitude that education can still be used to influence and shape things. Therefore, it is 'worthwhile' preserving it as a public asset and not privatizing it.

the fields of therapy and education shrank their spheres of reference to only what is measurable (despite the failure of behaviorism). People served by these fields ceased to be human beings and are now defined as "cases" and as "pupils" when they arrive and as "output" when they leave. But nowadays we are experiencing the pinnacle of the process as consumerist logic completes its total control over the last holdout of the establishment, by defining the activity of the social institution in terms of consumerist reality: people can only fall into one of two categories—either they are consumers or they are suppliers. It is astounding to see the speed with which the welfare and educational institutions adopted the customer-supplier language, thinking, and planning and, at the same time, how the change in language has affected the way in which people who operate in these institutions adopted a self-image that fits with the new terminology. Particularly important to note are those places where the conformity to customer-supplier concepts posed a challenge and required the narrowing of meanings: the pupil-teacher relationship (or patient-therapist relationship) is far broader and more complex than that of the customer-supplier. Thus, in order to turn the teacher into a provider, education's sphere of legitimacy has to be reduced and given a professional basis that suits the activity of a supplier. This reduction manifests itself in the various components of communal life in the school, for instance, in the area of responsibility: In the framework of the customer-supplier relationship, the supplier's responsibility is limited to the transfer of merchandise. But the way in which the merchandise is "consumed", the extent to which the customer uses the merchandise, as well as the purpose for which the merchandise is used are all the customer's responsibility and do not concern the supplier. Once we reduce the teacher-pupil relationship to that of customer-supplier, it is obvious that the immediate meaning of the reduction is that what is transferred from the teacher to the pupil is no more than merchandise. This merchandise can be varied; it is usually perceived as "information", but can also be a skill, even an emotional skill (today, we "buy" sensitivity, love, and creativity through participating in a wide range of workshops, nicely packaged, at a hefty price, and they can sometimes be returned within fourteen days).

However, the further implication is that the teacher bears no responsibility for what the pupil does with the information and skills transferred to him by the supplier. Moreover, the supplier is responsible for marketing his merchandise, but does not sell it to somebody who is not interested in it. In the school context, this means that the new terminology directs the teacher to invest in those pupils who most loyally "consume" the teacher's merchandise and do not demand anything beyond that merchandise from the teacher.

Teachers have no need for pupils who do not think and operate as consumers, who do not "know" how to consume. Consumer logic goes on from this point to extend to parents who are also defined as consumers, sometimes as the school's real consumers (as the children are not yet trained in all aspects of consumerism because they have insufficient control of economic resources). Here, not surprisingly, we can define a person who knows how to be a consumer as someone used to consumer logic and activity, namely, a person of means. Indeed, we see how, at every school, the influence of high-income parents is expanding. Their communication with the school framework produces the classic ingredients of consumerist logic, such as being demanding, being partisan, individualist insistence on customer rights, seeking the best merchandise at the lowest possible price for their children, and so forth. Not generally represented in any forum, neither the class forum nor the systemic forum, are the children from low-income families, who are less skilled at consumerist activity.

This is only one of many examples in which the reduction of language affects the definition of professionalism, self-image, patterns of activity, and the overall atmosphere in the school in a range of ways, all of block the way to mentoring. In this sense, mentoring as actualization is a subversive activity since it cannot accept the reduction of the child-adult relationship to a consumer-supplier relationship. Generative mentoring is not merchandise, and mentors do not have customers. It is a human encounter between subjects that is based on a principled insistence on actualizing the other to the fullest extent of his or her humanity. Consequently, mentoring works in a radical way against the overall objectification tendency, against the total reduction of everything into merchandise, against alienation and depersonalization of the process of being educated.

Part IV

The Idea of Radical Compassion

CHAPTER 7

COMPASSION

A problem arises from the discussion in the previous Part: if the only meaningful way of creating values is that dictated by the neocapitalist reality (namely, the reduction of everything, including people, into goods) and if the meaning of mentoring is creating a self-image of being of value, what can warrant that the value that is created in the personal encounter between mentor and child will not be the accepted social value? After all, both the mentor and child live in a totally neocapitalist world that leaves hardly any room for values that are not reducible to commercial dimensions. What can ensure their ability to create an intimate space in which a different conscious and emotional process can take place? Particularly when this process, as I described it above, is so radical?

The problem is, of course, connected to the broader question of the existence in principle of an alternative: Is there a real alternative in the form of human relations, of recognition that these relations should be "authentic", outside the firing range of destructive social forces?

The answer to this question is by no means simple or uniform. It oscillates between absolute pessimism and prudent optimism, but with respect to the discussion on education, it seems to me to be settled *a priori*. For anyone who chooses to work in education or believes in its importance, there must be the assumption that there is an alternative to alienation, because there is a dimension of reality, unrelated to the ontological status of that reality, in which people exist as people and not as goods.

A relatively optimistic alternative has been suggested by Habermas in response to a neo-Marxist analysis by Horkheimer and Adorno, whose critique of instrumental (or functional, in Habermas' words) capitalist rationalism led them to pessimistic conclusions regarding people's ability to find humaneness. According to Habermas, identifying capitalism as a totality and as functional rationality is too simplistic. Human reality is multi-dimensional and includes other sorts of logic. One sort of logic that was neglected by the critical theory is the rationality of communication. The human need to communicate and reach agreement creates (both in the historical and psychological senses) a dimension of reality that Habermas calls "the world of life" in which people can meet in an unmediated way and communicate.[1] The problem is that the reality that exists in the political and economic world is completely detached from the "world of life" (as part of an historical process of fragmentation that characterizes modernity). This is a mechanistic, alienated reality that attempts, and in many cases succeeds, to penetrate the reality of interpersonal communication (by means of the communications media, for instance).

The important task recommended by Habermas is to defend against alienation by strengthening the world of life against the intrusiveness of the economic and administrative systems that impose themselves on the individual and infuse mechanicalness where the activity is supposed to be spontaneous and based on mutual relations. The ability to strengthen the world of life, as a world of agreement, is, to a large extent, similar to the ability to achieve "global knowledge", which is the birthright of all participants in communicative action and on the basis of which it is possible to create common agreement.

Habermas argues that the difficulty in achieving global knowledge stems from the fragmentation and splitting between spheres of knowledge that become exclusive, with internal logic and intelligible only to those who specialize in them, and contribute nothing to overall knowledge. Thus, the way to cope with the alienation will always be to try to create knowledge, which is

---

[1] Habermas, 1984, Vol. 1, pp. 337, 383-399.

the shared birthright of groups of people and their shared creation and, in its essence, "synthetic" (generalized) knowledge that is founded on communicative, rational, and authentic action. If we could create a community (a school, for instance) directed at the creation of knowledge of this sort, then according to Habermas, there is a chance it would withstand what he calls the "colonialization of the world of life".[2]

Another possibility of release or emancipation was proposed by Freire in the form of critical-dialogue pedagogy. According to Freire, education, provided it is based on critical dialogue, is an act of emancipation. Freire claimed that the ability of the oppressed (and the children of the lower class are oppressed, according to Freire's definition) to cease to be objects and become, instead, subjects and free themselves from oppression depends on their capacity to understand and become familiar with the oppressive reality itself. By means of a dialectical-dialogic framework of apprenticeship, the apprentice will be able to reveal the oppressive nature of his knowledge of the reality, and this revelation will become new "knowledge" by means of which he will be able to redefine himself as an autonomous subject. Consequently, Freire argues, it is important to create an apprenticeship procedure that will enable the apprentice to achieve knowledge not by way of transmission, or what Freire calls "bank deposit", but by means of a dialogue directed at decoding the oppressive molds:

> By stimulating "perception of a previous perception" and "knowledge of a previous knowledge", decoding stimulates the appearance of a new perception and the development of new knowledge. The new perception and knowledge are systematically continued with the inauguration of the educational plan, which transforms the untested feasibility into tested action, as potential consciousness superseded real consciousness. [3]

According to the Freirean educational model, it is possible to exchange knowledge-transmission for conscious acts directed at

---

[2] Ibid. Vol. II, pp. 330-355.
[3] Freire, 1970, p. 108.

creating awareness of the reality, after which self-awareness develops, followed by praxis that changes the reality in practice as
emancipation approaches. This process can constitute the basis
for realizing the ontological objective of the oppressed person,
as subject and not object, functioning in the world and shaping
it, while constantly expanding life. The process reaches its peak,
according to Freire, with the formation of awareness ("concien-
ciation"), the full meaning of which is simply understanding political and economic contradictions and recognizing the necessity of action against oppression.

It seems to me that it is not hard to identify both the communicative potential, in Habermas' sense, and the dialogic "releasing"
presence, in the Freirean sense, of generative mentoring. The
problem is that in every dialogic, interactive process, a meeting
takes place in which the participants try to create themselves as
being of value for others. Freire mentions the oppressed's psychological state of a lack of confidence that is intensified in the
encounter with social forces that deny their understandings, their
feelings, and even their perspective of reality, creating in them
the tendency to be like the oppressors and not necessarily to release themselves from oppression and to seek an alternative
autonomy.[4]

If we add to this tendency the demand for shaping awareness
or learning as an educational goal, we very quickly arrive at a
model of apprenticeship in which the teacher's/mentor's values
and knowledge decisively dictate the way in which the children
form their self-images and perceptions of reality. Dialogic mutuality suddenly seems to be a sort of facade, since the educator
enters the process through an intentional view of the end-point.
And she holds the key to the apprentice's consciousness transformation, without being committed to undergoing any change
herself. The educational setting, even in its most liberal mentoring guise and even if it includes the apprentice's conscious relinquishing of "knowing the truth" and is instead directed at
"common" discovery of the knowledge, is still directive and

---

[4] Ibid. pp. 30-31, 49.

constitutive. When it happens in the intimate sphere of dialogue between a child and significant adult, it is even likely to be dangerous. Hence, the question of the educator's character, intentionality, values, and conscious decisions become the principal basis for determining the educational act of actualization. The figure of an enlightened, rationalist, skilled, democratic educator who is a "team player" with a developed social consciousness can be derived from Habermas' approach recommending an agreed, common search for global knowledge. The correct institutional model for apprenticeship processes will inevitably be a university-academic model. By contrast, the need to search for educators with a radical-critical outlook emerges from the approach that sees the deconstruction of oppressive reality as the goal of education. Freire's followers, like Giroux, for instance, proposed a renewed definition of the teacher as a critical intellectual who is committed both to a profound conception of the school as an instrument of social production in a capitalist reality as well as to an ongoing attempt, together with his pupils, to expose the processes of repression, stigmatization, discrimination, and racism.

In my view, these solutions are not serious, neither on the theoretical level nor on the practical level. There are a number of reasons for this. First, the requirement that teachers should be academic researchers, or critical intellectuals, is not realistic or fair. Second, understanding the apprenticeship process as a function of learning as a purpose removes the discussion from the epistemological basis on which learning can be built. If we wish to ensure the meeting between child and adult as an actualization meeting, we need to find a conscious foundation for it and not necessarily a purpose. Third, I am not at all certain that people who seek to do research and search for so-called knowledge or, alternatively, people who are critical intellectuals possess any advantage in terms of their ability to enable children to have a sense of substance, of presence, of self-value. In many cases, there is no difference between the next-door-neighbor, the grocery store owner, or the bus driver and the social revolutionary with critical awareness in terms of their abilities to communicate, to be sensitive to and love children. In many cases, it is precisely the revolutionary teacher who is in a problematic position in relation to the child's freedom, since his commitment to the autonomous subject, a commitment is welcomed by the establishment, frequently turns out to be a theoretical commitment alone. It adds up to little more than a "critical" intellectualization of the curriculum and, in practice, only intensifies and reinforces the school's reproduction of an opportunistic, quiescent, and, in time, compulsively consumerist consciousness, which plays into the hands of the social control mechanisms.

I suggest looking for the conscious, emotional, social basis of apprenticeship as actualization in the universal human ability to view reality through the eyes of others, which is the basic meaning of the concept "empathy" (under Winnicott and Kohut's definition). My argument is that empathy, particularly in its incarnation as compassion, could turn out to be a powerful tool in the creation of an alternative educational reality, because by means of empathy, the human encounter inevitably leads to a critical view of reality and, in many instances, also includes the imperative of praxis for social change.

Under this approach, revolutionary consciousness is no longer the starting-point from which to structure awareness of the need for change. It is the result of a conscious-emotional process that begins with an unmediated meeting that embodies what I call "radical compassion" and actually leads to the dismantling and redesigning of reality for others. The educator, under my approach, is not necessarily perceived as someone who is committed to changing the world or even to understanding and exposing the oppressive foundations of the neocapitalist reality. An educator is simply a person who receives legitimacy to realize her conscious and emotional ability to look at others. This looking at others, when it maximizes human talent to sense and think about other people's pain, includes the desire for change and will lead, in many cases, to the critical exposure of a lack of humanity, of oppression, and of reification. Empathic and compassionate looking at others means recreating self-consciousness; it means shifting from looking to a reality-changing activity; it means change to the viewer himself.

A. Divine Compassion and Human Compassion

Compassion, in the sense of the ability to become acquainted with other people's pain, is a universal phenomenon. All people are capable of feeling the real pain of others, and this sensitivity is possessed by men and women, children and adults, rich and poor, oppressors and oppressed. It appears in all cultures throughout the entirety of human history, and its appearance as a basic human quality has been used by thinkers, philosophers, and religious preachers from China to America to point to the good of man and of his being a social creature.

Compassion, which accentuates the place of pain and suffering of the beggar as opposed to the rich, of the slave as opposed to the master, of the child as opposed to the adult, has served in history as the basis for the radical call to change the world order, correct injustice, and battle for equal rights. But it has also frequently served as a political instrument in the hands of the powerful in society, who exploited the sense of calling that compassion arouses, in order to soften the nature of the oppression and conceal the immoral nature of social control mechanisms.

The overall presence of compassion as a universal phenomenon at the very heart of a cynical, cold, exploitative, oppressive, chaotic, and extremely unjust social reality has frequently been used as an optimistic argument in favor of humanness. We are most familiar with compassion through its use in the great religions, particularly Buddhism, Christianity, Judaism, and Islam. Over the course of history, these religions have used compassion and, in certain senses and contexts, continue to present themselves as religions of compassion. These religions maintain extensive establishments to care for the weak, the poor, the miserable, and the afflicted. They use compassion as a hallmark of their social and missionary activity (less so in Judaism and Buddhism, more so in Christianity and Islam). These religions attribute compassion to their founding fathers (Jesus and Buddha) and relate to it as a sublime application of the original religious purpose. These religions expanded the social manifestations of compassion, such as alms, anonymous donations, self-sacrifice, etc., from the moral sphere to the metaphysical realm. Compassion is presented as a road to redemption, as an attitude of sanctity.

In fact, in the monotheistic religions, compassion was originally not in fact considered a human attribute, but, rather, a facet of God's relationship with people. The prayers of all three religions include asking for God's compassion and mercy ("God full of mercy" in Judaism, "May God have mercy on him" in Islam). This compassion stresses God's power and virtue against the lowliness, insignificance, and sinfulness of man, who is incapable of meeting the divine demands. At the same time, all the religions incorporate the social demand to care for the weak, miserable, and poor. This demand was a religious injunction for the People of Israel even before they received the *Torah* on Mount Sinai. It appears in the Jewish sources as a practical demand: the believer is required to perform certain actions, and her feelings and her thinking are of no relevance—she must give to charity without any question or discussion of the matter.

Christianity developed both the idea of divine compassion and care for the poor and weak. The perfect personification of divine compassion was the figure of Jesus, whose words and deeds demonstrated the containing and healing power of compassion. The transfer of compassion from divine reality to people is ensured by accepting Jesus and his incarnation, his recurrent embodiment in material, sinful, and pitiful human existence. The idea of caring for the poor and weak was developed at different times in the various Christian traditions, since the main recruiting ground of the religion was and still is from among the weaker segments of society. In Christian theology, the overall concept of charity received the status of a virtue, indicating, on the one hand, a commitment to a series of activities related to the poor and weak and, on the other hand, defining certain types of relationship, recognition, and sentiment that characterize the worthy person, the good Christian.

Both divine compassion and care for the unfortunate are, of course, fittingly represented by the Christian Church. The Church, which bridges between man and his God, is a compassionate institution, and as we move up the Church hierarchy (that is, as we approach godliness), so the level rises of extent of

divine-Jesus compassion transferred by way of the priest, the
bishop, the archbishop, and finally the Pope. At the same time,
the Church takes care to implement what stems from Jesus' exhortation with regard to the poor and suffering:

> Then he shall say to them also that shall be on his left hand: Depart
> from me, you cursed, in everlasting fire which was prepared for the
> devil and his angels. For I was hungry, and you gave me not to eat;
> I was thirsty, and you gave me not to drink; I was a stranger, and
> you took me not in; naked and you covered me not; sick and in
> prison, and you did not visit me. (Matthew 25:41)

Within the sphere of this exhortation, the Catholic Church developed a vast (the largest of its kind in the world) establishment
of care for the poor, sick, and afflicted. In fact, it is hard to find a
social problem that does not fall within the ambit of the Catholic
Church establishment, although one could dispute the form of
care offered by the Church as falling under the heading of
"works of mercy". It is a range of acts and welfare services
given in the name of and for Jesus, in other words, as an expression of divine compassion translated into almsgiving.[5]

The reduction of compassion into terms of charity and
mercy[6] extends the concept beyond its divine sense and indicates
a kind of feeling and intentionality. In this sense, compassion
remains entirely paternalistic on the part of the strong in relation
to the weak and is still closely tied to the degree of faith and be-

---

[5] The word "alms" is derived from the Greek word alenmosyne,
which means mercy.

[6] The concept of mercy appears in Catholic theology as a type of
value, which affects a person's willingness to feel compassion toward others and, where possible, to improve his situation. According to Thomas Aquinas, mercy should be classified on the list of
Christian values as a special value. Despite being a spontaneous
outcome of generosity, it should be classified as the value 'justice',
because it relates directly to interpersonal interaction. Thus, the
scholastic theology gives authorization to understand compassion
as a human attribute belonging to human-relations and not necessarily to the context of God's relationship to man.

lief in the Church as a condition for its existence. Moreover, it is also still basically a divine attribute that the Church translates and implements for suffering people by means of certain spiritual activities (guiding the illiterate, consoling the skeptics, forgiving the sinners, praying for the living and the dead, etc.) and material activities (feeding the hungry, giving water to the thirsty, visiting the sick, burying the dead, etc.).

In Catholicism and Buddhism, compassion is frequently bound to the ideal of poverty. The believer, particularly the devoted one, sentences himself to a life of economic meagerness. He removes himself from the race for material achievement, dons the monk's cloak, relinquishes all property and luxuries, embraces asceticism, and engages in spiritual redemption, his own and society's. He is also a compassionate person who puts his compassion and spiritual "assets" at the disposal of the wretched and oppressed.

In the Christian context, the ideal of poverty appears as part of the clear antithesis between flesh and spirit, where material things representing wickedness and submitting to lust are subordinated to the soul, redemption, and spirituality.

In Buddhism, the separation between body and soul is not as clear, and in certain Buddhist streams, asceticism is not recommended: matter does not necessarily represent moral evil; rather clinging to desire in reality, which, in Buddhist terms, is simply an illusory reality. Accordingly, Buddhism recommends cutting oneself off from anything that holds the person, whether property or family, that creates an attachment to conventional reality and causes suffering.

Poverty, under this ideal, is not necessarily a state of suffering requiring change, but, rather, can constitute a purification medium and a basis for religious catharsis. From many perspectives, it is actually the poor person who is better prepared for spiritual redemption in Christianity and for being released from the cycle of suffering in Buddhism. The historical founders of the two traditions were people who consciously chose a life of poverty, and their poverty made their spiritual insight possible, followed by universal compassion toward other people. Compassion is offered by the enlightened, the holy person, as the bridge between people and all the spiritual possessions he acquired when he relinquished all material things, property, and constrictive and harmful attachments: it is the invitation to redemption presented by his image and modest way of life.

Despite the similarity between the ideals of poverty and compassion in Christianity and Buddhism, historically there have been significant differences between the two traditions with regard to the way in which the ideal is given expression. The Catholic orders, particularly the Franciscans and Dominicans, started out as beggar orders that strived to return to simplicity, to the spirituality of life without property, to seclusion, and to universal compassion personified in the figure of Jesus. Besides the fact that the monks in these orders really did manage with the bare minimum and although there were and still are wonderful, compassionate, and generous people among them, their sociopolitical history is not one of poverty and not always one of compassion. In a relatively short time, these orders became economic empires in their time, and the way in which they accumulated their wealth would make even the most avaricious jealous. Compassion fared little better if we recall, for example, the political power amassed by the orders, the dominant roles of the Dominicans in the Inquisition,[7] and the horrors of the conquest of South America, which at least in part, was carried out with the full knowledge of the Catholic orders (the Franciscans, Dominicans, and to a certain extent, also the Jesuits), who led it in collaboration with the political establishment.

Buddhist history is different. It involved the same amassing of power and property wherever it reached, and the political influence of Buddhism in Tibet, Southeast Asia, and Chinese soci-

[7] One of the classical examples of the cynical religious politics of compassion is the story of the Inquisition. The terminology of the justification of imprisonment, torture, degradation, and murder, among other things, included the claim that this was an act of compassion: the Inquisition, representing the Church, displays compassion toward its victims, because it releases them from pangs of conscience, from devil-worship, or simply releases the agonized soul from the burden of the body—all this is compassion!

ety and politics was dramatic and also destructive, but did not involve expressions of force, imperialism, or cruel repression on the scale and intensity seen in Christianity. This may be linked to the fact that Christianity was and still is part of overall European imperialism and that Asia, the birthplace and throne of Buddhism, was one of the victims of that imperialism and, in any event, the scale and intensity of the political forces operating there were not as great. It may also be linked to the unique history of Buddhism, which was banned from India and became the tradition of nomads throughout Asia, translated in each place into different lifestyles with no organizing establishment whose wealth and influence were a function of the political power of those who adopted it and not part of Buddhism itself. However, Buddhism, as a way of life, may have succeeded in better connecting between the anti-materialistic and compassionate ideology and the reality of human life.

There seems little point in delving into the full cynical extent of the religious politics of compassion. Religious politics perpetuates the state of the oppressed and poor and enables the strong and rich to develop a sense of morality and social responsibility; the Christian and Buddhist priests invariably functioned on behalf of the strong and rich establishment, even while they personally made do with the bare minimum. These were people who were never poor in the full sense of the word: deprived, tethered, depressed, and exploited with a sense of uselessness and lack of value.

Religious politics always has been paternalistic, regarding compassion as a unidirectional relationship from the strong to the weak, from the rich to the poor (even if "richness" is defined as spiritual richness) and preventing the poor and needy the ability to feel compassion, i.e., to be human. Religious politics justifies the existence of social and economic disparities in that it deliberately avoids confronting them or taking a stand with regard to their origins, while recruiting adherents and gathering political strength from amongst the very social classes who are its "granted" compassion. Finally, religious politics is reactionary and maintains social injustices: it replaces the angry, enraged response to injustice, inequality, exploitation and repression with compassion and so-called understanding. A compassionate person is not supposed to climb onto the barricades, protest, or rock the boat of the existing social order.[8]

As the antithesis to this religious, accepted understanding of compassion, I suggest something slightly different. My proposed understanding renounces both the metaphysical and the paternalistic aspects of compassion and foregoes symbolic philanthropic acts as an expression of compassion. It is a naturalistic understanding that views compassion as a definitive, perhaps even innate, human attribute.

As a European cultural phenomenon, this type of naturalistic stance prevailed among certain eighteenth-century British philosophers. According to Himmelfarb, philosophers like Shaftesbury and Hutcheson proposed accepting compassion as an inborn emotion, as the natural, and, therefore, also as the legitimate foundation for building human society. This approach stood in total opposition to that of their French colleagues, who clung to understanding and rationality as the only basis on which

---

[8] Of course, there have been many impressive links between religious compassion and social activism. They appeared in Buddhism itself as a social movement in India and throughout the history of Christianity, from father Vieira's resistance to slavery and racism in Portugal in the seventeenth century to the official Catholic resistance to the price of capitalism identified with Protestantism that continues to this day. Some of the most important reform processes in the history of the religions themselves are also linked to protest by activist groups, who opposed the alienated, indifferent character of the religious establishment they belonged to. It should also be remembered that religious compassion sometimes had great socio-political significance, such as the struggle against poverty by the Anglican Methodists from the eighteenth century onwards or the Baltimore anti-capitalist Evangelists in the nineteenth century, the Buddhist struggles against the Indian caste systems, against the military regime in Burma, and against drug addiction in Thailand. However, upon closer examination, it becomes evident that in each case, these groups operated outside the official religious establishments, at the initiative of local religious leaders and, generally, also against official policy.

the vision of modernity could be founded. The existence of compassion can explain both the need and success of human organization to move from a state of nature to a state of society and civilization, and as opposed to the views of thinkers such as Locke but similar to Rousseau, the organizational act should not be regarded as an act of understanding (agreement or covenant), but an act of emotion. This stance was employed by some of the British philosophers, particularly Adam Smith, to formulate an optimistic vision in which the "easing" of economic pressure is possible, human actions take place alongside the cold and sometimes cruel activity of the free market, and there is a certain distribution of resources, even to the disadvantaged, on the basis of moral impetus. Compassion as a moral sentiment was defined by Smith as

> ... the emotion which we feel for the misery of others when we either see it, or are made to conceive it in a very lively manner ... . By imagination we place ourselves in his situation, we enter, as it were, into his body and become in some measure the same person with him.
> The perfectly virtuous man desires not only to be loved, but to be lovely ... . To feel much for others and little for ourselves, ... to restrain our selfish and to indulge our benevolent affections, constitutes the perfection of human nature.[9]

In many respects, my proposed approach is very unlike that of the British philosophers. First, as I will explain below, I do not view compassion as a type of emotion, but as a broader concept whose field of reference includes many components from the areas of perception, understanding, and recognition, in addition to emotion. Second, the concept of liberal compassion remains a paternalistic concept that justifies the existence of inequality and advocates giving "gifts" to the poor and oppressed as a way of assuaging the conscience of the exploiter and calming the protest of the exploited. Third, in contrast to Himmelfarb, I do not be-

---

[9] Quoted from *Theory of Moral Sentiment,* in G. Himmelfarb, "The Idea of Compassion; the British v. the French Enlightenment", *The Public Interest* 145, Washington, Fall 2001.

lieve that a public policy of concern for the weak and needy ever
constituted any moral basis (in contradiction to what was posited
by the English liberals who excelled at such policy). Welfare
legislation was enacted for political reasons of economic efficiency, as a means of contending with class opposition and public opinion (although compassion did hold a respectable place in
public opinion and in the protests of members of the British Parliament who were alarmed by the dire consequences of the Industrial Revolution for the lower classes). Nonetheless, I agree
with the British philosophers who noted the presence of human
compassion as a primary and defining attribute of man (in contrast to their colleagues, Locke and Hobbes, who saw the satisfaction of personal needs as the natural basis of man, with Locke
attributing the possibility of compassion to education). In order
to examine compassion as part of an anthropological perception,
I will turn to the Buddhists, who are, in my view, the great epis-
temologists of compassion.

B. Buddhist Anthropology
In order to enable an understanding of the Buddhist attitude to
compassion, I will explain briefly what Buddhism is or at least
how concepts such as suffering and compassion are understood
as central Buddhist concepts.

One of the accepted ways of presenting Buddhist thought begins with a description of the "four noble truths", which are the
four affirmations suggested by the Buddha himself as the essence of his teachings. The first truth is the truth about suffering
or distress (*dukkha* in Sanskrit[10]). The Buddha based his entire
teachings on the fact of human distress and viewed the human
existence as one of misery. It is a perpetual, real, existential pain
that accompanies the person from the moment of birth until his
death (birth and death are both painful moments).

The second truth is that the root of suffering is craving or desire. Craving (or desire) is an inseparable part of human existence since it makes that existence possible: without desire there

---

[10]*Dukkha* is usually translated as suffering or misery. I prefer to
translate it as distress.

would be no sexual relations, for instance, and there would be no continuity of existence. In Buddhist terms, desire is the life impulse itself; it is the driving force behind the cycle of death and rebirth; it compels the person to be reincarnated in an endless cycle of suffering. At the same time, desire is a yearning for what cannot be attained. It is the inability to secure attachment to any object of our craving: all is fluid, reality is in a constant state of flux, and the desire can never be realized. In this way, desire causes pain.

The third noble truth is that in order to end the pain, the craving and desire must be suppressed, and this will bring an end to the state of suffering, the endless cycle of rebirth. Under the fourth truth, in order to achieve this, a person has to adopt a way of life that follows what Buddhism calls the Eightfold Path. This way of life includes eight moral, intellectual, and pragmatic foundations that enable the person to free herself from her desires and reach Nirvana—whose precise etymological meaning is "blowing out the flame".

Alongside these four noble truths, the Buddhist philosophical tradition proclaims two radical assertions that originate from the Buddha himself and appear in Buddhist intellectual history in various formulations. One is the assertion with regard to the absence of the self. According to this assertion, a person does not have any fixed spiritual basis, sublime or lowly, that unites his perceptions, thoughts, and feelings inside him. There is also no mental superstructure through which a person can get to know himself as having a continuous, ongoing identity.

The conditions of individuality and self-attachment are those same conditions that cause human distress, namely: craving, attachment to objects of desire, etc. Under the Buddhist perception, a person's consciousness, like his body, is in an endless process of change and any reference to the self in terms of a permanent and continuous entity is simply a deception and illusion. In fact, a person is nothing more than a collection of psycho-physical components (*dharmas*) that are similar to a group of physical foundations, a group of emotional foundations, a group of perceptions, a group of thoughts, etc., where each of these groups exists separately, without any causal connection among them, and each one undergoes an endless process of change.

The second assertion relates to the illusory nature of external reality. Reality as we perceive it (namely, the world) is no more than a collection of conventions based on the illusion of the self, on the one hand, and the agreed use of language, on the other. These two assertions together create in us an illusion of a real, sequential, permanent, cyclical reality. In fact, as is the case with the self, reality is nothing more than a changing and random collection of elements in constant flow. Behind these assertions lies the assumption that release from the grip of the self, as from the grip of reality, means release from suffering, since how can distress exist without a subject that feels it? And how can craving exist without objects to yearn for? These two assertions in conjunction with the four truths make clear the nature of illusory life as a life of misery and present an alternative in the form of a search for the "truth". The key to ending misery is exposure of the illusion of reality, recognition of the self's lack of substance, and the conducting of a moral way of life of scrutiny and meditation, all of which loosen the hold on the illusions of self and reality.

In accordance with the philosophical perception, various techniques of meditation intended to support a "correct" way of life developed in Buddhism. Some of these techniques are expressly intended to melt or deactivate the self and, at the same time, to deny or reduce the ontic status of the objects of reality. The Buddhist meditator trains himself for years through a process of special concentration that enables him to perform a sort of transformation of the ego and the world by distancing them and diminishing them in his field of consciousness. In certain Buddhist streams, the end purpose of the process is the achievement of an "empty" consciousness or complete "emptiness" (*sunyata*) whose exact meaning is Nirvana.

Against the background of this brief description, another element emerges in Buddhism: compassion. Under the Buddhist perception, compassion is the ability to feel other people's pain and distress and this is a universal way of relating, in two senses.

First, it is achievable by all people, particularly by a person who has been released from the illusory perceptions of the self and the world. The "dissolving" of the ego and the "emptying" of reality enable the person to enter the world of others and to identify the final element that survives the deconstruction test of reality. This is the "discovery" of compassion as the last essence and, therefore, the most authentic and as definitive of man as man. Second, compassion is a universal way of relating because it is addressed to all people without any differentiation between poor and rich, child and adult, etc. In fact, from the Buddhist perspective, compassion also relates to animals, plants, and so forth, and not merely to people. This lack of differentiation originates in the basic outlook on life in all its forms as suffering.

The appearance of compassion in Buddhist thought is linked to the social ideal of *Buddhisattva*—the person who has, through a long, exhaustive process, achieved Nirvana, deactivation of the self, and the illusion of reality; the person who has reached the "truth" but decides not to remain with it. He chooses, instead, to return to teach others the truth and the path to enlightenment and does this out of compassion—out of recognition of the suffering of others and the wish to see the release of all living creatures from pain and existential distress.

The first *Buddhisattva* was, of course, the Buddha himself, to whom the various Buddhist traditions attribute the decision to contend with people's distress and show them the way to Nirvana. The Buddha's decision to remain within the cycle of rebirth, in other words, to continue to be personified in human reality after his death as the founder of Buddhism, guarantees the current presence of compassion in the world. As more people succeed in approaching the ideal set by the Buddha, in turning themselves into the Buddha, so will the circle of compassion expand and the existential, personal, and general suffering diminish.

This last point seems to indicate a certain similarity between the Christian idea of divine compassion personified in the figure of Jesus, guaranteed to exist in the world through his reincarnation, and the Buddhist idea of a *Buddhisattva* who sacrifices

himself for the sake of redeeming others and whose current incarnation continues to accompany us. Upon closer examination,
however, there are discernible differences between the two. The
Buddha was a person, as opposed to Jesus, who is the Son of
God. The Buddha, despite traditionally being attributed a certain
aura of sanctity, was flesh and blood. He did not belong to any
extra-mental reality and did not act on behalf of any divinity,
rather quite the contrary: the Buddha's main power stemmed
precisely from his being a person and not a god, from his ability
to maximize his humanity as manifested in his compassion.
Even the Buddha's incarnations, in contrast to Jesus' incarnation,
do not imply any supernatural element. Indeed, they actually
define him as being of humankind, as a simple person subject to
the cycle of repeated rebirth, which is the Indian definition of
human fate. Hence, despite the similarities, the concept of Buddhist compassion should be understood in naturalist terms and as
a human attribute and not necessarily as divine.

In the *Prajna Sutra*, the Buddha explains the way of regarding a
Buddhisattva:

> They should act towards all sentient beings with the mind of
> equanimity, with the mind of compassion, with the mind that
> does not create differences, with the mind of humility, with the
> mind of peace and security, with the mind that does not hate ...
> with the mind of a parent, with the mind of a brother, and speak
> to them like that.[11]

However, the *Prajna Sutra* also states that

> [t]he status of a *Bodhisattva* is attainable through the mind of
> compassion; it is not attainable by merely meritorious deeds.

---

[11] *Smaller Prajna Sutra*, Vol. VI, Taisho, Vol. VIII, p. 563c, trans.
J.C. Cleary, "On Temporal and Spatial Adaptability of the Buddhisattva Percepts", in Wei-hsun Fu & Wawrytko eds., *Buddhist Behavioral Codes and the Modern World*, Greenwood Press, London,
1994, p. 7.

In other words, compassion is an intentional state of mind that strives for the benefit of others, but at the same time, its importance is not expressed in mundane activities and sometimes in Buddhism there is even criticism of excessive activism. The universalism of compassion actually makes action in favor of a living creature more difficult since it is liable to cause sadness or pain to another creature. Giving food to a hungry person is liable to end in that person being able to continue to harm others, for instance—thus excessive activism must be avoided, at least in those situations where there is no way of seeing the whole picture. Practically speaking, it is evident that in the Buddhist tradition, despite the fact that as part of their preparation, the priests are trained to act and think compassionately, the range of activity of Buddhist compassion is limited by definition and cannot easily be seen as comprehensive social activism.

The Buddhist attempt, particularly in Tibetan Buddhism, to point to compassion in order to raise the awareness of the apprentice to compassion's conscious presence was based principally on concentrating on senses like empathy and of "being with the Other" while taking care to avoid similar feelings, such as pity and sympathy. These latter feelings, although they do contain real concern for others, are based on a value judgment of the other person as unfortunate, needy, and more miserable, and they are basically misguided and passive. Compassion is a kind of judgment-free active empathy directed at anybody.

One of the famous Tibetan Buddhist masters, Tson-kha-pa (1357-1419), suggested two ways to prepare the mind for Buddhist compassion. The one is through meditation on images (the accepted form in the Tibetan meditative tradition), in which the pupil is required to imagine an endless series of incarnations, backward and forward in time, and to recognize that in such a series of incarnations, the possibility exists that everybody was or will be the pupil's mother at some time.

The so-called memory of motherhood by others in the process of meditative thought is initially attributed initially to friends, relatives, and acquaintances, but then transferred to enemies or people about whom the pupil has reservations. The success of the attribution of the compassionate, loving, maternal image to all people will necessarily lead to a recognition of their suffering through total, boundless love and to the awakening of Buddhist compassion.

The second way or preparing the mind for Buddhist compassion is through "identity-exchange" meditation, in which the pupil is required to imagine first other people's viewpoint and then slowly turn himself into other people (again, beginning with relative and moving to enemy) in the full sense of the word—actually to perform a transformation of the viewpoint and the personality by means of a conscious act of empathy. In this technique, "identity-exchange" is the basis for awakening compassion, since it exposes the pupil to other people's pain in an unmediated manner.[12]

Buddhist philosophy, like the Buddhist stance on compassion, can be criticized in a number of ways. The scope of this discussion does not allow a comprehensive survey of them all, but I will mention three spheres in which I contest the Buddhist perception, since my criticism in this context should clarify my previous assertion and demonstrate the reactionary dimension of the use of compassion.

First, I find it difficult to accept the four noble truths. It seems to me that the correlation of existence with distress is somewhat superficial, despite the fact that most people suffer and are in pain for much of their lives and despite the fact that Buddhism and Christianity are sincerely motivated to help them. In my view, life is freedom, joy, and creativity and can offer self-realization and happiness. The problem is that the majority of people do not have the possibility to live: it is not that distress is constitutive of life, but that they are robbed of their freedom. I also do not think that desire is the reason for existential pain. There is plenty of human suffering caused to people simply by the loss of their freedom brought about by others who oppress, exploit, and subjugate them and cause them pain. In a certain sense, this is the greatest pain, because it is needless, because it

---

[12] A. Weiman, *Buddhist Insight,* Motilal Banarasidas, Delhi, 1990, pp. 101-102.

causes both the oppressor and the oppressed to lose their humaneness, to lose life. Moreover, the Buddhist solution of suppressing desire seems to me to be futile. It might well be that auto-suggestion leading a person to a certain type of emotional empathy could ameliorate the feelings of humiliation and oppression inherent in loss of freedom. But at the same time, that person could also lose her lust for life, everything that, to her, is worth living for. From the Buddhist perspective (at least in Buddhist orthodoxy), this last point does not constitute a problem—a person is not supposed to yearn for life, since life itself, by definition, is suffering.

Second, the way that Buddhism presents desire as the cause of distress places the responsibility both for the suffering and its solution on the shoulders of the individual. In fact, what emerges from the Buddhist position is that "distress lies in the eyes of the beholder": distress depends on the way we insist on looking at reality, and this way is unnecessary—if we would look at reality differently, we would not be in pain. This is a distinctly reactionary position, since it places the responsibility for a life of poverty and pain on the individual, on the victim, and not on the agent causing the injustice. This position is more in line with puritanical philosophy, particularly in its American incarnation, which stresses values such as personal responsibility and freedom of choice. Namely, people are responsible for what happens to them in life. They "choose" to think negative thoughts, they "choose" to become victims, and the key to change rests with them, and only with them. It is not the responsibility of others, certainly not the establishment's, to bring about changes in their lives.

I do not contest these values in themselves. I contest the notion that people are responsible for what other people impose on them, what the establishment imposes on them, and what is inflicted on them against their will. Is the young woman who is raped "responsible" for being raped? Did she "choose" to be raped? Is the solution to her distress to cease holding on to her "ego"? Is a soldier who is killed "responsible" for his death? Did he "choose" to die? Is the unemployed person who became homeless after the company at which she worked dropped on the stock exchange "responsible" for her situation? If she relates to reality as an illusion, will it provide food for her children? (But lest we forget, there is no need for food for children, since everything is an illusion and having love for children is merely an egotistical holding on to the imaginary self.)

Most of us live in a reality that sets many limits on us with regard to the manner and extent to which responsibility can be taken, let alone with regard to choice, and members of the lower classes in society are, of course, in the worst situation in this regard. From the perspective of a poor person, while she is able to change the way she looks at reality, changing oppression is beyond her ability. What she can do is create the illusion of coming to terms with that oppression, which is very desirable from the perspective of the oppressor, whether a person or a state.

Third, in my view, the concept of compassion in Buddhism is overly sweeping. It does have great esthetic beauty due to its universal quality; it applies to everything and creates the propitious enchantment of totality. At the same time, it is difficult to accept the idea that after a certain number of years of meditative practice, one will feel exactly the same level of compassion toward the woman who has been raped as toward the rapist; that a war criminal is deserving of the same level of compassion as someone who has stolen an apple because he was hungry.

Nevertheless, although I am not a Buddhist and despite the criticism, it seems that Buddhism's presentation of the concept is of importance/relevance in the matter at hand, in a number of respects.

(1) Buddhist compassion is not the sole legacy of the contented or the wealthy, who are supposed to feel compassion toward the hungry and poor. Rather, it is achievable by everyone and is not based on patronage. Quite the contrary, it is precisely the poor, suffering person who has the greatest potential for dissolving the ego and recognizing the compassion he feels for others and not necessarily the wealthy man who is a slave to his craving. Thus, the social role of compassion in Buddhism is not condescending and patronizing, but inviting, sharing, and cooperative.

(2) Compassion is the most basic human attribute in people. The deconstruction process of the personality and of reality as a whole leaves the Buddhist meditator empty. His senses do not provide him with conscious data; his thoughts are not active; objects of reality are absent from his conscience; his feelings are extinguished. And in this state of emptiness, there is one last element that is not cancelled in the process: compassion. Since compassion is the only mental state that survives the deconstruction, it is the most worthy definer of the person. It is the anthropological meaning of humanity.

(3) Compassion is the basis for social mission, which is individual in nature. It is not "on behalf of" someone or something; it does not serve an external interest, whether institutional or divine, and it has no purpose or personification in the individual's redemption (on the contrary, it distances the person from his personal redemption). At the same time, it must be remembered that for the Buddhist, the range of activities attached to this mission is extremely limited due to the universality of compassion and its abstaining from value judgments.

(4) Compassion is not an emotion—or at least not a normal emotion. Emotions, under the Buddhist view, like anger, sadness, joy, sorrow, and mercy (with the latter, in the Judeo-Christian context, appearing as a synonym for compassion) are simply an expression of holding on to the self and are all some sort of craving. Compassion in fact emerges in a person whose craving has extinguished, who is no longer slave to his desires, who has released his self-interested grip on reality in the foolish attempt to realize his cravings—in other words, a man who has broken through beyond the emotional realm.

Compassion is a special conscious state whose conditions are dictated by deconstructionalist logic: they first and foremost include denial of the ego, diminution of the status of the self, which enables the "entry into the body of others" and the ability to feel the pain of others. In this sense too, compassion is different from mercy, which is a clearly egocentric and paternalistic emotion.

Chapter 8

Radical Compassion

Against the background of the Buddhist conception of compassion, presented in the previous Chapter, I will now present a different way of dealing with other people's distress, what I refer to as "radical compassion". To this end, I will differentiate between compassion as a concept or an image and compassion as a state of mind, in the context of the chapter on Buddhism. My contention is that these two senses of compassion have inexhaustible and unexploited potential for educational work and that in a certain sense they are the best definers of one-way action by the adult in relation to the child.

In order to clarify this contention, I propose radical compassion as the basis for intentional action by adults with children. Radical compassion is compassion translated into real action. It is the extreme realization of the call, of the invitation, detected by a person who feels other people's pain. Radical passion is not Buddhist compassion. It represents taking a stance based on a reading of reality and the context in which other people's distress occurs and the need to act in order to change that reality. It is a state of "taking a stance" that has a special attribute: it is not based on judging and pigeonholing others, nor does it rest on a causal analysis of the distress factors. Quite the opposite is true: it is the taking of a purposeful stance directed at a future situation where the distress will disappear, with no dependence on the ability to identify the distress factors.

A person can be in distress for various and complex reasons, and we are used to thinking that only by identifying the causal process and dealing with it will we influence the result. Causal logic, accepted by therapeutic perceptions, derives from the sci-entific-mechanistic understanding of reality, and it has enormous explanatory force. At the same time, it is very limited practi-cally: there is generally no simple way of referring to a specific reason for specific distress unless it is a case of a physical mani-festation of a distress event (someone beat someone else and the result is pain). In most situations of mental distress, there is a wide range of reasons connected both to what has happened in the recent physical reality as well as to the way in which what happened is interpreted by the person who is suffering the dis-tress, in other words, to the complex mental dimension, which is partially hidden from view and partially belongs to what hap-pened in the more distant past, which is, any event, inaccessible.

If we add to this the fact that, even in relation to the immedi-ate distress factors, to "what happened in practice", a number of contradictory explanations will almost always emerge from those involved (*Rashomon*), we can learn how problematic it is to take a stance on the distress of others in reliance on an analy-sis of the distress factors. In the face of this complex situation stands the compassionate person with a clear sense that, "This situation does not merit continuance, and I cannot come to terms with it."

Radical compassion is the unwillingness to come to terms with a given state of affairs in relation to others, irrespective of its environment, which is translated into an intentional action to change the reality. There is a certain similarity between this definition of radical compassion and the manner in which we act to change the reality in concrete danger situations, particularly with respect to children. Most people sensing that a child is in real danger will pull her away and save her[1] without relating to this action to the reasons for which she reached the present situa-tion. Radical compassion is the extension of this pattern to less

---

[1] The Confucian wise-man Meng-Tze used impulse to come to the aid of "a child who has fallen into the well" as an example of the instinctive and universal human tendency toward "the good", based on which a comprehensive ethical perception can be proposed.

dramatic, more complex situations in which involvement requires prolonged investment of energy and time. Children who come to school hungry or tired need adult intervention that will change the reality for them. This change could be founded on an attempt to affect the home situation from which the child comes to school each morning, to change it without analyzing the distress factors in depth, without abandoning the family, without necessarily labeling the parents as neglectors.[2]

It is important to recall that the adult has additional options for action, ones that do not relate immediately to the home as the cause of the distress. There is no reason why the school should not offer nutrition and rest (on the assumption that the school does not serve meals, for example), since changing the child's situation for the child can also entail a change in the institutional situation, despite the fact that it is frequently more difficult for the adult.

The theory of radical compassion expands the concept of compassion beyond the emotional realm, characterizing it as a universal, human imperative with social implications. This expansion appears in the various features of our mental map as people. I will consider the main ones:

A. The State of Compassion
Radical Compassion as Impulse: Under the theory of radical compassion, people have an impulse to respond to other people's distress. This is a basic impulse that counterbalances the survival instinct, the tendency toward self-preservation, and as familiar to us in dangerous situations, people are frequently paralyzed by conflicting impulses. The examples of cases in which the impulse arises are simple and trivial. In the case of a person crossing the road and about to be run over by a car, it is easy to iden-

---

[2] I am not claiming that a causal analysis is not important. Quite the contrary: it sometimes has great importance and any progress toward a partial solution can certainly be of help. My entire contention is that this sort of analysis is not necessary; it is not a precondition for the intervention.

tify the two conflicting impulses: on the one hand, there is an inclination to leap out and save him, yet on the other hand, there is an inclination to avoid injury and survive.

On the theoretical level, which is influenced by the Darwinian and Freudian debates, the self-preservation instinct is normally identified as an integral part of a person's biological-genetic legacy (which has a survival dynamic if you are a Darwinist and an individual needs-gratification dynamic if you accept Freud's pleasure principle). By contrast, the inclination to help, the impulse known as altruism, and the willingness to endanger oneself for another person are simply the results of social conditioning originating from cultural superimposition that requires the person to be considerate, relinquish his or her natural inclinations, and do something for the sake of others.

The theory behind radical compassion has different presumptions. The altruistic inclination, the impulse to help and endanger oneself for the sake of others, exists in people to the same extent and intensity as the self-preservation instinct. In many cases, particularly in alienated, competitive societies, the situation could be the reverse: it is precisely the desire to help that is part of the impulse that appears to be natural, immediate, and instinctual, and the self-preservation and self-gratification impulses are the manifestation of a comprehensive, broad, cultural inclination that shapes us as individualist egoists[3].

---

[3] The similarity between this argument and Comte's (1851) altruistic theory is not accidental. Comte proposed recognizing social impulse as a basis for human ethics. The main points of his position can be formulated as follows: a. emotion controls people's lives, and we have to accept the superiority of emotion to reason; b. people are under the control of two emotional impulses—the personal or egoistic, and the social or the altruistic; c. the condition for the existence of a successful society is the subjugation of the self-love impulse and its subordination to the social emotion; d. accordingly, the primary moral principle is the regulative superiority of social sympathy over the self-preservation instinct. My position is, of course, different with regard to the superiority of emotion and moral principles, but in relation to the existence of the two im-

Compassion as Awareness: As noted above, under the epistemology of compassion, the basis for compassion is the ability, in principle, to perform a conscious act of empathy in the sense of entering the bodies of others. Compassion, which is based on the ability to feel another person's pain, is merely the additional aspect that complements the basic need for creating a self-image. It is a direct outcome of our dependence on others, with the interpretation of the way in which others look at us forming the backbone of our evolving self-images. As such, compassion develops into a concept, into part of the images of others as we perceive them. Since the construction of a self-image must rest on the presence of an observing person and on an interpretation of that observation, it forces us to recognize others, to be able to imagine them, the way they gaze, feel, think, and intend—in other words, to create their images. Having this ability means that every person has the inclination and practical possibility to envisage both the pain and joy of others. In this sense, compassion is no more than the development of other people's images, which we produce on the way to our constructing of our own self-images.

Compassion also appears as a state of mind. This is the state of being "inside" another person, of the practical experience of seeing the world through other people's eyes, of the actual physical and emotional feeling of their pain and joy. It is a compassion that does not appear to us to be a concept, but rather a feeling, an experience. The experience contains much emotion, but is also a conscious state, a state of forming a foundation that exceeds the individual's private experience, as it is based on someone else's senses and mind. In other words, it creates knowledge. The moment we formulate concepts, we achieve "knowledge", and therefore the action, in principle, creates also

---

pulses, at least on the intellectual level, I can agree with Comte, although I do not think this is a reference to social sympathy. A. Comte, & G. Lesner eds., *Auguste Comte and Positivism: The Essential Writings*, Transaction Pub., 1998.

knowledge. Specifically, this is knowledge of the unique way in which others grasp reality, a familiarity with the "world" of others, which is necessarily different from "my" world, and it is formed when I succeed in looking through the eyes of those same others.

The two different meanings of compassion—one, as a structured concept and, two, as an experience of a conscious act—make it possible to define the differences between adults and children. Generally, and not surprisingly, we are able to recognize the relative ease with which an adult can be enveloped by the concept of compassion, for instance, when someone is exposed to a painful, heart-rending story of distress and uses her concepts, knowledge as an adult, and the new information one obtains from the story, to set forth emotions.

By contrast, most adults have genuine difficulty becoming acquainted in an unmediated way with other people's feelings and their outlook on the world. Children, on the other hand, have the ability to enter into a conscious state of compassion. This can be easily discerned in their compassionate attitude toward babies, puppies, and pain of others in general and their considerable willingness to stay in this conscious state for relatively long periods of time (before they learn to feel confusion, before they recognize it as a vulnerable state). Here, we can detect the opposite tendency: how from an emotional, sensual situation produced by entering into the "body" of another person, we can build a concept, and how knowledge is built up "about" the other person's world.[4]

Radical Compassion as an Emotion: The conventional distinction made in the history of Western thought between emotion and intellect, between feelings and reason, between the rational and irrational, has traditionally placed compassion in the realm of emotions. As such, it is suited to emotional people, to impas-

---

[4] Obviously this is not a so-called real presence in another person's skin, rather, only what the child imagines the other person's "skin" to be, although for purposes of clarification, it does not matter.

sioned situations, to various kinds of religious pursuits, and to parents (particularly mothers). It is excluded from the definition of a rational person, who is in control of his or her emotions by dint of his or her intellect, and it is not part of the so-called scientific analysis of human society along with its materialist developmental processes. However, actually relating to compassion as an emotion is much more difficult than the simplistic manner in which it was presented, for instance, by the British philosophers in the seventeenth and eighteenth centuries, who were under the influence of religious rhetoric. If we try to break down into emotional terms what people feel in the face of other people's pain, we will discover a series of feelings and emotions, which sometimes contradict and sometimes complement one another. Radical compassion is a feeling of pain, a desire to act, and a sense of rage and is often accompanied by an acute sense of helplessness. All these feelings can appear simultaneously and with great intensity. At the level of emotional experience, they cannot be broken down in the conventional way by means of religious rhetoric, which differentiates, for instance, between pain and helplessness (supposedly authentic, and hence legitimate, emotions) and the impulse to act and exhibit rage, which originates in being over-judgmental and, therefore, should be repressed, ignored, or left to the discretion of a supreme being.

Under the theory of radical compassion, to the extent that compassion is an emotion, it cannot be dismantled. It is primary and simple (in the sense of a "simple entity", "atomic"). Consequently, there is no place for differentiating between experience and interpretation (or judgment, in the case of radical compassion). Empiricist logic dictates that perceptual and emotional experiences, like the experience of pain or looking through the eyes of others, could lead to thoughts on injustice in the world, on the need to do something to change this, and various other interpretations, responses, and judgments that rest on the norms and values of the person who has undergone the experience. This logic does not apply to radical compassion, which refers to the simultaneous presence of pain, the desire to act, and the sense of injustice or rage, which are not judgment in retrospect, but a structured part of the experience-awareness.

It is perhaps superfluous to note the importance of religious rhetoric and empiricist logic in the framing of compassion as "merely" an emotion, which is what enabled radical compassion to be swept into the margins of the neocapitalist social experience, its neutralization, and its theoretical and practical deconstruction, because it had the potential to threaten everything that was arbitrary, unjust, and a cause of pain.[5]

Compassion as Action: Radical compassion encompasses the imperative to take real action to change the reality in which other people live. "Looking through other people's eyes" involves an experience of reality that is sometimes intolerable, impossible, and painful. The unwillingness to come to terms with the reality of other people's lives is sometimes stronger than the manner in which compassionate people perceive their own realities. People are frequently prepared to live with very high levels of arbitrariness and injustice to themselves, but are not able to tolerate it when it applies to others (the simplest example is parenthood). Throughout history, this psychological-social state has led to radical social movements, despite their frequent denial of the compassionate nature of their action and their preference to regard themselves as rational or scientific in nature.[6]

---

[5] On this matter, it is easy to distinguish between the legitimacy given historically to action out of radical compassion in the face of natural disaster and cruelty, for instance, as opposed to the lack of legitimacy of action of this sort in cases of human disaster, with regard to radical change of social institutions or the mechanisms of power and manipulation.

[6] One of the classical examples of the radical-compassionate character of social-political thinking is to be found in the very heart of the "scientific" socialist literature, in Marx's *Capital*. Throughout the three volumes of *Capital*, one can discern rage, pain, and the will to act against atrocities and injustice. Marx gives many examples of various kinds of injustices and quotes from the discussions of the British Parliament, for instance, claims and stories by liberal leaders who expose unpleasant facts about the intolerable life of the working class, to which Marx adds a psychological analysis and the

However, radical compassion as an action toward social change is often on the margins of official social discourse. It is unique to groups of world-rectifying revolutionaries or religious missionaries who take too seriously the idea that things can be changed and people can be helped. Yet it also is inherent to most people, although almost never translated into a lifestyle or even into concrete action.

What is special about radical compassion as a society-changing action is that it does not require a complete understanding that delves into the overall reasons for social distress. It does not emanate from the demand for social justice, from an organized ideology, or from an obvious model of Utopia. Rather, it is a realistic, practical response to the distress of others. My argument is that if we enable people to realize their basic ability to exercise radical compassion, they will reach a point where they need to contend with a complex reality and take a more analytical look at the reasons for distress. The imperative to act effectively will lead many of them to select strategies for change that exceed the conventional patterns in official social discourse. The combination of the process of conceptual development and the development of realistic operational strategies means shaping a language game and a reality whose parameters, in great part, will be significantly different from the current neocapitalist reality.

Moreover, it is not very important from where a person arrives at radical compassion. Many people begin their activity out of commitment to the religious aspect of compassion, but the way of life involving encountering the reality of the lives of poor, depressed, and socially rejected people inevitably leads them to the demand for overall social change and to taking a radical stance with regard to themselves and reality, even if it contradicts or exceeds the original debate from which they came. Familiar examples of this phenomenon can be found in the works of Christian priests like Ivan Illich, whose work in educa-

---

effect of exploitation on man, as well as the overall social connection.

tion in the Third World led him to formulate a radical educational perspective; Mother Teresa, who, from a quiet missionary, turned into a social-activist; the priest Joseph Wrensinsky, who founded the Fourth World Movement, a movement of people committed to living together with people in extreme poverty and which, over the years, has become a movement fighting for social change; Buddhist practitioners, whose preoccupation with compassion led them to recognize the necessity of realistic, material action within the general movement of Engaged Buddhism.[7] However, this social phenomenon also includes hun-

---

[7] The term was coined by Thich Nhat Hanh in the 1950s and, since then, has characterized a general, current Buddhist tendency, particularly in Western countries, to display more social involvement and to take clear stances on the issues of poverty, distress, war, and ecology. The American social-activist Bernie Glassman lists three conditions for compassion in the spirit of Active Buddhism. This relates to the serious limitation that prior knowledge, theory, or intellectual analysis places on compassion. In the terms of the present discussion, it could be said that a compassionate meeting with a child is conditional upon being direct and not mediated by a story, diagnosis, or knowledge of the child's background, conditions, and history, particularly as it is told by adults. Indeed, this would only lead the person to arrive at the meeting with a defined perspective, rationalizations, and detachment from empathic possibilities. Another problem posed by prior knowledge is the attachment to the self as the one who knows, a preoccupation with what one knows about the other, which is manifested in the fundamental inability to put one's ego aside, one of the obvious conditions for compassion.
Bearing Witness: This describes the psychological state of the compassionate person. From a Buddhist point of view, the expression includes having reservations about a rapid, instinctive response to the pain of others. A person who bears witness prepares himself to turn into a kind of text, film, tape, monument, or any other form of documentation and to bear other people's pain, without any commitment to act. In a certain sense, Buddhists like Glassman are right in thinking that this type of willingness is too heavy to bear, but is essential for preserving compassion and preventing the im-

dreds and thousands of devoted people for whom radical compassion is a way of life, whether in the framework of a movement or individually, whether overtly or covertly, and who have a receptiveness to an inner voice of commitment to others, by translating it into real, physical action[8], led them to recognize the necessity for overall social change.

Thus, the radicalism encompassed in the term radical compassion has three meanings. The first meaning is that it is basic, primary compassion, intrinsic to all people. It is the root, the "radical", of our humanity. The second sense of radicalism refers to the activism in the attempt to translate the awareness into

---

mediate move to action that will supposedly release the compassionate person from distress in relation to other, as well as for preventing hasty action that is liable to cause damage. My stance on this matter is, of course, different. In my view, the act is part of the compassion itself and does not replace "bearing witness", but, rather, is joins it. Moreover, I do not think that an actual act constitutes an escape from the pain of others, but only from the feeling of helplessness in relation to that pain. This is an ego-feeling, which there is no reason to nurture.

Loving Action: This is, again, a beautiful expression that describes the legitimate motivation, from Glassman's point of view, for real action. Here, too, the Buddhist fear of the bad results of rage, of anger in the face of iniquity and injustice, can be discerned. Care must be taken to see that when we get to real action, it is soft and loving, and not violent and destructive. From my viewpoint of radical compassion, this is tactical advice. In most cases, it is good advice permitting change without too much resistance, but some cases require forceful intervention to stop real iniquity. In any event, the anger contained in radical compassion also has many advantages: it is an important source of energy. It is there anyway, so if we invest all our energy in repressing it, we might throw the baby out with the bathwater and eventually distance ourselves from compassion generally. B. Glassman, *Bearing Witness*, Bell Tower, N.Y., 1998.

[8] This is in contrast to all the philanthropic acts, for instance, which do not involve real action and are built to "protect" the philanthropist against radical compassion.

184 *The Idea of Radical Compassion*

action and not to leave it as a "game" of emotions, senses, and concepts. The third and, to my mind, most important meaning of radicalism hints at the quality of the action: radicalism is an action intended to change reality for other people. In other words, radical compassion is an intention with regard to other people that includes a decoding of the reality and identification of those elements that, if changed, would lead to relief or perhaps disappearance of the distress.

There are a number of implications for the possibility of educational action in this definition of radical compassion. First, an interaction that uncovers pain and promotes a compassionate relationship exists in the actual mentoring encounter between adult and child. Second, the very encounter between a child and a significant adult means a change in reality, since it is an encounter that generates the child's self-image as being of value for others. Third, on the assumption that the adult is exercising radical compassion, with regard to certain children, the encounter will arouse the feeling that action that exceeds the bounds of the interpersonal interaction is needed. Identifying the children's distress brings the adult face-to-face both with their pain and their unwillingness to come to terms with the existence of that pain. Nobody can confront a child suffering from severe abuse or hunger, for instance, look into her eyes and not feel the urgent need to change reality for her. The mentor's job, as someone acting out of radical compassion, is to find a way of doing so!

At this point, it is important to recall that there is a difference between radical compassion as defined here and the mentoring activity of generating the child's self-image. While the generative process, as an emotional and conscious process, is, a dialect process that assumes mutuality and dialogue between child and adult, radical compassion is unidirectional in intention. It is directed from the adult to the child, but is not intended to become the child's legacy in the sense of arousing a sense of compassion toward the adult. The mentor is not supposed to reveal his pain to the child or even to call on her to act toward changing reality for the mentor.

There is an obvious reason for this: educational activity is basically an activity committed to protecting children, and exposure to the pain of adults could damage and frighten the children. A second reason is related to the distinction made between conceptual (protected and rational) compassion, with which the adult comes to the encounter, and the child's vulnerable, exposed position. One possible benefit to children from the mentoring encounter that is potentially included in the dialectical process of generating a positive self-image is the manner in which the encounter enables the children to build concepts of "others" and acquire knowledge through their naïve ability to feel compassion, yet also offering them a protected environment in which they can shield their vulnerability from unmediated exposure to others. However, these two processes cannot be based on the child's exposure to the pain of an adult and remain a didactic challenge to the adult alone.

An invitation to act to change the world order is inherent in the concept of radical compassion. But, not all compassion is radical. Radical compassion distinguishes between reality that requires change and a reality of distress that does not call for intervention. I have already mentioned above that apparently the "call" to effect change is merely a taking of a normative stance based on and stemming from a value judgment by a compassionate person with regard to reality. It does not derive from the sense of compassion itself. This appears particularly true in relation to Buddhist compassion, which is supposed to be universal. It applies to the poor and the rich to the same extent. Thinking that we should act to change the poor person, particularly if at the expense of the rich, is simply taking a social-ethical or ideological-political stance, which bears no similarity whatsoever to being compassionate.

My contention is that distinguishing between taking a social stance and being compassionate is an erroneous distinction. Radical compassion means taking a social stance. On the epistemological level, there is a principle difference between the ways in which compassion arises in people. Not all compassion enjoins us to change reality. For instance, seeing a homeless person in the streets of New York can induce radical compassion in us directed at changing the life of that person in practice. By contrast, meeting an industrialist exasperated by a shortfall of a few million dollars in his bank account would arouse a different sort of compassion in us, which is not radical at all, since it is not directed at changing reality for him. Working with a privileged child who is frustrated because she has received only a grade of 90, instead of 100, on a test can arouse compassion, but not radical compassion. There is a principle difference between the former type of compassion and compassion stirred by a tired, hungry child who cannot read, never mind get high marks. To help this child, the world has to be changed, and herein lies the real sense of radical compassion—the call to change.

B. Anti-Compassion

School, certainly elementary school, is a place where compassion exists. The human contact generates many situations in which adults and children are exposed to the pains and joys of others, situations in which feelings are externalized and warm, where empathic and containing communication takes place.

At the same time, from a bird's eye view of how adults function in schools in relation to the children, it seems that compassion plays a very minor role in prescribing behavior. This is particularly noticeable with regard to what I call radical compassion, although teachers do feel sorrow and anger and are sometimes not prepared to come to terms with the reality of the child's life to which they are exposed. Indeed, in practice they do virtually nothing. The question is: Are there identifiable processes and phenomena unique to school life that prevent compassion from turning into a pattern of activity? I think there are.

Emotional Dullness: For many children, school is not a place that prompts emotional expression. In the event that it is expressed, it appears alongside the school activity and sometimes in complete contrast to it, in the form of a sort of defiance. A child who goes to school learns very quickly that it is not a place where he is expected to express his emotions, and if he does happen to express them, the response will not necessarily be a fitting one—it may be drawn from various kinds of communication, but not from emotional communication.

What lies behind the emotional dullness that characterizes the way the school institution relates to children is, for the most part, the modern school's commitment to rationality and keeping a distance from emotions, which are regarded as the "great enemy" of scientific awareness. This commitment, which has slight and generally contradictory manifestations in the curriculum, is an integral part of the teacher's image: a teacher is supposed to teach study material, to train, to impart information, and to prepare children at the cognitive level. Under this image of the teacher, children are young adults and their youth is expressed primarily in their inability to overcome their emotions, as opposed to the adults, who are rational and in control both of their impulses and their emotions.

Emotions are the enemy of science, as they distort the so-called objective world-view that science tries to convey to the world. Emotions leave people in a mystical, intuitive reality where there is no meaning to learning, but only to feeling, where there is no learning, only belief, no certainty, only vagary, no control, only chaos.

In this sense, children are "primitive": they are like people at the dawn of history, like children in tribal societies that conducted themselves emotionally and sentimentally. The teacher's job is to carry the children through the stages of human development, from the ancient primitive stage in which man's emotions controlled him and his science was infantile, misguided, and based on the mystification of nature, to the scientific, rational, logical present whose substance is measured by the demystification of the world view.[9] Hence, the most important me-

---

[9] In the history of educational thought, there has been no lack of important theoreticians who held onto the view that draws a parallel between the stages of a child's development and the various stages of man's development in history. The most famous are Rousseau, of course, and Stanley Hall, who defined "adolescence" for us as a special period, unique psychologically—parallel to the Renaissance in European history. G.S. Hall, *Adolescence*, Appelton, N.Y., 1916.

dium in a teacher's work with children is the rational, and the manner in which the teacher is supposed to "educate" is simply the application of the rationalization of the child's emotions and his emotionally influenced thoughts. In other words, each time a child responds to a situation or expresses himself emotionally, the teacher's job is to rationalize the emotion, to stress the critical role of thought, and to point out the child's "error" to him: "Think about what you are doing before you act." "Your responses are not appropriate for your age—you are too old to have such outbursts," "You must control your reactions." "Think before you answer."

Another style of rationalization, dictated largely by the impact of psychoanalysis on education and significantly supported by school counseling, is to reflect back to the child his own responses—to label with another name the same response: "You are responding now because you were insulted, but when you think about it, you will see that you have no reason to feel insulted." "You think you are angry with the teacher, but actually you are not handling the study material." "Take note that every time we talk in class about rules of behavior, you ask to leave the room." And so forth. The school process of rationalization is an attempt to transform children's feelings systematically. It manifests itself both in the denial of the authenticity of children's feelings and in the relative paucity of possibilities for emotional communication within the school's bounds.

One instance of the emotional dullness of schools that I encountered during the course of my work arose when I became acquainted with the various attempts to introduce violence-prevention programs into schools. The programs I came to know can be classified into two groups: programs with an administrative, procedural emphasis and emotional communications programs. Not surprisingly, the schools preferred the procedural programs to the communications programs, but even in cases where the school management chose to work with an intervention program based on emotions, there was tremendous difficulty adjusting to its requirements. One of these programs was Marshall Rosenberg's NVC program. The program seems to have simple operational lines and is intended to change language from cold, judgmental, and causal to cooperative, emotional, empathic, and judgment-free. Judgmental language, which Rosenberg calls "jackal language", is a language bereft of compassion; it is violent and blocks the possibility for empathic identification with others. A language that does not control others, that does not judge them, which Rosenberg calls "giraffe language", is a language that enables and even creates empathy, solidarity, and compassion. Rosenberg's interesting focus on language and the attempt to change reality by means thereof is, in itself, a worthy and important effort. But, at least in my experience (which is definitely limited), it is virtually inapplicable within the bounds of the school, although its effectiveness in the realms of family and relationships, for instance, is considerable.

Without going into great detail about Rosenberg's model,[10] I have chosen one example that is typical his model: the "why" questions. When they appear in the context of interpersonal communication, questions of this type form blocks to communication. These questions generally contain disguised violence, reprimand, and judgment under the guise of an innocent question and supposedly causal investigation: "Why were you late for school today?" "Why were you rude to the teacher?" "Why did you hit him?" These questions are often followed by "Explain to me, I want to know why!" But in most cases, the teacher does not really want to know the reason for the tardiness (just as a spouse does not really want to know why the other came home late from work today). It also does not interest her to know *why* the child hit someone else. What she is really interested in is to express anger, to reprimand, and to attempt to exert psychological pressure on the child by inducing a sense of shame.

The hidden message that accompanies the "why"-type of questions is harsh and judgmental, unrelated to investigating the motives and reasons. The alternative is simple: instead of asking, "Why did you come late?" the teacher can simply state, "I am angry" or "I am insulted." This appears simple and logical, but

---

[10] M. Rosenberg, *Non-violent Communication: A Language of Compassion,* Puddle Dancer Press, 1999.

in practice, there is a gap between the willingness of partners to adopt this kind of emotional communication and the great difficulty teachers have in relinquishing "why" questions. It simply does not happen, and teachers feel stripped of communication tools the moment these questions are taken away from them. This is complicated when this demand is accompanied by the suggestion to demonstrate emotion. In many cases, it emerges that the teacher's language of emotions in the school context, namely, in front of children, is surprisingly poor. There are very few words of emotion, particularly those indicating emotions that are considered by society as expressing inferiority to others (jealousy, fear, anxiety, insult, etc.), that teachers are prepared to use in talking with children. For the most part, this kind of usage is perceived by them as injury to their dignity, as a sign of weakness, as helplessness, and as a loss of authority—in short, those very emotions that every teacher fears and that, more and more, are becoming part of her professional life.

In my opinion, this is one of the obvious examples of schools' clinging to language that is supposedly scientific, linked directly to the image of the teacher, as part of the school's modern meta-narrative. It is a language that investigates the reasons, but whose deep structure assumes that every event, behavior, and situation are a fact, and facts have causes. Under this logic, it is clear that knowing the cause means "understanding" and, consequently, also having control over reality and over others.

In the reality of most schools, emotional expression is not legitimate, since this kind of expression is permitted only to children and, even then, is perceived as an expression of weakness. Beneath this reality there are strong undercurrents of veiled violence, fear of losing control, and a sense of helplessness on the part of the teachers. And none this emotional baggage is expressed or released. Quite the contrary, it slowly takes the shape of a demon that controls the teacher's imagination and hinders her from noticing the child facing her. It is a reality with no room for working compassionately.

Disregard and Denial: Working through compassion, particularly radical compassion, requires looking at reality in a straightforward way. For a person to be able to feel the distress of another and to act on his behalf, she must recognize the existence of this sort of distress. One of the problems in schools in this context is the difficulty teachers have in becoming acquainted with children's distress.

Facing a child's pain requires courage. It requires the adult to have the ability to face a whole world of helplessness with which children's distress is liable to confront her. The actual exposure to pain could arouse her will to act, driven by the instinctive, animal urge, familiar to all of us, to protect the child and expel his "demons", by the desire to be relevant and of value for the child, by the fantasy to be a savior, a person who, with a wave of the hand, can make the pain disappear and enable the child to have a better life. But have any of us ever succeeded in meeting the demands of our childhood fantasies? How can one turn into a savior? In listening empathically to the child's tribulations, am I not raising his hidden hopes for something I cannot deliver?

The difficulty of facing other people's pain and distress exposes the cruel aspects of radical compassion. It is sometimes more difficult to bear the pain of others than our own ("If only I were in his place, I would manage"), and the need to act to change reality reveals us as insignificant, incapable, paralyzed, and scared that even if we do act, our actions will have implications we cannot handle. Radical compassion is analogous to the demon or the genie: the moment we let the genie out of the bottle, we can never put it back in. We have a problem the moment we agree to talk to a small child who arouses our sympathy and, in that talk, it turns out that in an hour, when she goes home, she is going to be beaten black-and-blue.

The solution to the problem at the school level is generally simple. It is better not to know and not to ask, and even if we do get to know, it is better not to focus attention on the child's pain, as it will arouse radical compassion in us. Here, three parallel processes are at work. One process is connected to the systematic attempt not to be exposed to information directly and in an

unprotected fashion. In order to avoid "seeing", we have to reduce the points of personal contact with children to the necessary minimum, distance ourselves physically from them. In this
regard, it is astounding to discover how few personal talks and
individual interactions there are in the school, where children
and adults spend a very significant part of their lives. If we try to
recall the number of meaningful personal talks we had with our
teachers in elementary school (meaning talks about "life" and
not reprimands or disciplinary clarifications), we would discover
that they were scandalously few, in unreasonable number relative to the amount of time we spent in school together with those
adults—particularly considering that we, the children were their
raison d'etre for being there.

The second process, which supplements the previous distancing process, is the creation of emotional distance or what is referred to in the adult world as "perspective". In cases where the
first distancing process has not succeeded and, unfortunately,
information about a child's possible pain has reached the teacher,
the teacher has another possibility available to her: having failed
in distancing the child, she can distance herself from the pain.
The ways in which people distance themselves from the pain of
others are many and varied and generally based on avoiding
looking through the child's eyes. It is similar to observing a terri-
fied deer in flight from a tiger: if we were to allow ourselves,
even for just a moment, to feel the deer's terror, we would be in
actual distress. The solution is to close your eyes, tell a joke,
always remain "outside"; to look at both the deer and the tiger
through "scientific" eyes, to rationalize the situation ("this is the
way of the world", "nature is cruel", etc.). Teachers have a
broad, firm foundation for this sort of distancing. First, professional caretakers are supposedly at work in the immediate environment of teachers, and these caretakers bear clearer responsibility for children's "distress" than do the teacher; thus, it is always possible to transfer the pain of witnessing that distress to
them (even if the transfer is in the imagination and not an actual
process: "I don't need to be involved in this—there is a social
worker for this."). Second, teachers have available to them the
therapy rationalization that emotional "identification" is not nec-

essary and even liable to be harmful to the child in distress. Children need an adult who can look at them from the outside without getting involved or feeling any sense of identification A sense of identification and, therefore, compassion are perceived as indication of a lack of professionalism, as unnecessary and even harmful.

The third process is the acquisition of a selective gaze—a gaze that sees only a certain part of reality and systematically disregards the other parts. This universal human process, described so convincingly by Freud, is uniquely present in the school reality: teachers practice daily at ignoring some of the children. The reason for this lies in the need of teachers to identify those children who will assist them in realizing their teaching abilities—those pupils who respond "correctly" to what the teacher says, who give the right answers, on time, and enable the teacher to progress with the material at the required rate, while preserving the self-image and professional image of a teacher who lets her pupils participate, who listens to them and gives them a chance to express themselves, etc. Both the direct and indirect segregation processes in teaching find simple and direct expression in the disregarding of those pupils who put up their hands but are almost never given a chance to answer, whose presence upsets the orderly course of the lesson, who learnt very quickly that they are not part of the class game the teacher plays with the privileged pupils.

This process is accompanied by a rationalization: "How can I relate to everybody in a class of thirty-five children?" "It's not my fault that there are differences between children—some know and some don't." "There are some children who are simply not interested in learning." And so forth.

Not all teachers have the benefit of these processes (sometimes not even the majority), but they are current and real in a school reality in which there is potential for teachers to distance themselves and deny and disregard children and their distress. This is the anti-compassion potential of schools.

Fear of Children: As has become clear from the discussion on compassion thus far, choosing compassion as the way to look at others requires a great amount of confidence and courage. The greatest enemy of compassion is fear, which is rife in schools. There are two reasons for this phenomenon: one, because fear is an accepted mode of operation in every social institution that claims to partake in socialization, to impose norms and values, and to do so uniformly and purposefully; the other, because to-day's schools are characterized by an anxiety-ridden existential situation in the face of the loss of control in the chaotic reality schools are progressively falling under.

But the great fear of every school is the adult's fear of the children. This has serious implications, since a person cannot become a significant adult for a child if she is afraid of the child. A teacher who is afraid of children and cannot teach them will try to make them afraid of her. Adults in schools are scared of the children. They are scared of wild, rude children who inter-fere with their conducting of the lesson and constantly remind them of their loss of authority. They are scared of children who are involved in criminal activities, who are likely to inflict direct or indirect harm on them. They are also scared of children whose parents might put pressure on the school against the teacher. They are scared of children whose distress is too great. They are scared of children who see them in their wretchedness and their weakness.

The truth is that fear of children does not begin in the school. Rather, it is a more far-reaching social phenomenon, perhaps even a cultural phenomenon that is linked to postmodernist con-fusion and the change in the definition of childhood in general. The full extent of this change is felt in the population group that has experienced the postmodern situation at its most severe: middle-class children of today are simply not what they used to be. They mature physically more quickly; they are more in-formed, faster, and with greater access to information; they are independent in many senses (particularly in their feelings) are more exposed to violence, sex, drugs and ideas; they are used to staring passively at television screens, to unbridled consumer-ism, staccato thinking, and video clips. They are more critical and less accepting of society's dictates and more aware of their rights as individuals. At the same time, their youth is longer, as they leave home later than their parents did, and they struggle with interpersonal relationships. Their behavior seems capricious and unpredictable, but they clash less with their parents. Their communication patterns are limited and immature, exemplified by: their participation in chats on the Internet, their imitation of the poor language on television shows, their limited verbal skills in social encounters, and the fact that they do not read books. Their economic dependence on their parents is greater, and their adolescent moratorium sometimes continues well into their twenties. And all this by no means exhausts the list of characteristics of postmodern middle-class youth and children.

These changes are not unidirectional. Changes have also occurred in middle-class parenting, at least as it is presented in the mass media. Parents of today are unlike their parents. They accept their role as late-twentieth-century parents: they are more empathic, more containing; they try to display interest in their children and are more involved in their children's lives; they insist on a certain level of friendship with their children. They turn to various kinds of "guides" for parents, mainly those prevalent in popular literature, and take seriously the parental ethos by which they bear responsibility for their children's personalities and functioning. Yet today's parents are more bewildered, more anxious about their rate of success, the inconsistency of their children, and about their inability to predict the behavior of their children and control them. They are frightened by every sign of faulty communication and are easily affected by the moods of the mass media, with the sense that they cannot guarantee stability and protection for their children in the rapidly changing reality.

These features of the middle-class parent-child relationship are determinative in shaping the feelings of adults working in the postmodern city schools, first, because most of them are parents or due to become parents and most belong to the middle-class. Second, middle-class life in post-industrial big cities has taken on the meaning of "real life", both for people living in a remote village and those living in a metropolitan slum. This is the life that is broadcast day-in and day-out on television, in every home, in a wide range of programs and films; this is the life about which movies are written; this is the life of the people who constitute the backbone of the consumer society. And if the parents are bewildered and feel helpless, if they are concerned about their children's loss of values, and if they report on their fear of loss of control and inability to predict their children's behavior, what can teachers do, when they are not trained for situations of "not knowing", who can only operate as part of a control mechanism all of whose power derives from the security of "knowing", from the ability to predict what is going to happen.

As in most situations of fear and uncertainty, the road to social paranoia is very short. The transition from "I can predict his intention" to "he certainly intends to do damage" and the transition from "I cannot understand him" to "he seems to be a different creature—perhaps even a monster" are very smooth. The transition can most easily be made in American society, where the public thinking reflects and, to a large extent, is shaped by television and the film culture, where the "average" American family is the Simpson family and where the misbehaving child facing the teacher can be anything from a monstrous psychopath to a brain-damaged, violent child to an childish egoist.[11]

---

[11] Henri Giroux analyzes the American paranoia with youth, as reflected in the American media: from Tarantino's violent movies, through Disney's cartoons, to radio programs and talk shows, as well as the influence of the media on shaping the self-image of American youth. H. Giroux, *Channel Surfing*, Palgrave, 1997.

Part V

Alternative Schooling

Chapter 9

The Possibility of a Paradigm Shift

I hesitated greatly before writing this Part: Is it even possible to propose an alternative to conventional schooling? Is the institutional and curricular structure of existing schools not an inevitability? Is it possible to devise another kind of school that can also be realized? Is current schooling although bad, perhaps the best that can be done, with all its conflicting and coexisting detriments and merits: the coexistence of its segregated reality and class reproduction with its humanistic image of "imparting knowledge" and "shaping the individual"; of the various and conflicting types of teaching activities with the latent and violent curriculum; of the clinging to "knowledge" as the most concrete expression of the essence of school activity with the disintegration of knowledge and the legitimacy of adhering to it in the social reality; of the adherence to rationalization out of fear and conservatism with the chaotic, violent, and alienated reality; of the fantasy of autonomy and values with the intolerable dependence on unrealistic public expectations. Perhaps the conclusion should be that the conventional school can be helped, improved slightly or even reformed, but cannot be revolutionized?

This gains force in view of the reformatory fantasies of the various liberal and radical educational reformers, which frequently are met with approval and support in intellectual circles, but run into great difficulty when introduced in the school and most are not realized. Perhaps the right tack to take is to leave the school as it is, examine the "natural" disintegration processes it is undergoing in the neocapitalist reality, and add mentoring to its activities, for example, which would exist as a supplement to school life in the hope of influencing that life. And even if mentoring does not change the school, it would offer a better opportunity and a different meaning to school life for those children it is intended for. Moreover, the disintegration processes might expose the hopelessness of school images and set future schools their true functional place as public babysitters. This type of possibility is not necessarily bad. It would reduce the harmful effect of schools on widening social disparities, and even if it does not eradicate them, it will at least not exacerbate them. It will enable future schools to attempt to forge a different identity in a reality in which the expectations of them are lower, more realistic, and less stifling. It will also obligate schools, for the first time in their history, to be genuinely concerned with the welfare of the children.

With this realistic possibility in mind, it appears to be worthwhile to try to propose an educational alternative, if only to suggest an idea of alternative schooling and perhaps only as a possible prospect whose very existence constitutes a source of energy and conveys to people that "things can be done differently". However, before embarking on this intellectual experiment, I would like to stress that in this forum, I am unable to present an orderly and structured alternative education doctrine, for I have more questions than answers, more quandaries than certainties, and I, in any event, believe that educational realities must be established by the people dealing with education in practice and cannot arrive from the outside through intellectual discussion or an eclectic collection of ideas. Therefore, this chapter will present a collection of personal opinions, of stances with regard to schools and their functioning. This collection is not a suggested program of action for schools; at most, it will form a sort of theoretical scheme from which real operations can be gleaned. I will divide the schematic into two parts: In the first part, I will submit the stance that I advocate in relation to the school's operation in practice and as aspired to in educational theories, that is, the school as a place that deals with instruction, learning, and knowledge. In the second part, I will describe the ramifications of adopting generative monitoring as a different, additional basis for school practice.

The basic assumption underlying the stance that I will present is that serious thought should be given to the social promise the school holds. Indeed, the school has the potential to be a social institution that strives for the reduction of social disparities, the eradication of social and personal alienation and of oppression and the disavowal of the weak, those who are different and "otherly". This alone is a worthy moral goal justifying the existence of schools and education in general in the neocapitalist reality in which we live. On the one hand, this line of thought is based on the view that schools, particularly elementary schools, still constitute a place of hope, especially for lower-class families who send their children to school in the hope that it will serve as a kind of social "jumping-board" for their children. On the other hand, this approach is based on the recognition of the existence of alternative, powerful social reproduction mechanisms that reduce the general need for schools as an instrument of social segregation.

Under this position, the possibility of creating another type of schooling depends on two complementary steps:

(1) Relinquishing three of the most vital components of the school as it exists in practice and as it is envisaged by teachers, parents, and propagators of educational theories. The first component is that "knowledge" is the goal of schools; the second component is the assumption that teaching is the most important activity in schools; the third component is the striving for results of the school activity (teaching) in the performance of the children. If we assume that relinquishing these components is possible and that they can be replaced with various combinations of generative mentoring, it might be possible to envisage a basis for an institutional, educational alternative.

(2) *The introduction of generative mentoring as the formative basis of schoolwork.* This will mean that the school shapes its organization, contents, and work methods in accordance with the specific objectives derived from the personal interactions, especially from the mentoring relationship between the children and adults. This "redesigning" will lead to a renewed definition of the objectives of school education, with such concepts as wel-

fare, liberation, equality, and "fighting for the children" included in the definition of the teacher's function and task.

A. The Problem of Knowledge

In every discussion on schools and education, the question of knowledge inevitably arises. Schools are perceived historically and concretely as a framework for transferring knowledge. Children, parents, educators, and public dignitaries all assume that anybody who enters school at a certain age will leave it after a number of years in possession of knowledge. The great debates in educational thought were and still are about the nature and status of knowledge and the way in which it is acquired, but there is dispute over school being the place where you learn. There also is no dispute over the fact that the intentional part of school activity concentrates on teaching, despite the many reservations about the connection between the act of teaching and its academic results.

It is very likely that children do not learn what teachers think they learn and the teaching may not match the children's learning processes, or at least of some of them. It may well be that much occurs in the school aside from learning, but teachers get up in the morning and go to work in order to teach and children attend school in order to learn.

The postmodern critique casts doubt on the emergence of a rational coherent method of knowledge. It regards the attempt to achieve "objectivity" and "truth" as a pathetic endeavor to restore order to a chaotic reality, as a type of naïve response to existential fears, as the manipulation of an aggressive, commercial, white, Western culture in order to force hegemony on other cultures through the diffusion of scientific knowledge, objective technology, and the Protestant ethic.

However, it is important to note that we cannot conclude from this criticism of the status of knowledge that there is no such thing as "knowing". The fact that the evolutionary theory does not have a firm foundation of objectivity and knowledge means that there is no justification for clinging to it or for preferring it to the Biblical theory of creation, for instance. However, it does not mean that the biologist who prefers the theory of evolution does not have any knowledge of the evolution of different species. Even after it becomes clear to an historian that the way in which she tends to present the French Revolution is simply an expression of a defunct bourgeois ideology and even if she struggles to meet the challenge of methodological and content reorganization, she will still have at her disposal skills, information, and experience that are not available to someone who is not an historian. The fact that it is hard to identify a criterion for preferring the way I read a text as opposed to the way my two-year old daughter reads it does not mean that she knows how to read. In other words, the main point of the criticism, as well as its great value, lies in the sphere of the status of knowledge. The criticism does not question the actual existence of knowledge, information, and skill or even their accumulation into a "body" of knowledge in the disciplinary sense. After all, people know more today than in any other period in human history. People possess destructive and constructive technology and skills on a scale and at a level of accuracy and reliability that was difficult to imagine only twenty years ago. There are two main points to this criticism: the one is the questioning of the status of knowledge—mainly the way in which we relate to Western science, the outcome of the scientific-epistemological revolution, as superior to other kinds of knowledge; the other is the claim that there has been a loss of meaning that is connected to the fragmentation of knowledge. This latter point refers to the simultaneous existence of many disciplines, each of which defines the method as well as the "object" of learning differently, making the possibility of integration very doubtful. In its extreme form, the criticism raises the possibility that such a long series of disciplinary views of actuality implies the construction of many "actualities" that are foreign to each other and the loss of a single actuality. Thus, the important challenge facing schools with regard to knowledge is not whether to teach, but what to teach, since there are so many types of knowledge, so many disciplines, each of which prescribes what learning is and the right way to achieve it. The disappearance of the learning "hierarchy" means that we do not have a criterion for choosing one sort of learning over another. Is mathematics more important than drama? Should we study music? And if so, what music is "worthy" or "good"? Or should we be teaching and learning all types of music in order to be politically correct? And with regard to learning a causal explanation of reality, should the sort of explanation given by physics, for instance, be preferred to an Indian mythological explanation? Or a Muslim religious one? After all, even the scientific pretense of modernity, built on the attempt to obtain knowledge of the nature of reality by means of physical theories, seems to have lost its validity.

First, there are serious doubts as to the "suitability" of the causal model for the demands of our understanding. Do we understand something better if we are given material causes for its presence? What sort of understanding is derived from an explanation of this type? Is this the only possible understanding? What is the price of choosing this sort of understanding instead of others? Indeed, it is evident that in many cases, the scientific explanation does not enlighten us at all, whereas other types of understanding, like a good story or intuitive understanding, could be more meaningful and even more fruitful.

Second, embracing the modern scientific approach means rejecting other perceptions of reality; it means embracing a hegemony that leaves no room for other explanations and creates a hierarchy between what is "scientific" and therefore "correct" and "good" and all things that are not scientific and therefore not good or correct.

Third, the scientific project of modernity, particularly in the form of physics, got bogged down by some severe difficulties in the twentieth century. Not only is it unable to provide a theory of "everything", but also the language in which it is couched today deviates significantly from the concepts and mechanistic and deterministic explanation patterns understood by everyone that characterized science during the period of the scientific revolution. It is an esoteric language that employs inaccessible syntax, whose world of concepts is intelligible only to a small, exclusive group of "scientists", and whose purpose is far from clear. The modernistic image of open, transparent, and democratic science seems to have failed abysmally. Fourth, serious doubts are now being cast on the "holy" inductive principle, which constituted the fundamental substance of scientific empiricism. Under this principle, scientific theory is a theory based on facts, on empirical data, which, when they correspond with the theory's predictions, confirm it or at least do not repudiate it. Under this principle, when there is a lack of correspondence between the laboratory or reality data and the theory, the theory can be rejected or at least can undergo substantial revision.

Philosophers of science have for many years pointed to the fact that this is not the way in which science works. The manner in which theories are accepted is different and is affected by many factors—social, psychological, and political—and not necessarily by correspondence with facts. But even when science tries to operate according to the empiricist image, the concepts of "fact" and "datum" emerge as not at all clear and seriously disputed.

Paul Feyerabend, for instance, has claimed that the conservatism that characterizes empirical science is so great that there is now no similarity at all between the way in which science operates and its self-image. He proposes relinquishing the monolithism of the inductivist model of science (a model that, in any event, does not exist in practice) and adopting a new type of scientific investigation that is counter-inductive, namely, based on the assumption that "anything goes", and that considers any type of explanation, including non-scientific ones (religious, for instance) as part of the investigation's structure. Only in this way can science come close to the desired ideal of open, transparent, and free investigation.[1]

But if science disappoints and there is no procedure by which we can set up a rational, hierarchic, and justified model of learning, how will schools be able to structure their curriculums? How will we be able to tell when a pupil knows and when he does not? And does "anything goes" mean the end of systematization, analysis, practice, measurement, and estimation, all of which originate in the rational, scientific methodology?

---

[1] P. Feyerabend, "Anything Goes", in Anderson, 1995, pp. 199-203.

In my opinion, the problem is less serious than it would appear. When hierarchies are leveled out, knowledge does not disappear; it only changes its status—which is a good thing. The issue of the status of knowledge is important and must be approached with great gravity, but the addressing of this issue does not rule out the possibility of achieving knowledge, certainly not disciplinary knowledge. Moreover, in the various disciplines, particularly the social sciences, culture, and physics, fairly impressive attempts are currently being made to reorganize both research methodology and the status of "facts" as opposed to "theories" in a critical, creative way. This reorganization is characterized by the relativization of learning and by the advance agreement to renounce hegemony by recognizing the complexity of the subject of knowledge and by becoming more clear-headed about the naiveté and narrow-mindedness of science in its infancy stages. More and more we are witnessing up-to-date curricula in the subjects of world history, gender studies, anthropology, and even in the exact sciences and mathematics, which permit new types of understanding, interaction, and definitions of knowledge and a more cautious and complex way of relating to the status of knowledge.

Let us assume for the moment that we wish to structure a curriculum to teach what an apple is. We would discover very quickly that in order to know what an apple is, we need to recognize it as an object of experience, namely, a type of food. Research into an apple as "food" would expose us to a long series of study tasks, starting with gaining familiarity with the apple's chemical composition, its botanical lineage, the way it grows, the different tastes to an apple, etc. However, this is only the beginning of the investigation. To get to know the tastes of an apple, for example, we will need to know how the human sense work, the human digestive system, and so on. We will need to branch out into an investigation of taste itself as a sensual experience, as well as a psychological experience, with the latter requiring us to "understand" psychology.

Our curriculum, in its attempt to convey what an apple is, will not be able to pass over mythology and literature, since the apple in the story of the Garden of Eden is an integral part of the monotheistic religions and cultures. This immediately raises the question of the apple's meaning in other cultures, which requires conducting literary research and investigating the customs and perhaps the eating habits and tastes of those other cultures. An investigation of this sort cannot avoid a crucial discussion on the way a culture uses the apple as an erotic symbol and how symbols generally can reflect power and manipulation structures. The apple also has other expressions: it is an esthetic object; it arouses responses that are not necessarily rational; and perhaps the best way to get to know it is by eating it and not by investigating it. It raises questions and philosophical ponderings; it is a physical object with time and spatial properties; it grows in various geographical regions around the world and has an appreciable history that is closely tied to developmental processes in human society and culture in general.

Two contradictory conclusions should emanate from this brief description (one could go on and on with a list of learning challenges). One is that it is impossible to what an apple is, either from a practical point of view—since learning all the contexts and appearances of an apple could continue for years—or from a theoretical point of view, since in each of its guises, the apple is a completely different object. There is no connection whatsoever between the apple of the Garden of Eden and the laboratory chemical formula for apple juice. The fact is that there are many apples, and in this type of learning process, the apple itself is lost—it has simply disappeared and no longer exists. What remains is a collection of specific apples whose existences depend on the specific "language game" of the discipline we adopt. But it is also possible to reach an essentially opposite conclusion, namely, that this is the proper way to learn what an apple is—via an interconnected system of disparate contexts and different perspectives. Even if the learning process continues for years, we have not lost anything except for the apple itself. The path is fascinating and crosses through various fields of learning, even though it is disciplinary and its language is in total contradiction to any other field of knowledge. Moreover, we cannot ignore the fact that while we are engaged in the learning and investigation process, we could be building a new and general understanding of the apple, one that integrates the whole plethora of "interpretations" of the apple and leads us to the creation of a new "apple idea".

However, whatever the conclusion may be, the apple curriculum—say, a six-year curriculum—is an example of a possible school curriculum. It is a curriculum that deals with the issue of knowledge in a manner that takes into account criticism, but does not easily renounce the desire to know and understand. If we add to the apple curriculum the assertion inherent to the basic assumption as presented above, namely, that schools have an *a priori* obligation to the values of freedom and equality, we can then also propose criteria by which disciplinary knowledge can be related to and judged. One is the way and extent to which specific disciplinary knowledge is the underpinnings of social injustices; another is the possibilities that the discipline offers for social change. For example, an investigation into the apple's botanical and geographical aspects could reveal that the way in which certain agricultural crops moved across the globe, from continent to continent, is simply part of a broad economic process connected to colonialist exploitation and domination. A continuation of the investigation might reveal the various ways in which today's Third-World farmers are being duped by the giant corporations, who are using them to test pesticides, thereby causing the destruction of the land, agriculture, and sources of livelihood in those countries. However, the investigation will also reveal the various ways in which the apple or other species of crops could constitute energy and nutrition sources for starving populations and how humanitarian, egalitarian, and proper use of agricultural technology could eradicate hunger, on the one hand, and preserve the planet, on the other.

In the alternative school, knowledge is not important in and of itself. Rather, knowledge is the means of reaching what is human in the sense that it permits a systematic revelation of repression and is a convenient and interesting tool for collaboration between adults and children in opening up egalitarian possibilities and in enabling the potential expansion of the world embodied in it. Hence, the curriculum is not at all important in terms of its contents—it can start with apples, movies, arithmetic, or personal experiences. The only elements that should remain are the "peeling" method that uncovers *every* topic (including arithmetic, for instance) in the same way that we peel an onion; the willingness to structure the learning undertakings on the basis of association, interest, and the common needs of adults and children; and the willingness to relinquish consciously preconceived outcomes.

B. The Problem with Teaching

Teaching is the means with which schools are most familiar for the generation of knowledge in children. However, when we examine this preoccupation with teaching more closely, two levels of structural contradiction become apparent: one, the contradiction between the various possible, or desirable, kinds of teaching; two, the contradiction between the recommended type of teaching and the reality in practice. There are a number of teaching models familiar to us from the school reality and the educational literature. I will outline briefly three of the better-known ones.

The first and most familiar model is that of old-style teaching, which is the target of most of the criticism, both its contents and methods. Old-style teaching is frontal, with the teacher standing in front of a group of pupils, sometimes on a raised platform, and talking. The talking is a sort of didactic speech, sometimes learned and sometimes vapid, generally based on quotations from textbooks and including references to books as the place where the "knowledge" is deposited. What the pupil has to do is listen to the lecture, read the book, memorize it, and be able to regurgitate its contents at the right time in accordance with the predetermined rules of regurgitation.

This type of teaching, termed "banking education" by Freire because it "deposits" the knowledge accumulated by the teacher and the textbook into the pupil's "vacant" brain, is always accompanied by a series of questions addressed by those who supposedly "know" to those who supposedly "do not know". These questions always have a correct answer, which the teacher knows, but it is the pupils—those who "do not know"—who have to answer them.

This type of teaching has been lambasted by educational reformers. It has been presented as foolish, inhuman, authoritarian, and indoctrinatory. It has been castigated for fostering imitation and memorization, for being boring and not really contributing anything to the pupil, and for perpetuating unquestionable power-situations. It is a form of teaching that purports to teach children formally; that is, it defines "learning" as what can be found in books, as "learning about" and never as "knowledge that—". It does not direct children to experience things in practice and rejects their emotional and physical sides as essential elements in the learning process.

The second model, which is simply a collection of behaviors intended to respond to some of the weaknesses of old-style of teaching, is formative teaching. Under this model, teaching is performed by the teacher, who takes into account the pupils' situations, feelings, and physical alertness and, in extreme cases, also ideas she brings with her from home (particularly if her parents are teachers, for instance). The techniques of this kind of teaching include various attempts to break the frontal format, whether by changing the setting of the classroom or by distributing material to the pupils to work on their own, with the teacher wandering among the various groups.

The curricula corresponding to this kind of teaching are generally arranged in workbooks in which the children are supposed to paint, draw, cut and paste, and, at later stages, to write down answers, generally short. In this way, the model expresses recognition of the "findings" of developmental psychology and tries to adapt the teaching process to the various stages of the development of juvenile cognition—from the sensory-motoric sphere, through the operational stage, to abstract thinking. It focuses on the concrete before the abstract and sometimes prefers the known to the unknown. The theoretical basis of the formative method recommends giving an actual place for children's personal expression as well as to teachers' deliberate manipulation of their conversations with children, from the place where the child chooses to express himself to the place the teacher wants to get to, without the child being aware of it. In this way, the children think they have reached the right answers, that they have chosen a certain path, and that they have an influence on the learning process. The teacher's "shaping" is critical particularly in the normative sphere, where it is recommended to the teacher to constitute a kind of "model for imitation" or, alternatively, to use historical figures as desired models, through which the children will internalize the desired moral code.

The third model of teaching is dialogical teaching. This model is not operative in schools, but has many theoretical reverberations in the critical literature as an alternative mode of teaching. In fact, there are three sub-models of dialogical teaching. One is the sub-model of the Socratic dialogue. In this dialogue, the adult allows the child (or in the case of Socrates, his interlocutor) to express his positions and views on any subject. While critically examining the pupil's stance (and criticism in this sub-model means the test of logical consistency), the teacher identifies the essential internal contradictions in the pupil's views and refutes them and, by doing so, is supposed to create in the child an appreciation of logic and cause the adoption of rationality as a tool for testing knowledge, as well as create motivation to continue intelligent research and investigation.

The teacher in this type of dialogue works on behalf of reason, of the idea of "knowledge", which, even if not achieved in practice, constitutes the supreme purpose of education and of a person's life generally.[2] (This type of dialogue also characterizes

---

[2] In fact, two types of Socratic education appear in Plato. The one I mentioned above appears in most of the Platonic dialogues. The second type, beloved by advocates of the educational view, is identified with Plato's *Meno*—where Socrates gave birth to, by means of well-structured questions, a series of answers from an uneducated slave boy, at the end of which, it turns out that the boy "knows" the Pythagoras Theorem. From this birth process and from the possibility suggested by Socrates that the ideas have been in the

various types of religious learning, where a deity appears in lieu of the "idea"). The second type of dialogical teaching is the Buberian dialogue, which was proposed by Freire as a mode of teaching. It is based on the mutual actualization of the participants in the dialogue, where the dialogue itself is nothing more than a sort of human encounter directed at dialectic mutuality and the generation of conscious acts that replace "bank" knowledge. This type of teaching respects the experiences and personal biographies of both the teacher and pupil, with the teacher's tutoring job being to direct both of them toward critical investigation, to expose the external social forces that are responsible for the pupil's situation, thereby freeing him and enabling his autonomy. This type of dialogue is, to a large extent, similar to the generative mentoring interaction presented in Chapter 5. The third sub-model of dialogical teaching is that recommended by the humanistic psychologists: it aligns the job of the teacher with that of the therapist, who is supposed to be watching "behind the curtains" and leaving the stage to the learner to experiment on his own. The teacher in this sort of dialogue is "just" a director, a facilitator, who enables the child to learn by himself, to investigate and experiment, while she reflects the process to him, enabling the child to reflect and look at himself.

The history of educational criticism and theory took care to arrange the various models of teaching according to chronological order, from the old to the new, and to create a sort of synchroni-

---

soul forever and the teacher's hob is "just" to expose them, the interpreters conclude the Platonic "recalling myth" as the basis of an educational view that stresses the pupil's self-knowledge and the teacher's relative passive place. In terms of the present discussion, Socrates, in his two appearances as a teacher, is a bad tutor. He does not work compassionately, but, rather, on behalf of the sacred idea of learning, and even when he deals with procreation, a thorough study of the dialogue reveals a whole manipulative set-up that does not correspond with the idea of the "pupil who knows".

zation between what is old and what is "bad". The newest models, particularly those that have not been tried and tested and which are not at all possible to implement, are, of course, considered the most prestigious. They are the ideal to which we supposedly must aspire.

I do not agree with this contention. In my view, this is nothing more than different techniques that represent nothing more than technique. I have never feared the dangers of frontal teaching. The only danger in a lecture is that it might be bad. But to assume that children must be deprived of the possibility of sitting, listening, and being carried away to worlds of contents and drama by a good, interesting, fascinating lecture seems to me a great sin. I cannot accept the assertion of passivity that frontal teaching supposedly imposes. I have known too many pupils who were carried away by their imaginations, who were active, excited, and underwent a real sensual experience just from "passively" watching an interesting play or listening to a good lecture. I reject the idea that children do not have intellectual needs when they are young, that all they need is to cut and paste, as long as they do not talk, ask questions, or argue and try to manipulate the language signs not included in their workbooks. For many children, intellectual stimulation is important from an early age. Emotional contact is important for all of them, and it cannot be found either in the workbook or in the teacher's movements around the classroom space. It is important to children that they be listened to, not be contradicted, be given their own place, are spoken to and not activated all the time. It is important for them to feel important and nurtured at school and to feel that others are also important, also have a place, and also are nurtured. There should be no need to trample over anyone in order to be heard or to secure a place. The sort of needs that children have and that determine their learning possibilities is not in any way connected to the teacher's teaching techniques. It is connected to the way in which the teacher looks at the children and the way in which they understand that gaze. The teacher can teach frontally, while inviting the children facing her to join in a common journey that expands to reading texts that seem important to her and valuable to the children, because they are directed to it and participate in it. The various assertions made at school with regard to any given child's access to "knowledge" are not determined by teaching techniques, but, rather, by interpersonal interactions if they exist and, if they do not, by a system of hidden messages not found in the manual of teaching techniques.

The most important thing in teaching, in my view, is that the teacher should feel comfortable with it. There is no point to a teaching technique that does not express the teacher's inclinations and social and verbal talents, as well as her preferences. The real ailments of teaching are the clumsiness with which good frontal lecturers try to conduct a talk with a large number of participants for which they are not prepared and which they do not want to give, the boredom resulting from listening to a frontal lesson of a person who is a wonderful one-to-one interlocutor or an excellent group conductor but does not perform well in front of an larger audience. The desperate feeling of being forced into a technical straight-jacket of a "method" and the shameful habit of education thinkers of proposing and forcing teachers to become dependent on methods they did not invent harm teaching much more than does conservatism or clinging to convenient, familiar patterns. Moreover, it is precisely the new methods of teaching that sometimes provide effective tools of repression and for denying the presence of some of the children (those who do not like cutting and pasting; those to whose hands the glue always sticks). Even methods that are not practiced in school, like Platonic dialogues, are dangerous and manipulative (as Socrates himself demonstrated in *Meno*) in certain cases and can cause frustration and emotional damage.

It is assumed that the various teaching models ultimately contradict each other. It is said that there is no way a teacher can adopt more than one style of teaching, since the different styles of teaching are based on different perceptions of knowledge and on a different understanding of "what learning is" for children. They are connected to different educational outlooks, based on different values and on a completely different reading of professional identity and of the teacher's function.

I do not agree with this assumption either. A teacher can combine many different techniques in her teaching, in accordance with the time, place, and nature of the lesson, pupils, or her talents and motivation. There are many good teachers who can offer fascinating combinations of techniques and even secretly invent new types unfamiliar to the accepted theories. The problem is that their voices are not heard. Just as in the case of the children, teachers are sometimes an oppressed group, comprising mainly women, whose social status is low and not recognized by the official narrative as creative, innovative, having expertise, or as being a place to develop optimal communications.

I believe that if we give teachers the room, if we leave the search for a desirable teaching methodology to them, we will discover very quickly that unique, combined patterns are formed together with a return to existing standards—only that they express teachers' real place and professional vitality. We will discover that when they are relieved of the burden of the ever and rapidly changing "method", the sparkle will return to their eyes. The children will respond to this sparkle with responsiveness and excitement, which have much greater personal and social value than does the teacher's consideration of the cognitive abilities and limitations of the children.

The conclusion that can be drawn from this belief is that the desired teaching technique is the one with which the teacher feels good, by means of which she is able to express what she wants to say to the children. Some of my colleagues who deal with educational theory may regard this as strange. As a technique, it depends totally on the teacher and must be returned to her and be her professional concern. It is not a function of the "method", of the theory, and not even of the children.

C. The Problem with Vicarious Dependence

In the previous sections, I presented a position according to which education clearly does not consist only of a teaching technique. From the child's point of view, education in the alternative school reality is a series of avenues in which it becomes possible to live as a subject of value to others. For adults, education means a social mission driven by radical compassion. In the neocapitalist society, it means the struggle against alienation and social reproduction, manifested in a reduction in social disparities, in giving a place to deprived children, and in schools taking renewed responsibility for the children's well-being. This is the commitment of adults in the school, and they must take responsibility for that commitment. Part of this responsibility is to recognize the (perhaps significant) extent to which concern with knowledge could affect lower-class children's sense of equality through having a self-image of value, which may be significant. Teachers are also obligated to examine the various avenues at their disposal for dealing with this knowledge with all the children and whether to deal with it uniformly or differentially. At the same time and without any causal connection, teachers will find the way in which they want to meet with groups of children; they will clarify what they think they have to say to those children (something that, amazingly, never occurs in schools) and choose the best, most vital and fascinating path that they know (or that they want to get to know) to express themselves in front of the children.

The problem of vicarious dependence, as I have frequently hinted in the course of the discussion, is that teachers are judged and are used to being judged according to the children's performances. This reality, which stems from the seemingly logical connection between teaching, learning, and knowing, places teachers in the impossible position of being in an inevitable instrumental relationship with the children as a means of achieving actuality and social success, as a tool by which the teacher will or will not get a sense of being of value, when most of its outcomes are completely out of the teacher's control. This connection has to be unraveled if we want to achieve a more reasonable, humane, dialogical, and equal education.

What is interesting is that it is easier to refute theoretically the connection, which I call the connection of vicarious dependence, than to renounce it in practice. In order to refute the logic underlying the connection, we only have to look at the complexity and unintelligibility of the simplest learning activity. Learning, even the simple learning of the linguistic signs that syntactically comprise the sentence "I want to eat", is an amazingly complex enterprise. It extends way beyond what is known as "learning" in the animal world, for instance, where instinct and direct imitation work overtime to create in the young the desired species pattern that will ensure their survival. In the case of language, we are dealing with the manipulation of symbols, with an abstract symbolic process whose very occurrence permits innumerable further impromptu abstractions. This feature of human language and regarding learning as a language activity, in the sense that it always takes place "within" language confront us with a complex problem: How can the strange linguistic creature of the "I" be generated, for instance? When does a child learn to say "I"? Why does she learn to do this? Is it imitation or mimicry? Is this inborn grammatical pattern? The number of theories and explanations for this "simple" phenomenon could fill three heavy volumes. We certainly cannot expect consensus or certainty on the subject, but it is completely clear that it is important for every speaker of a language to identify the subject in the basic grammatical mold in order to construct sentences, and most children, other than those suffering severe organic impairments, can do this easily.

The attempt to define learning immediately indicates its being a complex, multi-dimensional activity, which, as far as we know, also is unlimited. People learn more than one thing from a single learning activity. Some of our learning is conscious, and some occurs in unconscious ways. However, learning is not restricted to the verbal or the conscious spheres. It also occurs on the emotional and the physical levels, and each of these levels has its own learning conditions that influence the possibility of learning at a parallel level.

For instance, it is hard for a tired or angry person to concentrate on arithmetic exercises, and the pleasure of discovery or creation of something new might have a decisive impact on the quality and ability of later learning. Moreover, precisely what type of learning are we talking about? Does learning mean practice, memorization, and the ability to do a long, complex mathematics exercise or perhaps copy the same operation to another mathematical matrix? Or is learning perhaps the ability to strip the mathematical law of the memorization and repetition activities?

Other issues can be added to these. Perhaps we should distinguish between different sorts of learning according to a hierarchy, such as, for instance, the distinction between meaningful learning and unmeaningful learning. Would the criterion for this distinction be the extent of abstraction in the learning, namely, the level of control over the symbolic dimension? Then we would prefer the learning of general rules to specific information. Or should we choose the criterion of utility? Perhaps we could call mathematics studies meaningful learning only if they contribute to a person's recognition of herself as a "learner", only if they enable her to understand her limitations and possibilities, to examine her relations and value vis-à-vis others, to cope with arbitrariness, authority, and power, and to understand its effect on her critical abilities.

But if we are not clear as to how learning occurs and if there is a structural difficulty in defining what learning actually is and if it is not sufficiently clear to us when learning has any meaning, how can we structure a process that is supposed to create learning in others and to ensure that there is a direct causal relationship between the activity we are performing and the generation of desired learning? We apparently must repudiate immediately the unjustifiable connection between learning and teaching and separate the two activities.

However, this separation does not occur, for two reasons. The first reason is that although we are unable to define learning precisely on the epistemological level, many think it can be defined on the operative level in terms of its manifestations in human behavior. Under this approach, we therefore know quite a bit about learning. We know, for instance, that people learn and are learning all the time. It is clear that there is a wide range of common learning among people who have had similar experiences: from people who have learned about pain and trauma who show similar behavioral symptoms to people who were in the same class at school, who were exposed to the same teaching, and performed similarly in exams. We know that there are differences in the speed at which different people learn to manipulate linguistic symbols and that not all people approach abstraction in the same manner and with the same ease. We can clearly identify a number of obvious blocks to learning, such as lack of motivation and low self-image. And despite the fact that it is generally in the context of statistical data and a very operational and partial definition of learning, there is an astonishingly high correlation between the way in which children are expected to succeed at demonstrating knowledge (which, in a certain accepted sense, is the visible aspect of learning) and the way in which they demonstrate that knowledge in practice years later, in the sense of a self-fulfilling prophecy.

The second reason for the continued existence of the vicarious dependence connection between teaching and learning is political in nature. The systems dealing with "learning" are public systems financed by public funds. In other words, they are dependent on favors from politicians and other people in power. This dependence creates the demand to bend the school to the capitalist mechanical logic that dictates that every action has a single identifiable cause. Under this logic, the payment made to teachers for their "work" obligates them to perform a series of operations, which, at the end of either a short or long (short is, of course, preferred) causal process, will yield results that will reinforce the positions of those in power, whether through class reproduction, or through the satisfaction of the consumer public, namely, the middle class, which is the source of neocapitalist political power.

Under my position, the alternative structure for schools (a structure that stems from taking the value-oriented stance I presented above) requires the rejection of the indirect dependence connection and the separation of the way we relate to teaching from the way we relate to learning. Teaching is the experience, concern, and source of livelihood of teachers, whereas learning is the physical, emotional, and intellectual experience of children. There is, of course, a tight and complicated set of connections between them, but if we want to establish humaneness and dialogical and mutual recognition of schools, we have to separate the dependence of the teacher from the performance of her pupils. This separation does not mean that we will be totally re-

jecting the possibility of a causal link between the teacher's behavior and the child's feelings, thinking, and learning. Rather,
this link exists, and it will be demonstrated fully in the mentoring activity as an activity that enables learning. The meaning of
this separation is that we consciously sever the teacher's dependence on the children and try to allow the teachers professional,
personal, and social space to determine internal criteria for
evaluation. In evaluating the work of the teachers, there is no
need to look at the performances of the students. Rather, the
evaluation of teachers can be done in one of the following ways:
either by establishing teaching as a profession (something I am
not in favor of, but is certainly possible), with set professional
criteria for evaluation and measurement, or, alternatively, teachers will be evaluated according to their degree of intentionality
and degree of impact on the social objectives of the school, with
no connection at all to teaching activities or any other activities
they employ.

D. Mentoring and Learning

Alongside the propositions presented above—to relinquish the
hegemonic status of knowledge in its instrumental sense as the
purpose of education, to allow teachers to choose their method
of teaching, and to sever completely teachers' dependence on
pupil performance—we find mentoring as the basis for the alternative education process. In a mentoring school, the teacher's
place is founded on his place vis-à-vis the children. It does not
depend on the curriculum or on the performance of the children
in relation to an external index. The starting point is in the children's actualization process, from which a number of simultaneous processes should occur, some connected to a redefinition of
knowledge, some to the design of the teaching, and some to
learning.

   Generative mentoring offers a dialectic process of the mutual
growth of the adult with the child, where the child's self-image
enables him to identify the adult as being of value for him,
thereby enabling the child to see through the adult's eyes, to feel
and think like him or her. This point is very interesting because
it puts the educator in the place she hoped to be in when she first

turned to teaching. It is also a dangerous point because it obligates the adult to take a stand vis-à-vis the extent to which she takes the child into the adult world. This "taking" is socialization, and the more institutionalized it becomes, the wider the social consensus it requires. On the other hand, it must be remembered that socialization of this sort, in which the mentor himself, by virtue of his personality, constitutes the cultural mediator and significantly reduces the social hierarchy and enables the child to get to know him on equal footing.

Mentoring is a conscious process, but is also emotional and sensual. It mediates between the child and others in a way that is sometimes experienced as direct; in other words, it combines self-building and socialization and the private and the social dimensions and, in fact, wrests those participating in it from the individual-society dichotomy. It is difficult to define this learning process as either socialization or individuation; it is simply both yet neither one.

Generative mentoring in a formal framework of actualization means being summoned to undergo an inner experience that enables external learning. The evolving self-images of both the child and her mentor enable both of them to choose to enter the teacher-pupil relationship. It enables the child to choose an image of a learner in order to achieve successes of other types, with other adults, and in new places. It also enables the mentor to appear in other circumstances, in front of an audience, for example, as a more complete person, certain of his objective, feeling, at least for a moment, that he can be as sort of model for a group of children. In other words, he can constitute a suitable foundation for forming the teacher image and positively affect the formation of teaching.

Adopting mentoring as a preferred mode of operation or as an accompaniment to the renovated school activity has far-reaching significance in terms of the definition of learning, because it constitutes the foundation that provides both the adult and child with the possibility of testing the matter of "knowledge acquisition" from a broad perspective. This testing could lead to various personal conclusions in relation to every child, adapted to the totality of his life, consciousness, emotions, and wishes. This ability, when structured according to a significant time-span of years, can lead to various kinds of learning experiences, in terms of learning strategies, time and place of the learning, and the study medium (personal, individual, group, instrumental, literary, dialogic, passive, active, etc.). As an integral part of teaching, mentoring can also provide the mentor with the legitimacy to implement changes and adaptations, including in the way in which he defines his place in relation to the child's learning and to his own learning.

But perhaps the place where generative mentoring is unique in terms of the self-definition of the educational institution is that place where the uniqueness of mentoring as a generative process is determined. Generative mentoring is a process of generating self-image, which also entails the generation of concepts. It may serve to define knowledge differently from the accepted definitions, since it does not relate to knowledge in terms of its contents, nor in terms of its performance. It represents relating to knowledge in terms of its potential as a conscious and social event, in terms of its generative conditions. Again, what emerges from this way of relating is that there is a significant difference between teaching and learning, as learning is no longer defined as "behavior change" or as performance potential. Learning means generation of a new concept, a new context, a new entity in the person's cognitive field. The meaning of this definition is that the child's possibility for learning is identical to the possibility of a new entity or concept arising in her world.

However, when discussing this possibility—namely, the possibilities and limitations of generating concepts in the cognitive field—we must be aware of the fact that these possibilities and limitations are not of one piece. They include: the logical rules of language, which are the general, universal generation conditions for all of us; culture's rules of the game; and every person's personal and social ability to prevent generation of concepts and images (for psychological and physiological reasons, amongst others, and where the prevention of generation itself could be part of the game). The rules of culture are stricter for adults than for children. I live in a world where you cannot invoke demons and spirits as actual entities, in complete contrast to the world of my orthodox religious neighbors, who have total belief in angels and spirits. We all live according to different linguistic-cultural game rules, which permit us to invoke different entities. Currently, children—and in this sense this is another definition of "childhood"—often (especially in their early years) live in a world with fairly flexible cultural game rules. They allow magic and witchcraft to remain in their worlds for a long time; they tend to personify objects and to change considerably their scope of belief in reality. Hence, children have great potential for learning, and it is the very attempt to expose them to culture, like the attempt to expose them to logical scientific thinking, that, in many cases, limits generation possibilities in their world or, to put it more precisely, restricts their learning. Yet adults may, in fact, have a certain advantage in the psychological-emotional sphere. Adults, particularly those with a suitable self-image, hesitate less to face up to things and explain their motives in terms of the subconscious (which, of course, is part of the cultural rules of the game), something that is frequently difficult for children to do.

At this point, which is perhaps the most important juncture of learning, the advantage of mentoring becomes apparent. The unmediated meeting between two consciousnesses has the immediate ramification of the expansion of the conceptual field of reference, the potential multiplying of the possibilities for generation, since at the actual point of meeting, at the very moment when actualization occurs, the conscious-psychological field of each participant is expanded by means of that of the other participant and two new possibilities are created simultaneously. The one possibility is that of being aware of the conditions for the other person generating concepts (that, his possibilities for learning); the second possibility is for the expansion of the awarenesses of the actual participants, which stems from the very expansion of the cognitive field into the consciousness of the other (namely, the creation of "knowledge").

.

Chapter 10

Mentoring as an Archimedean Point

The last question I will consider relates to the possibility of change in already-existing schools. The principal difference between a discussion of this sort and the discussion thus is that existing schools do not start at the same point from which alternative schools set out. Existing schools can wave, either intelligently or in a clichéd manner, banners of social commitment and ideology, but they cannot change the most basic parameters of their operation, beginning with the politics of knowledge, through to the mode of dependent teaching, to the ways of communicating, and ending with the relationships between adults and children, in the relating to parents and the community, and so on.

My claim is that even without far-reaching concessions on existing patterns of operation, it is possible to institute a far-reaching, long-term process of change in existing schools. This can be achieved by using generative mentoring as the Archimedean point, the lever for overall change. This contention, like the contention with regard to the radical meanings of compassion, is based on the assumption that the very introduction of mentoring into existing educational institutions will create ripples like a stone thrown into a pond, and the educational institution will not be able to ignore those ripples.

In order to clarify this contention, I will begin with a question that has troubled my colleagues and me in recent years: Should mentoring be suggested as a way of operating in public schools? Is this sort of activity suited to the teaching, organizational form, and budgetary structure of existing schools? Are the powerful

anti-mentoring and anti-compassion trends not a way of slam-
ming the door on the possibility of the average school becoming
a mentoring school? At least on its face, mentoring seems to be a
type of activity intended for some pupils but not for all, especially those who do not suffer from significant distress in school.
It is also clear that mentoring means a different kind of resource
allocation, particularly of time, a rare commodity in schools.
Generative mentoring is the adult's commitment to becoming a
significant figure for a child, thereby instigating a new sort of
responsibility, particularly if it is built on radical compassion
that purports to change reality.

To this must be added the fact that mentoring is a voluntary
activity; it cannot be imposed on a child and requires the consent
of her parents to engage in a process that will turn a strange
adult into a significant figure for their child. It must also be recalled that schools are designed to work with children on a large
scale, in groups. The ratio between the number of people working in the school and the number of children does not permit
systematic individual work on the part of one teacher with one
child. If, to this supposedly objective data, we add the academic
tasks prescribed by external entities such as the state and community, who fund the school, we will quickly reach the conclusion that mentoring is no more than a pleasant but impractical
and inapplicable fantasy. Hence, the proper place for generative
mentoring might be outside the school—but as an addition to the
school framework or alongside it? Is it preferable to situate it in
the sphere of welfare, in informal education, in the framework of
community centers, or in external therapy services?

At the same time, as I have argued throughout our discussion,
the public school has a serious problem with its humanistic obligations, and there is an intolerable disparity between the self-
image of people dealing with education and the way the educational institution dictates the interaction with the children. The
situation is particularly grim with regard to lower-class children.
Schools, which have never excelled at reducing social disparities
(and were not built to do so), seem to be moving further and further away from the possibility of meeting the needs of children
in distress. The combination of the sense of frustration and fail-

ure and the fear of postmodern chaos is making the lives of educators in public schools in the metropolitan slums intolerable. Against this background, new modes of operation are appearing, which are frequently unknown to the frustrated teachers and principals. The most important of these is the real possibility of taking responsibility for setting a new school reality, based both on the relative openness of the neocapitalist social reality and the school's loss of status as an implementing tool of social control.

Again, my question is: Can generative mentoring be structured as the Archimedean point for creating new educational possibilities in schools? I believe that it can, based on the fact that despite its difficulties, it is a relatively simple activity. Generative mentoring is an activity that because it can be conducted by virtually any teacher, it does not require any special, extended training, nor does it entail structuring as a "professional" activity. On the contrary, it in fact starts with the deconstruction of opaque models, of unfounded self-images, and of intolerable alienation toward others and ourselves and with the decodification of the world picture (in Freirean terms). Relating compassionately to children, being willing to take up their cause when they are in pain, and generating a self-image of being of value are all possible and, in many senses, quite essential to us as human beings because they are part of our nature, our humanity. If we could stop for a moment and silence the institutional voices, ignore the marketing aggression that surrounds us, slightly deflate our overblown consumerist egos—we would be able to hear other voices, particularly those of children. The moment radical compassion appears as a possible way of relating and generative mentoring is granted legitimacy, the ultimate situation of the realization of the educator's self-image will materialize. This realization may well provide a source of energy and renewal and will effect the reshaping of education activity and the human physical and administrative environment. With these assumptions as background, I will describe some of the meanings of adopting mentoring as a basis for changing the operation of public institutions.

A. De-Reification

Reification is the phenomenon of human institutions, created by people for people, appearing as external, alien, non-human phenomena opposing those very people. The analysis of the phenomenon of reification as a sort of fetishism appears in the writings of Marx, who examined the way in which economic, social, and administrative systems develop into a type of force that dictates people's behavior and exerts repressive force on them. These forces, which operate according to the logic of maximizing efficiency and productivity, do not show any sensitivity to people's needs and difficulties, despite having originally been created to respond to that distress. This is applicable to the Nation-State, the various social institutions of education, health, and the like, as well as economic institutions like banks or the media. The peak of the reification process is capitalism, which adapts people to market forces dictated by the private interests of capitalist economics, but is presented via the various institutions as natural, arbitrary forces, despite originally being nothing more than the action of man working against himself.[1]

In the 1960s, a number of studies were conducted on the estrangement between people and their institutions and, in a short time, became the authority. One such study is the analysis by Adorno and Hokerheimer that proposed understanding the alienation as a necessary outcome of the enlightenment approach, which, in its attempt to base human government on nature, a denial of human nature and formulated a language in which the phenomena of natural laws are included but their concreteness is lost. This linguistic construct creates a kind of artificial world in which people's culture (despite its accessibility and intelligibility) is separated from their feelings. The social institution is merely part of the supposedly objective, scientific reality, and, accordingly, it is arbitrary. It is subject to the modern mythology of the "objective fact", in which suffering, inequality, and oppression are justified by the immutable arbitrariness of reality.

---

[1] Karl Marx, *Capital*, Lawrence & Wishard, London, 1983, Vol. 1 Chaps. 1, 4.

Social institutions are what Adorno and Hokerheimer term "the intensification of the thought against its subjects."[2]

Another well-know analysis is that of Berger and Luckman,[3] who expanded the reification concept beyond the phenomenon of the way people relate to their institutions and showed that it is just an individual case of the alienation phenomenon, namely, people's alienation in principle from their creations, other people, and themselves. According to Berger and Luckman, after creating the myth, after establishing a society with laws, and after constructing ritual or an education system, people forgot they had established them. They invented other types of divinities and today worship them as though it invented them. As a rule, people are not aware of the fact that they live in a world that they created themselves.

> The basic "recipe" for the reification of institutions is to bestow on them an ontological status independent of human activity and signification. Specific reifications are variations on this general theme. Marriage, for instance, may be reified as an imitation of divine acts of creativity, as a universal mandate of natural law, as the necessary consequence of biological or psychological forces, or, for that matter, as a functional imperative of the social system.[4]

If we examine the reification process in relation to schools as a social institution, a number of interesting phenomena will emerge. For instance, it is clear that the school is a social institution created to serve people, but it is perceived by the children attending it as a natural, arbitrary, and unavoidable necessity, like an external force that can be "theirs" only if they shape their behavior according to its internal mechanisms—and never vice versa. The reification of schools does not end with the institu-

---

[2] Adorno & Hokerheimer, 1988, pp. 180-197.
[3] P.L. Berger & T. Luckman, *The Social Construction of Reality,* Anchor USA, 1967.
[4] P. Berger & T. Luckman, "The Dehumanized World", in Anderson, 1995, p. 38.

tion; it can certainly extend to people, like the principal or, frequently, the teacher, who cannot be perceived as a person, as flesh and blood, but, rather, as an object, a sort of "institution" representing power, knowledge, and morality. This is the image of the educator who has undergone the reification process by means of the ontology of "knowledge", on the one hand, and of school rationality working "for the children", on the other.

However, the reification of schools is not uniform. There are some children who attend the same school their parents attended, where the principal is the best friend of a parent's coworker or where the teacher is the daughter of a parent's business partner. These are the children who have no difficulty becoming attached to school, who do not feel any great foreignness, and who frequently operate well within the school's language and world of concepts, even prior to their entry into that world. Sometimes they feel they so confident at school that it seems to the teachers that they are disobedient, that they feel they are above the rules of the institution and not afraid of overt confrontation with the teacher. The contempt they feel toward anyone professing to bear authority over them is directly connected to the degree of contempt that neocapitalist reality dictates to all forms of ontology—be it of knowledge or of morality.

In contrast to these children, at the other end of the scale we find the children who suffer anxiety when they get to school. They are intimidated by the esthetics of the concrete and peeling plaster of the building, by the size and coldness of the corridors, of the forms and bureaucratic language. They know nobody, and when their parents come to school, they feel exactly like their children. Many of these children will experience school as an alien institution; they will experience the way in which the institution rejects them, denies them, and ignores them as people.

It seems to me hard to overlook the fact that there is a high degree of correspondence (and frequently identity) between these two types of experience and membership in a given social class. Neocapitalist reality prescribes a leveling of the hierarchies and, in many senses, works toward nullifying the reification with regard to whoever plays the overall consumer game well. It is difficult to be in awe of a teacher who I saw only yesterday morning being shown the exit to the supermarket by the cashier because her credit card was at its limit. It is hard to feel that school is beyond my reach when I grow up in a world where everything is apparently within the reach of anybody with a checkbook. At the same time, for those who did not grow up with the game or were thrown out of it shamefully when they did not succeed at the consumer roulette wheel, there is no procedure for nullifying the reification. School and, for that matter, any institution that provides social services, from the welfare department, to national insurance, to the income tax department, are a sort of threat. These institutions always exist "somewhere out there", and the logic that guides them is not accessible, not known, and not part of my world.

With regard to immigrants, minorities, homosexuals, the poor and unemployed, the strongest expression of social rejection appears in the form of the reification of institutions created to help them. Children of the socially rejected come to school from a reality in which their parents do not have friends on the staff, certainly not on the school administration. The language of school bureaucracy is simply an echo of the language of consumerism and acquisition, and these children are not fluent in it. Not surprisingly, it becomes apparent very quickly that these are also the children who are not the high academic achievers, who almost certainly will find themselves in the bottom half of the children who are below average.

An institution that adopts generative mentoring as the basis of its activity halts the reification processes. The adoption of mentoring means that the institution itself is realizing its professional objectives through personal contact and that it chooses intimacy rather than formality as the preferred mode of communication, and, in any event, this type of communication creates anti-reification familiarity and access. But there are two other senses, slightly more obscure and less taken for granted, in which mentoring produces institutional de-reification. The first sense is connected to the understanding of reification as necessary in the formation of consciousness. According to Berger and Luckman, reification cannot be regarded as a "distortion" or "misunderstanding" of social reality. It would be a mistake to think that people originally understood their social world in a non-reified manner and that this understanding was distorted over the course of history, thus distancing people from the "true" meanings of their social institutions. On the contrary, claim Berger and Luckman, psychological and ontological evidence supports quite the opposite assumption, namely, that the original apprehension of the social world is highly reified, both phylogenetically and ontogenetically.[5] If this is the case, it means that striving for de-reification is not a "return" to a more primitive, more humane situation, to a period when people listened to one another and when institutions were more accessible or more congenial. Rather, this situation has always existed in human society, and the ability to carry out de-reification depends on the ability to identify the existing reifications and fight them. This is a new type of ability, which, according to Berger, appears at a much later stage of our social and personal histories. Looking at it from this angle shows that generative mentoring has great potential for de-reification because it is based on the generation of a self-image of being of value. This generation operates in opposition to internal institutional logic and is, in fact, alien to it. It creates a situation where the institution itself produces the tool that unravels the apparently rational structure on which it is based and does not permit itself, as an institution, to exert its formative forces on the individual.

The second sense is connected to the structured mutuality of generative mentoring. As an institutional activity, mentoring requires the mentors to work on behalf of the institution. These people are exposed consciously and systematically to their feelings, thoughts, and the knowledge of people who thus far have been socially rejected. This exposure must affect the mentors' perceptions, emotions, and cognition, particularly because they are driven by the power of radical compassion, which obliges them to try to change school reality for the children they work with. If we regard mentoring as a process, we can assume with certainty that with time, the world of poor, rejected, lower-class

---

[5] Ibid. p. 37.

children will become part of the overall school experience, part of the school's contents and feeling. We can assume that the very existence of mentoring means that they will have a place and that their voices will be heard, both because their rebuilt self-images will make this possible and because the mentoring experience of the adults will henceforth include the life experiences and thoughts of these children. Thus, school de-reification means that a child who attends at a mentoring school can say, "It is mine too—I am here too."

B. The Waning of the Hidden Curriculum

The hidden curriculum is the way in which schools carry out the reproduction of the class division. In principle, the formal, "overt" curriculum applies equally to all pupils. Every pupil in the school is supposedly given the same access to the knowledge and social values presented by the adults. The critical position, as formulated in the "sociology of knowledge" of the 1970s, claims that a "hidden curriculum" as well is at work in schools. This curriculum comprises a series of assertions to the effect that knowledge is external to people, i.e., people have to become familiar with it and master it (in fact, the reification of knowledge); assertions that determine the study contents and value attached to various types of information (mathematics is more important than drama, for example); that establish a hierarchy of accepted, "formal" knowledge and the way pupils should be assessed, judged, and classified. Not only does this set of assertions make learning difficult and cruel for certain children, it also stands in the way of integration and mobility for lower-class children. As I have noted in the discussion thus far, in addition to the hidden curriculum, there are a series of further concealed elements in the school: administrative procedures and selective institutional violence toward some of the pupils; denial of the experience and reality of the lives of children living in poverty; the school language that grants hegemony to certain European values; and the school myth regarding the non-use of violence.

The adoption of mentoring as an Archimedean point in schools means revealing what is concealed. This means that there will be in the school a continuous and unbroken dialogue between adults and children with regard to their senses, emotions, and thoughts and the way children experience the school reality. But mentoring also implies action to change reality for children in distress through radical compassion. Mentoring in school is a planned, conscious action against the school itself or at least against that unconscious part that acts as a stumbling block for some of the children and prevents the adults from realizing their professional and humanistic images. Action of this sort does not end with the stripping of the mask of equality of opportunity and the revealing of the hidden institutional violence.[6] The action is committed to continuing to create new institutional patterns, to instituting new teaching methods, to restructuring knowledge, to eradicating the superfluous hierarchies, to creating an atmosphere of solidarity and giving, and to creating for the children a self-image of being of value.

In certain senses, in the event that a school manages to realize the potential embodied in mentoring, it could find itself in an accelerated process of almost total reconstruction. The dereification, deconstruction of the basic, elementary form of awareness and the struggle to eliminate the hidden curriculum, with its implication of deconstructing the curriculum, regulations, and interpersonal communication, all add up to virtually nothing familiar remaining intact in the school.

A total turnabout of this sort is not as frightening as it might seem to some people involved in education. If we peel away from schools all the structured curricula, the entirety of the so-called objective regulations and procedures, and the value-oriented pretensions, we could imagine a place where children whose parents go to work or elsewhere arrive each day, a place where they freely meet with a group of adults who are responsi-

---

[6] Since I do not accept the assumption, fairly widely accepted by radical thinkers, that the criticism itself is sufficient to create a released awareness (whether in the form of Theodore Roszak's counter-culture, Foucault's counter-memory, or Giroux et al.'s counter-narrative). Criticism is certainly a condition, but an insufficient one.

ble for their physical and mental safety. The adults receive a salary for their supervision and must take care not to harm the children. They must listen to the children and talk to them, promote their welfare when required, and act as significant adults for them when necessary. Does this sound so bad? It seems to me that many parents would be prepared to give blind support to a school that promises to take care of their children's physical and mental well-being, prevent them from getting hurt, and alleviate their distress. If we add to this imaginary description the attempt to deal with literacy, to teach reading and writing from a young age, and to study various texts (in the broad sense of text) and their possible interpretations with older age groups; if we add sensitivity and commitment to others, which emanates from the dialectic mentoring bond and which should expand to children becoming committed to easing the distress of other children—we will find that we have devised a rather decent school.

An Alternative Dialogue with Parents: An additional and important meaning of adopting mentoring is connected to the place of parents in school. In Chapter 4, I mentioned the increasingly prominent role of parents in the education system and I outlined what seemed to me the main reasons for this heightened involvement: fear of neocapitalist chaos and the sense that the school could constitute for the individual children of involved parents the jumping-board to a good bourgeois life. In recent decades, we have come to witness the dependence of politicians on public opinion processes becoming total. "Public opinion" is a type of communications game where it is not clear just how much the game is affected by what people think and feel and to what extent it shapes those very those thoughts and emotions (the reification process again). However, it is the only way politicians and decision-makers understand what they have to do in order to survive the political struggle, and it is almost entirely connected to the middle class, namely, the mass-consumption class. We are witnessing, as part of this familiar process, the maintenance and perhaps even expansion of public funding for education in industrialized countries, even though the school has, in many respects, lost its formative status with regard to the social division of labor and, in fact, there is no real need for it in terms of social reproduction (excluding, of course, the need for the school as a babysitter, to enable both the earning and spending of money).

Considering school mentoring raises another aspect to the presence of parents in the school reality: the academic (and, of course, detached) debate over whether the responsibility for children's education is borne by the parents or by the State. Although it strays from the boundaries of the present discussion, this debate is interesting in itself and has created and still creates strange alliances. For instance, liberals who criticize public education for its inefficiency find themselves joined by conservatives who champion "family values", in the demand for full responsibility for all aspects of children's education to be borne by the children and their parents. Opposing them is an alliance no less strange of the establishment defending the status of teachers as professionals (like doctors or psychologists) with social radicals who protest the neglect of children by their parents and the bleak future for children growing up in urban slums, both demanding the strengthening of the public system and the expansion of the State's responsibility for education.

Mentoring triggers a different way of settling this futile argument. On the one hand, it is clear that in order to become a significant adult for a child, the mentor has to have the consent of the child's parents. Being a significant adult is a deviation from the accepted public scheme of "teaching", which requires no consent at all, in that it ventures into the realm of intimate relations between the child and adult that cannot be made without parental consent. From a different perspective, it could be claimed that mentoring is the uncovering of what was previously concealed. After all, there was always a relationship between the teacher and the pupil that exceeded the bounds of "teaching". It included different types of manipulation and exertion of force, including intimidation, terror, humiliation, sexual tension, and sometimes also genuine intimacy and friendship. But each one of these arose in the dark, hidden domain of school life. Now, with the exposure and erosion of hidden processes, there is a need for a broader social basis to legitimize the adult-child bond, particularly if we are proposing that interpersonal intimacy be increased.

Generative mentoring also reinforces the school's status vis-à-vis the family, something that has deteriorated beyond recognition in recent years. This means that schools must renew the educational pact according to which they take responsibility for the children's welfare, even if this requires working beyond school hours. Ultimately, the implication is that the school must expand its scope to include the children's personal life and must be prepared to work toward a change where it is necessary.

Thus, mentoring has the potential for engendering a different sort of discourse between the school and the family. It would be based on cooperation and dialogue, on the resolute pursuit of children's welfare, and would redefine the concept of responsibility. In contrast to convention in commercial technocracy, responsibility is not shared: if one person takes responsibility it does not mean that the other person sheds or is relieved of his responsibility. This type of "responsibility economics" is practiced in neocapitalism as a prototype for what is called efficient management, in which there is a clear division of roles and responsibilities. It is totally unsuited to education, which requires collaboration, solidarity, trust, agreement, and shared responsibility that does not diminish by one iota the personal responsibility of each of the partners. Mentoring means looking at human reality in a dialogic way, implying a dual expansion of the concept of responsibility: first, in the sense that responsibility for children's welfare extends beyond the individual ambit of a parent or teacher and becomes joint, trans-personal and, second, in the sense that the very field of reference of the concept responsibility extends beyond responsibility and acquires the meaning of "to respond", which characterizes the dialogic experience, as Martin Buber has demonstrated.

C. The Institutional Meaning of Mentoring

From the above analysis, it emerges that the introduction of mentoring into schools means a change in various layers of the system. I pointed out before that I do not know what a mentoring school will look like in the long run, but its beginnings may already be discernible, at least at the institutional-organizational level. In my estimation, initial organizational models of a school adopting mentoring as an Archimedean point can already be considered. Without going into too much detail, I will describe three possibilities, at least one of which (the first) is very familiar to my colleagues and I and has proved to be workable and implementable. Its results are impressive from the perspectives of the children and the adults in the school.

(1) The first model is of an existing school that tries to add mentoring to its activities. This type of school does not need to unravel its structure; it does not have to commit itself to changing its timetable or curriculum. At this first stage, the only thing to be done is to add mentoring activities during the study week, while legitimizing and allowing a number of adults (who could be either staff members or people from outside the school) to work with children in distress on an individual level. The mentoring activity is to be carried out according to the parameters listed in Chapter 7 (Mentoring Conditions). It takes place in the children's territory; it is built on personal, dialogic contact; it establishes the place of the adult as a significant figure for certain children; and it is intended to generate a self-image of value for those children. At such a school, the regular lessons continue in their group format, with the mentors meeting the children during recess, at times when the children leave the classroom (either initiated or casually), and sometimes at a joint meeting with the child in the classroom. Organizationally, it creates a situation in which there are adults present in the school whose attention is directed at children's distress and whose great advantage in terms of the timetable is the fact that "they have time". This time is utilized for individual meetings with children, but could also be an Archimedean point for institutional processes if it is utilized sensibly, as well as being of benefit to the adults. These processes will be aimed at/will have the effect of opening the way for new possibilities for solidarity between teachers, and collaboration between them will lead to reflection, mutual learning, and experience to affect the redesigning of teaching meth-

ods, procedures, the school's organizational structure, and the school decision-making processes.

(2) The second possibility is a school that includes two separate tracks: mentoring and class teaching. The two tracks are separate in terms of the way they appear on the school timetable for children and teachers. Every child has individual mentoring time alongside group lessons. Each of the frameworks is conducted according to a totally different kind of dialogue, different language, and different interpersonal interaction and not necessarily connected to the parallel framework. The split between the teaching system and the mentoring is structured, enabling advance structuring of the timetables of all the adults and children at the school. In the framework of this possibility, one can imagine the work of two different adult groups with children (although some of the adults might find themselves in two groups). For the class teacher, the existence of the mentor is not an essential part of her work and her attention is still focused mainly on the teaching. For the mentor, the teacher is just another "fact" in terms of the child's life and she does not have a special status as a work "colleague". The teacher could well turn out to be yet another distress factor the child encounters during the course of his life, like family members, neighbors, or welfare workers. This model does not attempt to eliminate the basic alienation between children and school learning, but, instead, strives to contend with the alienation by means of parallel action directed at undoing the hidden curriculum. It should be noted that this model does not contain great potential for change: it leaves a lot of room for clashes and confrontations between mentors and teachers. It does, however, have advantages: it enables advance planning of the school's activities and allows the mentors to act on behalf of the children "cleanly", i.e., without having to consider or understand the teacher's viewpoint too much.

(1) The third model regards mentoring as the most important thing: its starting point is mentoring and only mentoring. It begins with a school situation similar to the one described in the previous model: a physical place attended by adults who receive

a public salary and where children whose parents are otherwise occupied gather. The one and only commitment of the adults is to see to the children's physical and mental welfare, seemingly a mere babysitter, but in practice, it is clear that things will not be as such. This model assumes that the unmediated meeting between children and adults, which entails a personal relationship but turns any other kind of meeting into one of low expectations, will necessarily give birth to new types of experience and learning that stem wholly from the children's needs and the adults' commitment to meet those needs. It will become apparent very quickly that certain children feel great distress because they experience themselves as lacking ability. Other children feel distressed because they are anxious about leaving home; yet another group of children experiences distress due to a lack of stimulation and interest. The adults will discover that a considerable number of the ways for responding to this distress and eliminating it work through dialogue, learning, familiarity with fields of knowledge, and the combined creation of new knowledge. They will also come to learn that the very fact of many adults and children being together will create a community with its own patterns of communication. The communication, which is created spontaneously, is merely a reflection of general social communication patterns, namely, of alienation, competition, violence, and hostility. The adults will learn that if they want to ensure that the evolving communication does not harm the children, they have to take control of it, manage it, and dictate its dynamics by taking a value-oriented stance in favor of equality and freedom. From this point onward, the group of adults and children will create a format of a "school", and it seems to me that despite the fact that an endless number of types of school communities apparently can be created, the commitment to the children's well-being and to the values of equality and freedom will ultimately dictate a very broad common denominator to all schools of this sort.

The last point I would like to mention with regard to generative mentoring as the educational center of gravity is linked to the external aspect of the school institution. If my hypothesis is correct about the necessary connection between contending with children's distress and a commitment to the unrealized values of modernity, i.e., of freedom and equality, then a mentoring school is bound to find itself in a completely different place socially from the existing conventional school. A mentoring school cannot continue to constitute a tool for class reproduction; it cannot simply integrate into the neocapitalist reality; and it cannot come to terms with violence, alienation, arbitrariness, and repression at any level of institutional life. It also cannot hide behind nihilistic "eye-rolling" and claim that this is the reality and nothing can be done about it or that that is the way of nature. All its activities must be directed at creating a tolerable, vital, creative reality that will ensure a real place and image of value for each and every one of the children, whether this proves simple or complicated and difficult; whether it means being aware of what is already out there and only needs to be exposed or if it is an action that is "against" nature or against people's biological, psychological, or social tendencies.

This all means that creating a mentoring school forms a kind of bubble: a social space in which a way of life is conducted according to game rules that are different from those prevailing in the overall social reality. It is a reality in which children's experiences, feelings, and thoughts are never denied; in which mutual human commitments are formulated and realized; in which adults are able to be compassionate and, in certain cases, are able to practice a radical actualization of compassion. There is no significant alienation in this place, but if there is, a way will be found to deal with it.

However, creating a bubble of this sort is not a simple task. It is not the bubble devised by the designers of the modern public school at the end of the nineteenth century, namely, a protected place creating an isolated world for the children where the basic conditions are different from those of the adult world in terms of responsibility, work, earning a living, coping physically, independence, and so on. In the case of the mentoring school, this quite another bubble, one that relates to the entire school community, including the families and the social and community services, as the basis of its legitimacy, as the field of reference for its concepts. This bubble differentiates itself from the external reality, but conducts a dialogue with that reality with the aim of influencing the latter's design and in recognition of the fact that it is only seemingly an external reality: it is present in the school at all times and in all places and should be the raw material for the learning processes, for criticism, and for creating opposition and devising alternatives out of that opposition.

In a certain sense, the mentoring school can be seen as revolutionary institution in social terms, because its very existence constitutes opposition to the reification processes and to the individual and general alienation in neocapitalism. It is an institution whose students and teachers work steadfastly to counter the overall trend toward global commercialization, by actualizing the human relationship of compassion and solidarity. It contests the official narrative of the consumer society, although its members are part of that society, by creating small, local counternarratives, and enables them to become important and significant. The chances of succeeding to set up a school of this sort or, alternatively, of undergoing the educational and organizational transformation required within an existing school are not great.

The reason for this is not the prosaic fact that public systems are not prepared to operate as a fifth column, against themselves, as I have already argued above. The way the public school operates is neither interesting nor important in the neocapitalist reality, for it is tested, but only according to its outputs. This aside, the mentoring school could have impressive outputs. In fact, its outputs will be so impressive that they are likely to create new types of resistance to the mentoring school itself, since in the mentoring school, more children will succeed in expressing their skills and the school will never supply a yardstick for the purpose of negating the social place of lower-class children. But only time will tell—at least at the first stage, the mentoring school will not constitute any sort of threat to the socioeconomic establishment.

Opposition to that establishment could well come from those very quarters where its main legitimacy rests—the parents, who are overawed by the preconception that school is supposed to provide their children with access to prestigious academic institutes of further studies, followed by economic status and wealth. With regard to these parents, most of whom are from the middle class, the mentoring idea might be perceived as a sort of threat, as making schools mediocre and holding back the exceptional and marvelous talents of their individual child.

My contention is—and here I will conclude our discussion—that if it proves possible to mobilize parents, citizens, children, and any people who care to create a new school reality, it is a certainly worthy endeavor and might be received with equanimity by the establishment, which will provide the nascent school with sufficient allowance to establish and prove itself.

Bibliography

Anderson, B., *Imagined Communities; Reflections of the Origins and the Spread of Nationalism*, Verso, London, 1985.

Anderson, W.T. (ed.), *The Truth about the Truth,* Putnam's Sons, N.Y., 1995.

Apple, M.W., *Education and Power*, Routledge, New York, 1995.

Aronowitz, S. & Giroux, H., *Postmodern Education: Politics, Culture and Social Criticism*, Minneapolis, 1991.

Aviram, A., "The Justification of Compulsory Education", *Journal of Philosophy of Education*, 20(1), pp. 51-58, 1986.

Aviram, A., "The Humanistic Conception of the University—A Framework for Postmodern Higher Education", *European Journal of Education*, 27(4), pp. 397-414, 1992a.

Aviram, A., "Non-Lococentric Education", *Educational Review*, 44(1), pp. 3-17, 1992b.

Aviram, A., "Personal Autonomy and the Flexible School", *International Review of Education*, 39(5), pp. 419-433, 1993.

Berger, P.L.& Luckman, T., *The Social Construction of Reality,* Anchor, 1967.

Berger, P.L. & Luckman, T., "The Dehumanized World", in Anderson, 1995.

Cooper, D., *The Dialectics of Liberation*, Penguin Books, 1968.

Devine, J., *Maximum Security*, Univ. of Chicago Press, Chicago, 1996.

Epp, J.R. & Watkinson, A.M. (eds.), *Systemic Violence in Education*, Suny, Albany, 1997.

Eppsteiner, F., *The Path of Compassion*, Parallax Press, California, 1988.

Erikson, E.H., *Childhood and Society*, W.W. Norton & Co., N.Y., 1950.

Erikson, E.H., *Identity, Youth and Crisis*, W.W. Norton & Co., 1968.

Ermarth, E.D., "Sequel to History", in *Postmodernism and the Crisis of Time*, Princeton, pp. 106-124, 1992.

Feyerabend, P., "Anything Goes", in Anderson, 1995.

Frankl, V., *Man's Search for Meaning*, Washington Square Press, revised & updated ed., rep.1998.

Freire, P., *Pedagogy of the Oppressed*, trans. M.B. Ramos, Herder & Herder, N.Y., 1970.

Gadamar, H.G., *Truth and Method*, Crossroad, N.Y. 1985.

Gergen, K.J., *The Saturated Self*, Basic Books, USA, 1991.

Gilligan, C. et al., *Mapping the Moral Domain*, Harvard Univ. Press, Cambridge Mass., 1988.

Giroux, H., "Postmodernism and the Discourse of Educational Criticism", *Journal of Education*, 170(3), pp. 5-30, 1988.

Giroux, H., *Channel Surfing*, Griffin, N.Y., 1998.

Giroux, H., Lankshear, C., McLaren, P. & Peters, M., *Counter-narratives*, Routledge, N.Y., 1996.

Glassman, B., *Bearing Witness*, Bell Tower, N.Y., 1998.

Gramsci, A. *Selections from the Prison Notebooks*, Laurence and Wishart, London, 1971.

Habermas, J., *The Theory of Communicative Action*, trans. T. McCarthy, Boston, 1984.

Habermas, J., *The Philosophical Discourse of Modernity*, Cambridge, Mass., 1987.

Hall, G.S., *Adolescence*, Appleton, N.Y., 1916.

Harris, R.J., *The Nurture Assumption*, Touchstone, N.Y., 1999.

Harvey, D., *The Condition of Postmodernity*, Blackwell, Oxford, 1989.

Hegel, G.W.F., *Phenomenology of Spirit*, trans. A.V. Miller, Oxford Univ. Press, 1977.

Himmelfarb, G., "The Idea of Compassion; The British vs. the French Enlightenment", *The Public Interest*, 145, Fall 2001.

Hinkson, J., *Postmodernity: State and Education*, Deakin Univ. Press, Geelong, 1991.

Hodgkinson, C., *Educational Leadership: The Moral Art*, Suny, Albany, 1991.

Horkheimer, M. & Adorno, T., *Dialektik der Aufklarang*, Frankfurt a.M, reprinted 1988.

Hyman, I.A. & Snook, P.A., *Dangerous Schools*, Jossey-Bass, San Francisco, 1999.

Henry, J., *Culture against Man*, Random House, 1963.

Illich, I. *Deschooling Society*, Harper & Row, New York, 1972.

Illich, I., "Why We Must Abolish Schooling", *New York Review of Books*, 15, pp. 1-15, July 2, 1970.

Illich, I., "Schooling, the Ritual of Progress", *New York Review of Books*, 15, pp. 10-26, December 3, 1970.

Jameson, F., "Postmodernism or the Cultural Logic of Late Capitalism", *New Left Review*, 146, pp. 53-93, 1983.

Klein, R., *Defying Disaffection*, Trentham Books, 2000.

Kozol, J., *Free Schools*, Houghton, Miffilin Com. Boston, 1972.

Kant, I., *Education*, trans. A. Churton, Ann Arbor, 1966.

Lamm, Z., *Contradictory Logic in Teaching*, Sifriat Poalim, Tel-Aviv, 1974 (Hebrew).

Lamm, Z., "Ideologies: Educational Factors Affecting Curriculum", *International Encyclopedia of Education*, pp. 2388-2390, 1985.

Lavi, Z., *Is Education Possible in Times of Postmodernism?*, Sifriat Poalim, Tel Aviv, 2000 (Hebrew).

McLaren, P., *Critical Pedagogy and Predatory Culture*, Routledge, London, 1994.

Mandel, E., *Late Capitalism*, trans. J. de-Bres, Humanities Press, London, 1975.

Maslow, A. & Sorokin, P.A. (eds.), *New Knowledge in Human Values*, Harper & Row Pub., 1959.

Marcuse, H., *One Dimensional Man*, Beacon Press, Boston, reprinted 1988.

Marx, K., *Capital*, Vol. I, Lawrence & Wishard, London, 1983.

McCarthy, T., *Ideals and Illusions: On Reconstruction and Deconstruction in Contemporary Critical Theory*, MIT Press, Cambridge, 1991.

McLaren, P., *Life in Schools: An Introduction to Critical Pedagogy in the Foundations of Education*, Longman, 1998.

Miller, D., *Worlds Apart; Modernity through the Prism of the Local*, London, 1995.

Morley, D. & Chen, K.H. (eds.), *Stuart Hall; Critical Dialogues in Cultural Studies*, Routledge, 1996.

Naisbitt, J., *Megatrends in Asia*, Simon & Schuster, N.Y., 1996.

Perelman, L., *School Is Out*, Avon Books, N.Y., 1992.

Peters, M. & Lankshear, C., "Postmodern Counter-narratives", in Giroux et al., 1996.

Postman, N. & Weingartner, C., *Teaching as a Subversive Activity*, Delacorte Press, New York, 1975.

Postman, N. & Weingartner, C., *The Disappearence of Childhood*, Vintage Books, N.Y. 1982.

Read, H., *The Education of Free Men*, Freedom Press, London, 1944.

Rose, M., *Post-Industrialism and Postmodernism*, Routledge, London, 1991.

Rosenberg, M., *Nonviolent Communication: A Language of Compassion,* Puddle Dancer Press, 1999.

Rosenfeld, J.M., *Artisans of Democracy*, Univ. Press of America, Maryland, 2000.

Rousseau, J.J., *Emile*, trans. W.H. Payne, Appleton, N.Y., 1912.

Sarup, M. et al., *Identity, Culture and the Postmodern World*, Univ. of Georgia Press, 1996.

Sassen, S., *Globalization*, The New Press, N.Y., 1998.

Shapiro, S., "Beyond the Sociology of Education", *Educational Theory*, 38(4), pp. 415-430, 1988.

Sharp, R., *Knowledge, Ideology and the Politics of Schooling*, Routledge & Kegan, London, 1978.

Sollors, W., "The Idea of Ethnicity", in Annderson, 1995.

Tierney, W., *Building Communities of Difference*, London, 1993.

Toffler, A., *Power Shift*, Bantam Books, 1990.

Tite, R., "Who Knows? Who Cares? Schools and Coordinated Action on Child Abuse", in Epp, 1997.

Van Cleve, M., *Existentialism in Education*, Harper & Row, N.Y., 1969.

Wallerstein, I., *The End of the World as We Know It*, Univ. of Minnesota Press, Minneapolis, 1999.

Watkinson, A.M., "Administrative Complicity and Systemic Violence", in Epp, 1997.

Weedon, C., *Feminist Practice and Poststructuralist Theory*, Basil Blackwell, Oxford, 1987.

Wei-hsun Fu & Wawrytko (eds.), *Buddhist Behavioral Codes and the Modern World*, Greenwood Press, London, 1994.

Weiman, A., *Buddhist Insight,* Motilal Banarasidas, Delhi, 1990.

Wood, E.M. & Foster, J.B. (eds.), *In Defense of History*, Monthly Review Press, N.Y., 1997.

Young, M. & Witty, G. (eds.), *Society, State and Schooling*, Falmer Press, 1977.

Index

self-consciousness, 105, 154
self-discovery, 37-38, 40
self-image; compassion and,
177, 184,193; generation
of, 98-117, 120-128;
language and, 142-144;
mentoring and; 98-108,
110-117, 220, 223, 232,
234, 238; of value, 106,
114, 216, 238; poverty and,
xii, xiii, 131-134; the
impact of school on; 25-27,
41, 45-46, 133, 149, 216,
218;
self-realization, xxvi, 76, 100,
137, 169
significant adult, xii, 101, 125,
127, 153, 184, 194, 236; *see
also* mentor
Smith, A., 162
social analysis, 55, 73
social classes, 16-17, 40-41,
80, 160
social forces, 32, 62, 149, 152,
212
social frameworks, xi, xix, 55,
57, 75, 79, 118, 122, 127
social institutions, xiii, xxix,
15, 128, 142, 180, 228, 232
social life, 22, 91
social reality, xiii, xxiii, 17,
51, 73, 77, 81, 100-101,
141-142, 155, 199, 227,
231, 241
social situation, xxiii, xxvii,
51, 60, 128
social value, 46, 65, 71, 149,
215
socialism, 56-57, 64
socialization, xxi, 6, 8, 14, 30-
31, 34, 38, 40-41, 44-46,

48, 65, 115, 135, 137, 193,
220-221
sociology, 41, 110, 233
Socrates, 37, 98-99, 211, 214
subconscious, 83, 223
suffering, ix, 10, 138, 155,
157-158, 163-166, 169-171,
174, 184, 217, 228
superstructure, xxv, 16, 49,
164
supplier, 90, 143, 144
survival, ix, xxvi, 113, 119,
175-176, 216
systemic violence, *see*
violence
teachers, *see* adults; teachers:
the school-
teacher-pupil, xxvi, 44, 50, 99,
143, 221
technology, xix, xxvi, 56, 70,
74, 84, 202-203, 208
television, xxi, 3, 5, 56, 75-76,
80, 87, 104, 122, 124, 130,
139, 194-196
territory, 123-125, 140, 238
Tite, R., 20-21
tradition, 3, 35-36, 160, 164,
168
Tson-kha-pa, 168
unemployment, xi, 78, 84
value; being of-, xii-xiii, xxiv,
xxvi, xxviii, 25, 43, 46, 70,
98-103, 106-108, 111, 115-
116, 120-123, 125, 132,
149, 152, 184, 215-216,
220, 227, 232-234, 238,
240-241; commercial-, 104,
113; self-, ix, xiii, 153;
sense of-, xi, 116
values; absence of, 6, 87 ,138,
195; assimilation of, 34,
137; capitalist-, 42, 62 ,81,